Eight Paths to Leadership

Eight Paths to Leadership
A Guide for Special Educators

by

Belva C. Collins, Ed.D.
The University of North Carolina at Charlotte

·P·A·U·L·H·
BROOKES
PUBLISHING C⁰ ®

Baltimore • London • Sydney

Paul H. Brookes Publishing Co.
Post Office Box 10624
Baltimore, Maryland 21285-0624
USA
www.brookespublishing.com

Typeset by BMWW, Windsor Mill, Maryland.
Manufactured in the United States of America by Sheridan Books, Inc., Chelsea, Michigan.

Unless otherwise stated, examples in this book are composites. Any similarity to actual individuals or circumstances is coincidental, and no implications should be inferred.

Throughout the book, the Voice of a Leader features include excerpts from interviews with special educators and advocates. Interview material has been lightly edited for length and clarity. Interviewees' responses, real names, and identifying details are used by permission.

Library of Congress Cataloging-in-Publication Data

Names: Collins, Belva C., author.
Title: Eight paths to leadership : a guide for special educators / by Belva C. Collins, Ed.D.
Description: Baltimore, Maryland : Paul H. Brookes Publishing Co., 2018. |
   Includes bibliographical references and index.
Identifiers: LCCN 2017049688 (print) | LCCN 2018005225 (ebook) | ISBN 9781681252742 (epub) |
   ISBN 9781681252759 (pdf) | ISBN 9781681251714 (paperback)
Subjects: LCSH: Special education teachers—Professional relationships. | Educational leadership. |
   Special education—Administration. | Children with disabilities—Education. | BISAC: EDUCATION /
   Leadership. | EDUCATION / Special Education / General.
Classification: LCC LC3969.45 (ebook) | LCC LC3969.45 .C65 2018 (print) | DDC 371.9—dc23
LC record available at https://lccn.loc.gov/2017049688

British Library Cataloguing in Publication data are available from the British Library.

2022   2021   2020   2019   2018

10   9   8   7   6   5   4   3   2   1

Contents

About the Author

Belva C. Collins, Ed.D., Professor and Chair, Department of Special Education and Child Development, The University of North Carolina at Charlotte

Dr. Collins is currently Professor and Chair of the Department of Special Education and Child Development at The University of North Carolina at Charlotte and is former Professor and Chair of the Department of Early Childhood, Special Education, and Rehabilitation Counseling at the University of Kentucky. She began her career as a rural special education teacher in 1974 and became a professor in higher education in 1990. Dr. Collins was the 2017 recipient of the Eagle Award for outstanding service and leadership in special education from the American Council on Rural Special Education (ACRES). She also is a former Chair of ACRES and currently serves as an Associate Editor of its journal, *Rural Special Education Quarterly.* Dr. Collins's research interests include systematic instruction for students with moderate and severe disabilities, special education personnel preparation and teacher leadership, and inclusion of people with disabilities in their faith communities.

About the Downloadable Materials

Purchasers of this book may download, print, and/or photocopy the full transcripts of the Voice of a Leader interviews for educational use. These materials are also available at www.brookespublishing.com/collins/materials

Introduction

When people think of educational leadership, they often think of administrators—principals, special education directors, superintendents—but becoming an administrator is not the only way for an educator to lead. Teachers can be leaders without leaving the classroom.

This idea is not new, but its specifics remain unclear. My aim in writing this book is to provide special educators with paths to leadership they can follow as teachers.

The impetus for this book began when I was a professor at the University of Kentucky in the Department of Early Childhood, Special Education, and Rehabilitation Counseling. The Kentucky Professional Standards Board mandated that all master's degree programs in education in the state be shut down by December of 2010, redesigned, and resubmitted for approval by the board as Teacher Leader programs. This caused a great deal of discussion across the state as faculty groped to define the role of a teacher leader and determine what graduate coursework in a Teacher Leader program would entail.

My colleagues and I spent months discussing this and redesigning our program. In the end, we were the only institution of higher education in the state to design an individual program for a master's degree in Special Education Teacher Leadership instead of designing a general graduate leadership program across all areas of teacher licensure. We did so because we believed special education teachers have opportunities to serve in leadership roles that may not be available to all teachers. Special education has a unique mission. Teachers work with students with disabilities from birth through the transition to adulthood, a role that requires them to interact extensively with families and provide them with a good deal of support. We reasoned, moreover, that special education teachers often enter a leadership role by default. Other colleagues in the school turn to special education teachers when they need specific expertise. Often special education teachers are known to be experts in managing behavior, designing and adapting curricula, providing evidence-based strategies specific to various types of disability, using accommodations, providing specialized intervention in communication, providing physical management, working with special health care needs, and making data-based decisions using formative data. Special education teachers often must take on the role of consultant as well as collaborator when students with disabilities are included in general education classrooms, and they must take the lead in designing individualized education programs and transition plans.

We designed our new program for the Master in Special Education degree with this knowledge in mind as we referred to the advanced standards set by the Council for Exceptional Children at that time (these were updated in 2015). As we selected courses to include and developed coursework, we decided we needed a specific course in Special Education Teacher Leadership. I volunteered to develop and teach the course. My limited knowledge of the leadership literature led me to review the special education literature to identify areas in which special education teachers could exercise leadership. I assigned readings from my review to the students who later took my course. Each week, we discussed a different aspect of leadership after hearing a presentation by a guest speaker (most often an experienced special education teacher) who exemplified leadership in that area. Each student taking the course designed a leadership project that would help that student grow personally as a leader; students set benchmarks with dates to accomplish their individual goals.

A few years later, I left the University of Kentucky to take a position at The University of North Carolina at Charlotte. Before I left, I worked with Dr. Melinda Ault, my colleague who then took over the course, to survey the special education teachers who had completed the Special Education Teacher Leadership course. Our purpose was to determine whether they perceived that they had grown as leaders upon completion of the course (Collins, Ault, & Leahy, 2016). The survey results showed that, although some of these special education teachers already were participating in specific leadership activities before they took the course, the number and type of leadership activities in which they engaged increased in subsequent years. At the same time, the levels at which some of the special education teachers engaged in leadership also changed; they went from participating in school, district, and local community activities to participating at a state, regional, or national level. Other variables that affected their growth in leadership, such as maturity, opportunity, or confidence, cannot be ruled out. Still, the survey results were promising, and the comments students made in response to open-ended questions suggested that the course was a positive experience that played a part in their growth as special education teacher leaders.

This text is based on the Special Education Teacher Leadership course that I developed. Although the references have been updated and expanded, the topics remain the same. This book is not about how to develop leadership qualities such as persistence and confidence—as a special educator, you already possess leadership qualities and call upon them in your day-to-day work. Rather, this book is about specific activities in which special education teachers have an opportunity to be leaders. Participating in these activities will build upon your existing leadership qualities and skills while also greatly benefiting the students, families, and communities with whom you work. Each chapter of this book discusses a different pathway to leadership and provides guidelines specific to that path. It is my hope that this book will inspire special education teachers to share the practices they have developed in their classrooms and schools with others and to reflect on ways they can influence others in developing special education policies and implementing evidence-based practices in the field.

I used to joke with colleagues that, if everyone is prepared to be a leader, there is no one left to be a follower. In retrospect, I can state that, although no individual special education teacher can be a leader in all that he or she does, each has the opportunity to make a difference in at least one area of leadership. It is up to each teacher to determine what that area is. I hope this book will guide you on that professional journey of discovery as you determine where you can make a difference.

About This Book

The eight chapters of this book explore eight different paths to leadership that special education teachers can follow. (Each chapter title focuses on the specific leadership activity addressed therein.) As you read, you might discover one path that suits your experience, skill set, and ambitions particularly well, or you may find you are interested in multiple paths toward leadership. Chapter 1 discusses how to be a leader in the classroom by reading and conducting research and making data-based decisions. Subsequent chapters discuss how to move beyond the boundaries of your own classroom to become a leader within your school, your local community, and the broader community of educators and specialists who work with students with disabilities.

Each chapter begins with a rationale for the leadership path discussed therein, supported by a literature review addressing specific related activities in which you might engage. Key terms are listed at the start of each chapter, bolded and defined within, and compiled in the Glossary. As part of my research, I also conducted interviews with special education teachers who have demonstrated outstanding leadership in each area discussed. Excerpts from these interviews are featured throughout each chapter. (The full transcript of each interview is included in the downloadable materials for this book.) Throughout each chapter, reflection questions are provided to stimulate your thinking about the different principles and practices discussed. Each chapter concludes with guidelines for special education teachers who want to become leaders within that specific area, followed by activities that may help you to reflect on your experiences and learn more about the topic.

Your journey to leadership will transform your role as a special educator and increase your positive impact on the students, families, colleagues, and communities with whom you work. Let's begin.

In memory of my parents,
Vernon and Sara Cole, who were
always proud of my accomplishments.

1 Make Data-Based Decisions

Learning Objectives

After reading this chapter, readers will be able to

- Explain the rationale for a special education teacher's demonstrating leadership through data-based decision making in the classroom

- Distinguish among evidence-based practices, research-based practices, and promising practices

- Explain why fidelity of implementation is important and how this can be monitored

- Identify various types of formative data collection systems and the types of behaviors for which they are appropriate

- Use evidence to show that an instructional or behavioral strategy is effective within the context of a single-case research design

- Disseminate data on effective and efficient practices to others in different ways

Terms to Know

AB design	Duration data
ABAB (withdrawal) design	Effectiveness
Adapted alternating treatments design	Efficiency
	Event recording
Alternating treatments design	Evidence-based practices
Chained task	Fidelity
Discrete task	Formative data

Frequency data	Partial-interval data collection
Interval data collection	Permanent products
Latency data	Promising practices
Momentary time sampling	Research-based practice
Multi-treatment design	Summative data
Multiple baseline design	Task analytic data
Multiple probe design	Whole-interval data collection

INTRODUCTION

Leadership begins within the classroom. As a special education teacher, you need to have the skills to provide competent instruction and manage classroom behavior using effective practices. To do this, you must know how to collect data on the practices used, how to analyze and reflect on the data, and how to use the story that the data tell to make decisions for changes.

There are numerous instructional and behavioral strategies that sound research has shown to be effective. However, you may not be familiar with these strategies, based on where and when you completed your licensure program, the type and quantity of professional development provided by your school district, and your own ability and motivation to stay abreast of best practices through familiarity with credible professional sources of information (e.g., professional journals, web sites of professional organizations). Even special education teachers who are familiar with and use available resources may sometimes need to be innovative and try a new twist with a procedure or strategy; thus, you can serve as a researcher within the classroom as practices are evaluated for effectiveness. This chapter highlights the ways you can demonstrate leadership within the classroom through data-based decision making.

CONNECTION TO PROFESSIONAL STANDARDS

The teacher's role as a classroom researcher is supported by a number of professional standards. This book reflects standards for leadership developed by the Teacher Leadership Exploratory Consortium (TLEC, 2012) and the Council for Exceptional Children (CEC, 2015).

Teacher Leader Model Standards

Although not specific to special education, the Teacher Leader Model Standards (TLEC, 2012) list several standards under *Domain 2: Accessing and Using Research to Improve Practice and Student Learning* that support teachers becoming consumers of research as well as classroom-based researchers. These include relying on research to select appropriate learning strategies, analyzing and interpreting student data to make instructional decisions, collaborating in the research of educators in higher education and professional organizations, and collaborating with others in classroom data collection and analysis to improve practices.

In addition, standards under *Domain 4: Facilitating Improvements in Instruction and Student Learning* state that teachers should collect, analyze, and use classroom-based research to improve practices. Standards under *Domain 5: Promoting the Use of Assessments and Data for School and District Improvement* state that teachers should be knowledgeable about and collaborate with colleagues in using both formative and summative assessment data to improve student learning. (**Formative data** are collected as instruction occurs or as an intervention is implemented; **summative data** are collected at the end of an instructional session or unit.)

Council for Exceptional Children Program Standards

The Standards for Professional Practice developed by CEC (2015) state that teachers should be able to identify and use evidence-based practices (1.2) and collect data on the effectiveness of those practices (1.3). Specifically, Standard 7.0 focuses on research, stating that teachers should have the ability to interpret and disseminate the results of that research (7.3) and engage in research to improve practices and outcomes (7.5). The CEC Advanced Preparation Standards also focus on research in Standard 4.0 (Research and Inquiry) by stating that it is the responsibility of special educators to evaluate research to identify best practices (4.1), to use those practices (4.2), and to continue to improve instruction through engaging in research (4.3).

These standards might sound challenging for any teacher to meet, but the role of classroom researcher can provide a deeply satisfying path to professional leadership. One teacher who exemplifies leadership skills in this area is Carey Creech-Galloway. In the interview excerpt that follows, and in additional excerpts throughout this chapter, Ms. Creech-Galloway describes how conducting research and making data-based decisions have transformed her work as an educator. (The full text of the interview is available in the downloadable materials for this book.)

Voice of a Leader

Analyzing Data to Make Decisions

Carey Creech-Galloway is a special education teacher leader with skills as a classroom researcher. She has been a coauthor on several research publications that determined the effectiveness of systematic prompting procedures to teach core content in a meaningful way to students with disabilities (Collins, Evans, Galloway, Karl, & Miller, 2007; Collins, Hager, & Galloway, 2011; Collins, Karl, Riggs, Galloway, & Hager, 2010; Creech-Galloway, Collins, Knight, & Bausch, 2014). Ms. Creech-Galloway began using systematic data collection as a paraprofessional working with high school students with moderate and severe disabilities, and she continued working as a paraprofessional and honing these skills as an undergraduate.

After completing her degree, Ms. Creech-Galloway became a special education teacher whose caseload included students in both special and general education classrooms at the middle and secondary school levels. In this role, she continued to use data-based decision making to drive instruction. As she began taking graduate coursework, she became involved in more rigorous research in her classroom with her professors and colleagues. Here, she discusses the relationship between data and her classroom decision making. (Many of the specific strategies she mentions will be discussed further in subsequent sections of this chapter.)

Q: **How did data analysis guide your instruction? What type of instructional decisions did you make based on data?**

A: I made all my decisions based on data [smiles]. These are just a few of the types of decisions that I think I made the most often: *Am I providing enough reinforcement for correct responses? Am I teaching too many stimuli at once? Does this student need something different regarding materials or presentation? Have I provided what the student needs to communicate his or her response? Is the student making too many errors? Is the student stuck at a prompt level and is there something I could do to the task to get them closer to independence?* I have looked at my graph and determined that the skill was too hard and chunked it, or determined a different way to teach it, such as backwards chaining. I have also looked at the graph and determined that, even with wait training, this student needs simultaneous prompting because they are not able to wait and they are practicing too many errors. I've also looked at data and determined I needed to look at the environment again or decided to choose a different adult to train on that skill.

Q: **How did data analysis guide management of behavior in your classroom? What type of behavioral decisions did you make based on the data?**

A: Behavior management in my classroom was always heavy on the use of visual supports and continuous to variable reinforcement, depending on the student. Using the FBA [functional behavioral assessment] process and differential reinforcement was crucial, as well as being able to determine when to increase reinforcement or decrease it to shape behavior. For students that had very challenging behaviors, I always tried to remind myself that, if we didn't collect good behavior data and stay on a reinforcement schedule, then I would not be able to teach!

Sometimes, I would look at the data and determine a time of day, a person, an environment, or a day of the week that was toughest for the student. That allows you to tweak things for that student to increase student performance. I've had students that, on Monday, may not respond to a demand without physical aggression, so as the week progressed, I added more and more trials to their sessions, but in the beginning of the week, I required minimal participation to gain a reinforcer. I found structured work systems were valuable for teaching students how to complete a task independently. The more success students had in completing tasks without heavy adult support, then the more reinforcement they gained, and teaching became easier in a whole-group and small-group setting.

I could go on and on about all the variables that affect student behavior as I see it. Consistency in implementation is the most important part of managing behavior, and you have to collect data and analyze it in order to change behavior.

YOUR ROLE AS A CLASSROOM-BASED RESEARCHER

Even if you do not consider yourself a researcher (yet), you should be familiar with the concept of data-based decision making. In reality, being a teacher researcher is a fundamental requirement of being an effective teacher, especially in an age of growing teacher accountability for student performance. All special education teachers should complete their licensure programs with a foundation of knowledge of best practices in the field. Once in the classroom, however, they may find that they are confronted with issues for which they were not prepared.

For example, as a special education teacher, you may be responsible for students who exhibit challenging behaviors to which you have not been exposed, or students with whom the instructional procedures you have been taught do not seem to work. In reality, teacher preparation programs in special education attempt to provide aspiring teachers with a strong foundation on which to build skills, but these programs cannot cover every conceivable behavioral or learning challenge you may confront once in the classroom.

Meanwhile, students, paraprofessionals, general education colleagues, peer tutors, and other related staff may turn to you for leadership. You may discover that you have not been prepared with all of the answers. If you are a new teacher, this may be overwhelming. Even if you are a seasoned professional, you may find continual new behavioral and instructional challenges appearing as the years pass following completion of your preparation program. For example, special education teachers who received a foundation in functional skill instruction may struggle with teaching grade-appropriate core content, and special education teachers who are busy meeting their students' basic health care needs may find it difficult to keep abreast of continual changes in instructional and assistive technology.

Becoming a Consumer of Research

The first skill that all special education teachers need in order to become and remain leaders in their profession is the ability to find access to current quality research. A simple Internet search may result in a broad array of potential practices that may not be based on sound research. It is up to you to discern what is and is not evidence-based. For example, when Test, Kemp-Inman, Diegelmann, Hitt, and Bethune (2015) examined 47 web sites for evidence-based practices (EBPs), they found that 43% of suggested practices could be trusted because they were supported by explicit evidence, whereas 57% could not be trusted because there was no indication of such evidence. Specifically, explicit evidence on web sites stated criteria and their sources (e.g., Horner et al. [2005] criteria, Institute of Education Sciences criteria).

In evaluating practices, it is important to understand the difference among EBPs, research-based practices, and promising practices. According to Cook and Cook, **evidence-based practices** "are instructional techniques with meaningful research supporting their effectiveness that represent critical tools in bridging the research-to-practice gap and improving student outcomes" (2011, p. 71). They "are supported by multiple, high-quality studies that utilize research designs from which causality can be inferred and that demonstrate meaningful effects on student outcomes" (Cook & Cook, 2011, p. 73). Gersten et al. (2005) and Horner et al. (2005) outlined specific indicators that must be met for practices validated through group and single-case research designs to be considered evidence-based. Researchers have applied these indicators to a number of practices published in peer-reviewed professional journals.

A review of the professional literature in special education will identify EBPs that seem to consistently provide strong, positive effects on behavior and learning. For example, Hall (2015) identified EBPs in special education as including prompting, reinforcement, visual supports, social narratives, task analysis, PECS (Picture Exchange Communication System), discrete trial training, time delay, self-management, naturalistic intervention, extinction, functional behavioral assessment (FBA), differential reinforcement, antecedent-based interventions, video modeling, response interruption, and pivotal response training. More specifically, Ryan, Hughes, Katsiyannis, McDaniel, and Sprinkle (2011) identified EBPs for students with autism spectrum disorder (ASD) as including discrete trial training, PECS, social stories, and TEACCH (Teaching, Expanding, Appreciating, Collaborating and Cooperating, Holistic). Noting that they found three different lists of EBPs for students with severe intellectual disabilities (IDs), Courtade, Test, and Cook (2015) identified EBPs that included

- Systematic instruction (e.g., time delay, system of least prompts) and in vivo instruction for teaching academic skills

- Discrete trial training, functional communication training, modeling, and PECS for students with ASD

- Backward chaining, video modeling, and systematic instruction (e.g., time delay, system of least prompts, most-to-least prompting, simultaneous prompting) for students in transition

It is beyond the scope of this book to provide in-depth discussion of how to implement these EBPs. The point is that special education research literature has identified a number of specific practices that are consistently well supported by evidence, and it is the educator's responsibility to keep informed about these practices. If you are not sure if a practice is evidence-based, you can turn to such lists, found in professional peer-reviewed journals, for guidance. In some cases, you will discover that more than one EBP may be appropriate for teaching or managing the behavior of a student with specific needs. Cook and Cook recommended that "when more than one EBP fits one's needs, prioritize first by best fit, then by effect, then by level of evidence" (2011, p. 79).

Freeman and Sugai (2013) provided a decision tree for teachers to use in analyzing the graphed data from single-subject studies in professional publications to determine the effectiveness of an intervention that can be useful in selecting a practice. First, identify the problem—that is, what behavior is to be changed. Next, look for specific interventions in the research that have been used to address that problem and change the behavior. Once these studies are located, consider the following questions:

- Do the students identified in the study and your own students have similar characteristics?

- In what context was the study conducted (e.g., classroom, school, district)?

- How effective was the intervention in that context?

- How much clarity does the research design provide in terms of descriptions of the students, the setting, the intervention, and the data collection?

- Was the effect of the intervention repeated often enough to be convincing (e.g., across multiple students or behaviors)?

Finally, consider the outcome of the study in terms of effectiveness, asking whether it is believable that the intervention really did change the behavior. The more studies that can be located showing that a specific intervention was effective, the more confidence you can place in an intervention.

Compared to the criteria for an EBP, the criteria for a **research-based practice** are not as stringent. Research-based practices may be based on single studies, studies that have not been evaluated thoroughly, and studies whose effects were minimal (Cook & Cook, 2011). Although these studies may draw your interest, it is important to remember that they do not yet have a substantial body of research to support them. Thus, it's necessary to monitor their effectiveness when they are used.

Promising practices have even less empirical support and typically are based on "tradition, expert opinion, theory, and moral values—regardless of whether they are validated empirically" (Cook & Cook, 2011, p. 75). In your research to find better practices to meet behavioral and instructional challenges, you may discover in journals or web sites for practitioners some practices that do not have supporting data. The CEC Interdivisional Research Group (CEC, 2014) noted that, as EBPs are not yet available for all learners, teachers may turn to promising practices based on the best available data. If so, the use of such procedures should be monitored with care in the event the procedures cause harm or fail to improve student outcomes.

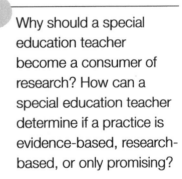

Why should a special education teacher become a consumer of research? How can a special education teacher determine if a practice is evidence-based, research-based, or only promising?

Becoming a Data-Based Decision Maker

Although special education teachers should be familiar with the need to use EBPs with their students, a number of variables influence their educational practices, including teacher preferences, the influence of colleagues in a community of practice, and teachers' training and comfort level with particular practices. For example, Johnson et al. (2014) found that, when teachers prefer a procedure, they are more likely to implement it with fidelity and continue to use it over time, whereas Hall (2015) found that teachers are influenced by others in a community of practice, making it imperative for teacher educators to build cohorts of students who are knowledgeable in their practice and support each other. Hall reported statements made by surveyed teachers in a community of practice. These statements demonstrated the teachers' conviction that better educational decisions are made when they are based on data and that data should drive modifications in instruction. As one teacher remarked, "Everything is evidence-based. We collect data, and change the way we introduce materials and tasks based on the data" (Hall, 2015, p. 36).

Finally, although it has become easier to identify EBPs from lists in the professional literature, special education teachers may not believe they have the training or background to use them. In a survey of 456 teachers across 89 school districts, Brock, Huber, Carter, Juarez, and Warren (2014) found that most of the teachers were not confident in their ability to use EBPs with students with ASD. Even when you are aware of an EBP and feel confident in its use, it is imperative to remember that all practices will not work with all students and that, to determine whether an EBP works with a specific student, the practice must be implemented consistently over time, and data must be collected and analyzed to determine effectiveness (Spooner, Browder, & Mims, 2011).

Voice of a Leader

Organizing Data and Training Colleagues

Regardless of what types of practices you implement, you will be collecting data— and when it comes to collecting data, organizational skills are essential. Below, Carey Creech-Galloway describes her system for collecting data and training her team to do so.

Q: *Special education teachers can be overwhelmed with monitoring student data. How did you organize your classroom to collect formative data? If others collected data, who were they and how did you prepare them to do this? What type of data did you or others collect in your classroom?*

A: I developed small-group binders as well as individual student data collection binders. The binders were in order of the student's schedule and, if you opened a binder, it [might] look like this: Student IEP [individualized education program], data summary sheet (where I transferred the raw data percentage for a quick glance), raw data collection sheet, raw graph where daily data were plotted, and probe data summary sheets (with all the stimuli selected to teach for that skill). This sounds overwhelming, but, after creating and revamping the process over time, this continued to be the most efficient method for my classroom. For vocational data and data collected on community-based instruction, I typically had clipboards with raw data sheets hanging in the designated location; then, the summary sheet and graph remained in the student binder, and we transferred the data to that location every few weeks. If you do not graph your daily data and organize the formative assessment in this manner, then you will not be able to make data-based instructional decisions about your everyday teaching practices.

I tried to be the individual providing the specially designed instruction and collecting the data the majority of the time, especially when it was the presentation of new information. I had paraeducators that collected data, and I trained them by modeling the group and how I would collect the data. I had them collect data simultaneously, and we would compare and discuss why the student response was recorded in a particular way. In the beginning, it is easier for paraeducators to provide "training trials" or use simultaneous prompting to teach. Then, they can provide the test probe without worrying about recording prompt levels. I slowly introduced response prompting procedures as the paraeducators gained confidence. For the most part, I found that the paraeducators were more comfortable providing instruction on discrete skills, and the chained skills were a little more difficult since they were trying to balance the prompt they delivered and reinforcement at the same time. I think you have to take baby steps and not expect paraeducators to do this without a lot of support in the beginning.

Maintaining Fidelity

Once an EBP has been identified, it also is important to implement the intervention with a high degree of **fidelity** (Cook, C. R., et al., 2012). *Fidelity* has been defined by Collier-Meek, Fallon, Sanetti, and Maggin (2013) as "how much of an intervention is delivered to the students as planned" (p. 54). Fidelity of implementation might encompass the ability of a teacher to provide directions, use instructional strategies (e.g., video modeling), and provide feedback as planned and as consistent with how the practices were meant to be implemented. Collier-Meek et al. noted that higher fidelity results in better outcomes. They also cautioned that teachers might not maintain a high degree of fidelity over time; thus, they recommended that teachers conduct periodic checks for fidelity. When teacher fidelity data are graphed, they can be compared to graphed student data, making it possible to determine if a lack of effectiveness can be attributed to the lax implementation of a procedure. Recognizing that not all procedures work for students with ASD, Witmer, Nasamran, Parikh, Schmitt, and Clinton (2015b) stressed that both careful progress monitoring and fidelity to the intervention are needed to determine which procedures will and will not work.

To convince consumers that they can have confidence in the results of published studies, strong researchers collect frequent fidelity data to show that a procedure was implemented as planned. Typically, it makes sense to collect fidelity data a minimum of once per week for each research condition (e.g., baseline, intervention, maintenance); the goal is for the agreement between an observer and the instructor to be 80% or higher (Billingsley, White, & Munson, 1980). (This means that a person observing a teacher conducting instruction or using a procedure would agree that the teacher implemented at least 80% of the steps accurately and as planned.) This stringent criterion may be impossible for busy special education teachers to meet. Just be aware that it is advantageous to conduct periodic fidelity checks for classroom staff who are involved in implementing instruction or behavioral strategies, such as special and general education teachers, paraprofessionals, peer tutors, and related service delivery personnel.

> What is teacher fidelity and why is it important? How can it be documented?

The process of collecting fidelity data is not as difficult as it sounds. First, make a list of the steps to implement a strategy. For an instructional procedure, this might include giving a task direction, providing a set response interval for the student to perform a behavior, delivering a prompt (as needed), and providing student feedback (e.g., praise, error correction). For a behavioral procedure, this might include performing a planned action each time a student displays a targeted behavior—for example, providing descriptive praise following each 5-minute interval that a student is engaged in a lesson. An observer watches you (or another instructor) use the procedure and checks each behavior on the list that you perform or that another instructor performs. After the observation, the data are summarized as a percentage; this is done by dividing the number of planned behaviors by the number of observed behaviors and multiplying by 100 (Billingsley et al., 1980). If the percentage falls below 80%, remediation on how to use the procedure is merited.

Choosing Effective, Efficient Procedures

There are two measures to consider in selecting a strategy. The first is the procedure's **effectiveness,** or how well it works. Keeping in mind "that some interventions may work differently in different situations" (Harn, Parisi, & Stoolmiller, 2013, p. 190), you may find that you need to adapt a procedure to fit the specific needs of students in specific contexts. For example, suppose you read that the constant time delay prompting procedure is effective for teaching reading, and you find a study in which a verbal prompt was used; if you have a student with hearing impairments, you may need to adapt the procedure to use text, pictures, or manual signs. When such adaptations are made, it becomes even more important to monitor the effectiveness of the procedure. Never assume that a procedure will work, even when research is available to support it; progress monitoring through formative data collection is always necessary.

To decide between EBPs that appear equally effective, comparison data can be collected on the **efficiency** of each procedure (Collins, 2012). Efficiency measures include

- How quickly a procedure results in criterion performance (number of sessions, number of minutes)

- How many errors a student makes over time in the process of learning (ideally, less than 20%)

- How much effort or cost goes into implementing the procedure

Although two procedures can be equally effective, you may select one over the other because it is more efficient.

Collecting Formative Data The first step to becoming a data-based decision maker is to have a solid understanding of formative data collection methods. Data collection should not be limited to a special education setting. For example, Vannest, Soares, Smith, and Williams (2012) pointed out the importance of frequent data collection using adequate measures, regular analysis, and data-based decisions when teaching science core content to students with disabilities in general education settings. Of course, summative data provide information on how well a student understands and maintains content after a unit of instruction. That said, collecting accurate and frequent formative data allows special education teachers to recognize when a student is not making progress and to make immediate changes in instruction before proceeding in a unit of instruction; thus, Westling, Fox, and Carter (2015) stated that it is important to collect student data through continuous direct assessment. Formative data may be more accurate if recorded immediately after a lesson rather than being recorded a few hours later, at the end of the day, or on the following day (Jasper & Taber Doughty, 2015; Taber-Doughty & Jasper, 2012).

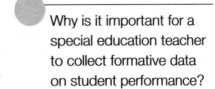

Why is it important for a special education teacher to collect formative data on student performance?

There are a number of ways to collect formative data to determine the effectiveness of an instructional procedure (Brown & Snell, 2011; Westling et al., 2015). Some methods of data collection produce precise information on a student's performance. These include three methods described next: permanent products, event recording during discrete tasks, and task analytic data collection during chained tasks.

Permanent products include student work samples, such as written sentences or paragraphs that provide evidence of skill acquisition. Special education teachers may collect and analyze permanent products looking for improvement over time. In contrast, a **discrete task** or behavior is a skill that can be recorded as a single behavior that is correct or incorrect. **Event recording** as a student performs a discrete task provides trial-by-trial data. Finally, a **chained task** is a task with a number of linked discrete steps, such as tying one's shoe, which involves performing several one-step behaviors in the correct sequence. **Task analytic data** collection during a chained task allows you to observe and record the number of steps a student performs correctly in a specified sequence of behaviors. The number of correct responses can be used to summarize data when there are a set number of opportunities to perform a behavior or a set number of steps in a task analysis, whereas the percentage of correct responses can be used to summarize data when the number of opportunities varies. For example, you might summarize the number or percentage of math problems answered correctly, or the number or percentage of steps completed correctly in a task analysis for a specific skill, such as using a calculator to compute sales tax.

Specific instructional strategies may require specific types of data collection that provide more detail than whether a response is correct or incorrect. My own prior work (Collins, 2012) explains data collection strategies and provides examples of data collection sheets for special education teachers who use response-prompting strategies. For example, when using a time delay procedure, it's important to record whether a student makes a correct or incorrect response before or after a prompt, and when using a system of least prompts procedure, it's important to record the level of prompt needed to elicit a correct response from a student (e.g., verbal, model, physical). The advantage to this level of data collection is that you can determine if a student is making progress (i.e., needing less prompting) even though the criterion has not been met.

Some types of data collection are more appropriate for monitoring the effectiveness of behavior management strategies, although some also may be appropriate for instructional procedures. Frequency data, duration data, and latency data are often collected for this purpose. Recording **frequency data** allows you to keep a running record of how many times a specified behavior occurs. Frequency data can be summarized as the number of times these behaviors occur within a specified amount of time—for example, the number of times a student talks out without permission during a 60-minute class. When the time varies across sessions, frequency data also can be summarized as rate—for example, the number of errors a student makes per minute when reading a passage. **Duration data** provide information on how long a behavior occurs, such as how many minutes a student is out of his or her seat during a class period. Duration data can be summarized as either the number of minutes (or other time units) or as the percentage of time. Finally, **latency data** provide information on how long it takes a student to begin to perform a behavior—for instance, how many seconds it takes a student to respond to a request to get out instructional materials. These data can best be summarized as the mean number of seconds or minutes across opportunities.

Other types of data collection produce an estimate of a student's behavior. When recording the occurrences of appropriate or inappropriate behavior, it may be easier to use **interval data collection.** This allows you to observe and record behavior once per interval instead of every time the behavior occurs. During **whole-interval data collection,** a behavior is recorded if it occurs for an entire specified interval (e.g., if a student is out of his or her seat for an entire 30-second interval, the out-of-seat behavior is recorded). During **partial-interval data collection,** a behavior is recorded if it occurs at any time within a specified interval (e.g., if a student is out of his or her seat at any point during a 30-second interval, the behavior is recorded). During **momentary time sampling,** a behavior is recorded only if it occurs at the end of a specified interval of time (e.g., if the student is out of his or her seat at the end of the 30-second interval). Interval data can be summarized as a number if the number of intervals is consistent across sessions; if not, interval data can be recorded as a percentage.

Monitoring progress is most important when students are acquiring new information or skills because it is crucial to making decisions on the effectiveness of instructional or behavioral strategies; once students have reached a set criterion, data may be recorded less often to measure the maintenance of a skill or behavior over time (Brown & Snell, 2011). Special education teachers also should be aware that technology can be used effectively to collect data (Vannest, Parker, & Dyer, 2011; Westling et al., 2015). For example, teachers may use an iPad with data graphing software (e.g., Behavior Tracker Pro, Skill Tracker Pro) to record formative data on behaviors as they occur, with the advantage that the software also may graph the data, thus facilitating analysis.

> Which methods of data collection are most useful for recording responses during academic instruction? Which methods of data collection are most useful for recording behaviors during behavioral interventions?

Documenting Effectiveness: Graphs and AB Research Designs A good classroom-based researcher often must collect data frequently, but it can be overwhelming to sort through a stack of data sheets and try to take in all of the accumulated information at once. For this reason, it is important to graph data periodically to identify overall trends. A graph should be an easily understood display of student performance over time, making it easier to see if a student is making progress, although Brown and Snell (2011) recommended retaining data sheets for when more specific information is needed (e.g., identifying the specific steps performed incorrectly on a task analysis). Graphed data allow you to see desirable and undesirable trends and note whether a student is making progress at an expected rate.

Data-based decisions may or may not indicate the need to change what you are doing. Browder, Spooner, and Jimenez (2011) suggested a number of possible data-based decisions:

- *Move to a new phase of learning.* When a student has demonstrated proficiency or acquisition, the special education teacher can move to a new phase such as fluency, maintenance, or generalization.

- *Simplify the behavior or task being learned.* When a student has made no progress for a specified period of time (e.g., 2 weeks), the special education teacher can simplify the behavior (e.g., by teaching smaller chunks of a task analysis).

- *Continue as is.* When a student makes adequate progress, the special education teacher can continue instruction as is.

- *Change the instructional strategy.* When a student is making inadequate progress, the special education teacher can change the instructional strategy (e.g., by providing a longer response interval).

- *Improve the behavioral strategy.* When data indicate a motivational problem, the special education teacher can improve the behavioral strategy (e.g., by using differential reinforcement for independent responses).

Although it may seem sufficient to begin data collection at the time an instructional or behavioral procedure is implemented, the process actually needs to begin sooner. The only way to document that a strategy is effective is to record baseline data on a student's performance prior to implementing a strategy (a method known as an **AB design**). Collecting and graphing baseline data (A) prior to collecting and graphing intervention data (B) will provide an indication that a practice is effective in changing a student's behavior. Because teachers cannot be positively sure that the intervention was what caused the behavioral changes, data still must be viewed with caution. Six single-case designs that build on a basic AB design are explained in the following sections. Although researchers seldom use these simple AB designs, they can be effective tools for special education teachers to determine the apparent effectiveness of a strategy (Brown & Snell, 2011).

Documenting Effectiveness: Six Single-Case Designs   The methods used in single-case research result in designs that can be used to document the effectiveness of a procedure beyond a simple AB design. Single-case designs (also called single-subject designs) are simple to implement in a classroom setting to show credibly that a specific practice does or does not work with a specific student within a specific context. Single-case designs are also useful for teachers who are consumers of special education research to understand, because they help teachers in evaluating data in the professional literature. Here, however, my focus is on how special education teachers also can employ these designs within their own classrooms to document the effectiveness of practices.

The following sections provide a simple overview of the ease with which six types of designs can be implemented within a classroom: ABAB (withdrawal), multitreatment, multiple baseline, multiple probe, alternating treatments, and adapted alternating treatments designs. It is beyond the scope of this book to provide a detailed description of these designs and the requirements for their rigorous implementation; for a more in-depth discussion, consult other resources (e.g., Gast, 2010).

ABAB Designs   When determining the effectiveness of a behavioral intervention on social behaviors, an **ABAB (withdrawal) design** is simple to implement. In this type of single-subject experimental design, baseline condition (A) is followed by intervention (B), providing an indication that an intervention may be effective based on whether the data reflect a counter-therapeutic change each time the baseline condition is in effect and a therapeutic change each time the intervention is implemented.

To implement an ABAB design, collect baseline data (A) on the occurrence of a behavior for a minimum of 3 days (the minimum number of data points needed to establish a trend). If, at the end of baseline data collection, the data indicate the need for intervention, implement the behavioral strategy (B) for a minimum of 3 days to determine the strategy's effect on the behavior. Once a change in behavior is established, withdraw the intervention and return to baseline condition (A). If the behavior also returns to baseline levels, you may conclude that the change in the behavior was due to the intervention; however, again reinstating the intervention (B) and seeing the effectiveness of an intervention for the second time builds believability in the procedure. If replicating this design across students can show the same effect, you can feel more confident in defending the use of a strategy in the classroom.

Multi-Treatment Designs   What if the procedure (B) is not effective or could be more effective? You can make the decision to try another procedure (C), again monitoring the data for effectiveness of the intervention. Again, a withdrawal and subsequent reinstatement of the newest intervention will increase believability in the procedure. When subsequent strategies are implemented in this manner, the design is considered to be a **multi-treatment design** and allows comparison to be made across procedures (e.g., "Was intervention B more effective than intervention C?"). Although researchers will be more stringent in controlling the variables of a multi-treatment design, it is a flexible tool for classroom teachers to analyze the effectiveness of more than one procedure.

To sum up, a multi-treatment design is a flexible single-subject experimental design in which baseline condition (A) is followed by two or more interventions (e.g., B, C, D), allowing the effectiveness of each intervention to be compared to the one that follows it. Interventions may be repeated within the design (e.g., A-B-C-B-C).

Multiple Baseline Designs   A **multiple baseline design** is a series of AB designs implemented in a time-lagged fashion. The design builds confidence in a procedure's effectiveness by showing that it is effective each time it is implemented. To use a multiple baseline design, begin by collecting baseline data across a number of students, behaviors, or settings. Then implement the intervention in only one of these contexts at a time. For example, you can implement a behavioral or academic intervention with one student until it shows an effect on the student's behavior, implement the same intervention with a second student until it shows an effect on the second student's behavior, and then implement the same intervention with a third student until it also shows an effect on the third student's behavior. At this point you may have enough data to be convinced that the procedure is likely to be effective each time it is implemented.

In another scenario, you could select one student and implement an intervention across three separate behaviors, one at a time. This might consist of implementing an instructional intervention across three distinct sets of vocabulary words (e.g., time delay), or implementing a behavioral intervention (e.g., self-monitoring) across three distinct behaviors (e.g., staying in the seat, raising a hand to talk, being on task). Again, you can grow more confident in a procedure each time it is shown to be effective.

Multiple Probe Designs   A multiple baseline design can be time-consuming because it requires continuously collecting and monitoring baseline data across other students, behaviors, or settings while intervening with only one at a time. Thus, the **multiple probe design** is a useful variation. When using a multiple probe design, instead of collecting continuous baseline data, you only collect intermittent data (e.g., weekly) until ready to introduce the intervention. If the intermittent data probes remain at the same level until the intervention is introduced, a case still can be built that the intervention caused the change in the student's behavior.

In brief, a multiple probe design is a single-subject experimental design in which a series of AB designs are implemented in a time-lagged fashion to show that an intervention is effective each time it is implemented following intermittent collection of baseline data. The intervention may be implemented across students, behaviors, or settings.

Alternating Treatments Designs   A useful design for comparing the effectiveness of one strategy over another is the **alternating treatments design.** In short, an alternating treatments design is a single-subject experimental design in which one intervention (A) is compared to another intervention (B) by alternating which intervention is in effect for a single behavior until one intervention appears to be more effective or efficient. This design is appropriate for comparing the effect of two or more behavioral interventions on a social behavior, such as being out of one's seat.

This design allows you to implement two interventions on a single behavior at the same time to see which has the most immediate or lasting effect. For example, you may compare the use of teacher-delivered reinforcement on staying in one's seat to student self-delivered reinforcement, by alternating which intervention is used each day. Once one procedure appears to be more effective than another, you can discontinue the less effective procedure. Replicating the design across other students will build believability and confidence in the procedure.

Adapted Alternating Treatments Designs When the targeted behavior is academic, you can use an **adapted alternating treatments design,** a variation on the alternating treatments design. An adapted alternating treatments design is a single-subject experimental design in which one intervention (A) is compared to another intervention (B) by alternating which intervention is in effect for similar equivalent behaviors until one intervention appears to be more effective or efficient than the other; it is appropriate for comparing the effect of two or more interventions on an academic behavior (e.g., vocabulary words).

Although you still would identify two interventions, it is necessary to also identify two similar behaviors (or tasks), such as acquiring two sets of equally difficult

> What is the most basic single-case research design that a special education teacher should use to document effectiveness? Describe a more complex single-case research design that would be appropriate for documenting the effectiveness of academic instruction, documenting the effectiveness of behavioral intervention, or comparing one procedure to another.

vocabulary words. You would then assign a specific intervention to each set of words (e.g., constant time delay versus simultaneous prompting) and monitor to see which set of words the student acquires first. Although both procedures may be effective, you may choose to use the most efficient procedure (i.e., the procedure that results in fewer sessions of instruction to criterion) with the student during future instruction.

DISSEMINATING RESULTS OF DATA COLLECTION

A special education teacher who takes on the role of researcher is in a good position to share data-based decisions with others. Here are just a few ways you can use the role to provide valuable leadership.

Train paraprofessionals. A classroom researcher skilled in identifying EBPs can teach paraprofessionals to use effective practices (Brock & Carter, 2015; Robinson, 2011).

Guide students' general educators and peers in inclusive settings. A skilled classroom researcher also can share effective procedures with general educators in inclusive settings (Musti-Rao, Hawkins, & Tan, 2011), especially when co-teaching (Conderman & Hedin, 2012) or when working with peer tutors or peer buddies who may provide support for students with disabilities in inclusive settings (Carter, Moss, et al., 2015; Hughes, Harvey, et al., 2013; Jimenez, Browder, & Dibiase, 2012).

Help colleagues gather data, interpret it, and make data-based decisions. McLeskey, Waldron, and Redd reported a case study of a highly effective inclusive elementary school and noted the importance of the special education teacher in sharing effective practices with others in a school where "data drive everything" (2014, p. 67). A compelling quote from the school administrator illustrating the importance of teacher data collection follows: "How can I have conversations with teachers about their students, how they're progressing, how well they're teaching without individual data about students? So we had to come up with ways to monitor student data" (McLeskey et al., p. 67).

Aid in transition planning. The special education teacher with research skills also can be a valuable asset in summarizing data for other special education teachers and members of transition teams planning future environments for students with disabilities (Shaw, Dukes, & Madaus, 2012). This role is considered so important for special education teachers that the journal *Teaching Exceptional Children* (Mazzotti & Rowe, 2015) devoted an entire issue to transition planning, instruction, and assessment. (See Chapter 6 for more information on transition.)

Share new practices and ideas with colleagues. A special education teacher who has researched the effectiveness and efficiency of a procedure to meet the needs of students with disabilities and has confidence in the results can exercise leadership by sharing his or her research with others, even if the data only can support the procedure as a promising practice. Remember that an EBP is like a brick wall that becomes stronger as each new brick is laid. Although a single brick may indicate a promising practice, the accumulation of enough promising practices to build a wall provides the foundation for an EBP.

Contribute to the body of research within a given field. As will be discussed in more detail in Chapter 8, two options for sharing research with a broader audience are through professional presentations and publications. It is important to remember, however, that no specific student data can be shared in a presentation or publication without the permission of the involved students, parents, and others who oversee school research (e.g., school- and district-level administration, research review board). Without permission, you will need to provide information about procedures in general (e.g., how to use a specific procedure); even with permission, student identifying information must be kept confidential.

The sections that follow provide more information about how you can contribute to the body of research within a given field through professional presentations and publications.

Disseminating Research Through Presentations

Many professional organizations, such as CEC and TASH, welcome teacher presentations at their annual conferences and also hold conferences at the state or regional level. State educational agencies and even college and university departments of education also may hold conferences at which teachers are invited to share the practices they have found effective. Teachers who wish to share their work through a professional presentation may want to begin at a local conference, such as a conference conducted by a community organization in a specific disability area (e.g., ASD, Down syndrome) or by a local school district.

A good way to develop confidence in making professional presentations is to collaborate with other educators. Sometimes, several teachers may develop a collaborative conference presentation for which they each present a practice related to a specific topic (e.g., behavior management, peer tutoring, transition). If you have a good relationship with a professor from an institution of higher education, you may want to approach this person about working together on a presentation; most will be glad to do so.

The exact steps for preparing a professional presentation will vary, but generally include the following:

1. *Identify a conference related to the practice you would like to share.* Most organizations will have a web site that provides conference dates and a Call for Proposals.

2. *Identify a colleague who is interested in the topic and would like to be a co-presenter.* Presenting with others has the advantage of reducing the number of minutes you have to speak and engage an audience.

3. *Read the Call for Proposals (or other guidelines) carefully and follow the directions to complete the presentation forms.* Note whether there is a conference theme that should be addressed.

4. *Decide on a short, catchy title that will draw the attendees' attention.* What would draw your attention and convince you to attend a presentation?

5. *Submit the proposal and wait.*

6. *If accepted, begin to plan as soon as possible.* Check to see if there are any additional conference guidelines or technology requirements.

7. *Prepare a presentation that will be engaging, and plan, plan, plan.* If using a PowerPoint presentation, limit the amount of wording on each slide to brief points in a large, easy-to-read font. Make sure that colored text is clearly visible on the background color. If using a hands-on activity, make sure that you have enough materials for all present, time how long the activity will take, and be prepared to summarize what occurred during the activity. If you are providing a handout, make sure that you have enough for attendees. (More guidelines for making engaging presentations can be found in Chapter 4.)

8. *Once the presentation has been developed, practice it and time its length.* Remember to allot time for technological glitches and for questions and discussion from the participants.

9. *Arrive early at the conference.* That way, you will know where your presentation room is located and how the room is set up. You can begin to set up as soon as the previous speakers have finished.

10. *When it's time for your presentation, take a deep breath, smile, introduce the topic and speakers, and begin.* Talk to your audience as one colleague to another. Be aware of time constraints, allowing all speakers sufficient time to make their points and the audience sufficient time to ask questions or share comments. Leave the room promptly so the next speakers can set up.

Disseminating Research Through Publications

Professional publication is another way to disseminate classroom-based research. Although writing for a professional journal can be daunting, being published and recognized for hard work can be a gratifying experience. *Teaching Exceptional Children*, the CEC journal devoted to providing promising practices, research-based practices, and EBPs for practitioners, is one example of a journal that welcomes submissions from special education teacher researchers. In 2013, Ludlow and Dieker provided guidelines for practitioners who are interested in sharing practices with other classroom teachers. Although their specific guidelines were created with *Teaching Exceptional Children* in mind, the general principles they recommend are relevant for any beginning writer planning his or her first submission to a professional journal. Ludlow and Dieker recommend following these steps:

1. Identify and share an EBP that the writer has used with success.

2. Review the journal's submission guidelines (often available online) and read through teacher-authored articles it has previously published with an eye toward finding one that can serve as a model.

3. Outline the article and then write a first draft with examples of how to use the EBP, as well as any needed tables, figures, or sample forms.

4. Create a polished final draft with careful proofreading and attention to spelling, grammar, and conventions of style and format.

5. Submit the article and allow time for editors to review the manuscript and to make a decision on publication. The editors may decide to accept the article for publication, ask the author to revise and resubmit it, or decide not to publish it.

If you are a reluctant writer, it may be wise to invite someone else, such as another special or general education teacher or a university mentor, to be a coauthor. Recognize that what you have to share is important and that publication is one way to share what you have learned and found from experience to be effective.

A final note on formatting: Journals in education and related social sciences often use APA format, guidelines for which are published by the American Psychological Association. However, various publishers and academic societies may also have their own specific guidelines or use another widely known format such as Chicago style. It's always crucial to review the submission guidelines a particular organization or publisher provides.

Later chapters in this book will cover other ways in which special education teacher researchers can share what they have learned with others, including ways to mentor (Chapter 3) or provide consultations, professional development, and in-service supports (Chapter 4).

Voice of a Leader

Leading Through Classroom-Based Research

Carey Creech-Galloway sums up how being part of a research community and sharing her findings has helped her to become a better teacher—and a leader.

Q: *What do you think are the benefits of being involved in research as a teacher? How can teachers who are not involved in formal research investigations still use data to determine appropriate practices in both special and general education classroom settings?*

A: First, you need those individuals [researchers] in your classroom keeping you on your toes and also for support. Any time I was asked to do research, I did it because it was invaluable experience that guides your teaching practices, gives you a professional community to use as a resource, and keeps you implementing the evidence-based practices you should as a special education teacher . . . a fidelity check of your teaching practices, if you will. As a teacher, it is important to continue to look at the professional journals for guidance, ideas, and practical application of skills. Sometimes, teachers get in a rut, or they are looking at the daunting core content and thinking, "How do I begin to break this down?" If I had not participated in research and MADE myself stay true to the use of systematic instruction, then I would not have been able to balance as a teacher the instruction on both the functional and the academic content for our students. This to me is the number 1 frustration of all in our profession . . . finding a way to teach what [our students] need to know and what is functional while still providing access to the core content in a meaningful way.

Q: *How did your skills in data-based decision making transform you into a teacher leader? What is your current position and how do you continue to use data to drive the decisions that you make?*

A: It allowed me to help team members make decisions, and it allowed me to spread the systematic instruction love [smiles]. I've taught more teachers response-prompting strategies than I can begin to count. When they see it works and it is just good teaching, then the data-based decision making comes much easier. A lot of times when I see a teacher with a lot of work samples, they are teaching daily but recording nothing. In my experience, when the teacher sees how powerful the data collection can be, they are usually quick to buy in to collecting such systematic formative data.

I collect data on all of our classrooms. I keep track of student performance on alternate assessment, and I try to look at that data along with student progress data from the teacher to see which teachers have the best results. Why? Which methods do they use? Do they use a lot of technology? Is their adult-to-student ratio low or high? The data collection system I described in a previous question is a district norm now. I have tried to use those teacher behaviors that were successful for my students and me when I was in the classroom and make those the focus for our professional learning community. The first question I ask when I am working with a team is, "What are the data telling us?"

BE A LEADER: BECOME A DATA-BASED DECISION MAKER

Benedict, Brownell, Park, Bettini, and Lauterback (2014) stated that it is the responsibility of teachers to cultivate their own expertise because they may not have access to appropriate professional development or have been provided guidelines on how this can be accomplished. The authors suggested that special education teachers analyze their own teaching, the feedback they get from their students, the knowledge they have in the subject matter they are required to teach, and the feedback they get from evaluations conducted by administrators. Benedict and colleagues recommend additional tips for what teachers can do once this analysis is complete:

- Become consumers of research

- Use strategies until a level of comfort is achieved

- Practice new strategies to a desired level of fluency and comfort before using them with students

- Problem-solve based on the analysis of student data

- Spend time reflecting on the effectiveness and efficiency of instruction

These are sound tips that align with the information offered in this chapter.

The heart and core of this text is the premise that special education teachers should become data-based researchers in their classrooms and that, as the interview with Carey Creech-Galloway illustrates, they *can* do this and can do it well. Becoming skilled as both a consumer of published research and a conductor of classroom-based research builds your credibility as a leader. When a special education teacher leader who is grounded in research and knowledge of EBPs shares expertise, others listen, practices improve, and desired student outcomes are more likely to be achieved. The following guidelines are offered to help you build your expertise as a data-based decision maker:

1. Practice formative data collection techniques to a level of fluency, and share these with others who work with the students you teach.

2. Search the professional literature for studies that conclude that a practice is evidence-based. When collecting formative data, remember that all EBPs do not work with all students, and make data-based decisions with this is mind.

3. When more than one EBP can be identified, analyze data to determine which procedure is more effective or efficient.

4. When using research-based practices that have not been established as EBPs or when using promising practices, collect formative data and consider the use of a single-case research design to document effectiveness.

5. Realize that it is your responsibility as a leader to share effective practices with others, whether this is through working with instructional personnel within the school or sharing with a larger professional community.

FOLLOW-UP ACTIVITIES

Throughout Chapter 1, you've learned about classroom research and data-based decision making as one path to leadership. For many special education teachers, this path is where they begin to discover their own potential as leaders.

Now it's time to take action. The activities below are designed to help you take the first steps toward becoming a data-based decision maker who consumes research, conducts classroom research, uses research to become a more effective teacher, and shares findings with a broader educational community.

1. **Review current research on a topic that interests you.** Visit a library and thumb through the issues of a special education journal, or download examples of refereed journals from reputable web sites. Examples of journals that provide studies on the effectiveness of special education interventions can be found on the web sites of professional organizations, such as CEC and its divisions or TASH. When you find a research article focused on an intervention that interests you, stop and ask yourself 1) what information the title and abstract provide, 2) who the participants in the study (e.g., age, gender, disability) were, 3) under what circumstances the study was conducted (e.g., special or general education classroom, clinical setting), 4) whether the descriptions of the data collection and intervention procedures are specific enough for a classroom teacher to replicate, and 5) what the results were. Is this a study that convinces you to try this procedure in your own classroom? Why or why not?

2. **Reflect on your own classroom data-collection practices.** If you are a special education teacher, reflect on the type of data you collect and how often you do this. Think of times when the data have caused you to make a change in your instruction or your behavior management strategies. Are the data you collect clear enough or displayed in such a way for progress (or lack of progress) to be easily explained to the student, parents, or others? If you do not currently have a classroom, interview another special education teacher about his or her data-collection practices instead.

3. **Reflect on the last professional presentation you attended on an educational practice.** Was the speaker convincing enough to persuade you to try an instructional or behavior management strategy? Why or why not? What did you like or dislike about the mode of presentation?

2

Effect Schoolwide Change

Learning Objectives

After reading this chapter, readers will be able to

- Identify ways in which special education teachers can serve as leaders at the schoolwide level

- Describe and apply strategies for facilitating inclusive school environments

- List and describe models of co-teaching and the steps effective co-teachers should follow

- Identify supports for students with disabilities in natural environments

- Explain ways in which special education teacher leaders can contribute to schoolwide systems of support and put these into practice

Terms to Know

Alternative teaching

Coaching

Collaboration

Co-teaching

Inclusion

Natural supports

Parallel teaching

Primary support

Response to intervention

Schoolwide positive behavior support systems

Secondary support

Service learning

Station teaching

Team teaching

Tertiary support

INTRODUCTION

Chapter 1 described how all special education teachers can begin to become leaders by thoughtfully choosing the practices they use in their classrooms. They should have inquisitive minds that lead them to

- Search for EBPs in the professional literature
- Adapt those practices in working with students with disabilities
- Assess the effectiveness, efficiency, and reliability of their instruction
- Share the results of the practices they have researched in their classrooms with others

By consciously applying this process as a special education teacher, you can build a strong foundation for leadership. Becoming a data-based decision maker in your classroom will increase your confidence, knowledge base, and sense of self-efficacy—important qualities for any educational leader to have. The next step is to extend your leadership skills through schoolwide involvement. Special education teachers have the opportunity to do this when they work in inclusive environments, collaborating with general education teachers and others in the school setting. For example, your involvement can take the form of supporting or providing direct instruction for students with disabilities in inclusive settings, collaborating and engaging in co-teaching with general educators, and preparing paraprofessionals and peers to support students with disabilities. As a special education teacher, you also have the opportunity to work with many school staff across multiple settings in implementing schoolwide levels of support for all students, not just for students with disabilities. Special education teachers can be valuable members of school teams because they have a strong foundation in differentiated instructional strategies; behavior management; physical management; and collaboration with paraprofessionals, peers, and related staff.

As will be discussed further in Chapter 7, special education teachers should be advocates for students with disabilities throughout the school setting. To be an advocate, you need the skills to develop collegial relationships and communicate with colleagues (Whitby, Marx, McIntire, & Weinke, 2013). This chapter provides information on how to be an effective leader at the schoolwide level.

CONNECTION TO PROFESSIONAL STANDARDS

The teacher's role at the schoolwide level is supported by a number of professional standards listed under the Teacher Leader Model Standards (TLEC, 2012) and the

CEC Standards for Professional Practice and Advanced Preparation Standards (CEC, 2015).

Teacher Leader Model Standards

While not specific to special education, the Teacher Leader Model Standards (TLEC, 2012) list several standards under *Domain 1: Fostering a Collaborative Culture to Support Educator Development and Student Learning* that support teachers having the skills to work collaboratively with others. These include

- "Helping colleagues work collaboratively to solve problems, make decisions, manage conflict, and promote meaningful change"

- "Model[ing] effective skills" in working with others

- Facilitating trust among colleagues

- Working to "create an inclusive culture"

- "Promot[ing] effective interactions among colleagues" across diverse backgrounds

Collaboration is also apparent in standards under *Domain 4: Facilitating Improvements in Instruction and Student Learning,* which call upon the teacher to "serve as a team leader" in working with colleagues to "meet student learning needs" and under *Domain 5: Promoting the Use of Assessments and Data for School and District Improvement,* which address working with colleagues to design assessments and analyze data.

Council for Exceptional Children Program Standards

The Standards for Professional Practice developed by CEC (2015) state that teachers should be professional colleagues (4.0) who recognize and respect the expertise of their professional colleagues (4.1), strive to have positive and respectful attitudes toward colleagues (4.2), and collaborate with general and special education colleagues to improve services (4.4). The CEC Special Education Advanced Preparation Standards also focus on collaboration in Standard 5 (Leadership and Policy) by stating that teachers should be able to create and maintain a collegial and productive work environment (5.3) and advocate for policies to improve programs (5.4). In addition, Standard 7 (Collaboration) states that special educators should enhance collaboration by using culturally responsive practices (7.1) and use collaborative skills to improve (7.2) and promote consensus across (7.3) programs, services, and learning outcomes.

Sara Stout Heinrich is an example of a special education teacher leader with skills to effect schoolwide change. She began this process as a classroom teacher by working for inclusion of the students that were on her caseload, and she now works with other teachers in a large urban school district to do the same. Recently she completed a research study on including students with disabilities in core content classes that was published in a refereed journal (Heinrich, Collins, Knight, & Spriggs, 2016). (The full text of the interview is available in the downloadable materials for this book.)

Voice of a Leader

Working Toward Full Inclusion

Sara Stout Heinrich is in her 8th year working as a special education teacher. She spent her first 5 years as a high school teacher for students with moderate and severe disabilities; currently she is in her 3rd year as a Low Incidence Resource Teacher for her district. In this role she provides programming support to students from preschool through high school who have been labeled with a low incidence disability. This support includes behavioral support, academic support, IEP development and implementation, attending ARC (admission and release committee) meetings, assisting with classroom set-up, scheduling for students and staff, assisting in determining the least restrictive environment for students, preparing and presenting professional development, and more. Here, Ms. Heinrich describes how she has worked toward fostering full inclusion and effecting schoolwide change throughout her career.

Q: *Special education teachers can be an influence on the schools in which they work. How have you worked to make changes in schools? Who have you worked with?*

A: When I taught in a high school classroom, I worked really hard to make my students a more integral part of the school. Before I came, my students were never included in general education classrooms. This was really important for me because I knew how much my students would benefit from interactions with their nondisabled peers, as well as having access to the content presented in those classes. I worked with my counselor, as well as the regular education teachers, in order to have my students participating more in the general education classrooms. By the end of my 5 years there, I had several students that spent more than 40% of their day in the regular classroom environment. This was achieved through a great deal of collaboration between the general education teacher and me, as well as training for my staff and peer tutors that accompanied the students to class.

Q: *What benefits have you found that collaboration with general education teachers has provided for the students with disabilities with whom you work?*

A: By collaborating with the general education teachers, I was able to make them more informed on various disabilities and learning styles. They became more open to having my students in their classes and would actually seek me out to include my students. I also felt that I gained a better knowledge of the core content material, allowing me to better instruct my students in it. My students also became more socially accepted by their nondisabled peers, as they were around them more.

YOUR ROLE AT THE SCHOOLWIDE LEVEL

As a special education teacher, you can have a role in creating an inclusive learning environment for all students through involvement in schoolwide systems of support. The following sections discuss how to achieve this.

Inclusion

Inclusion is defined as all students with disabilities being educated with their same-age peers without disabilities. Inclusion consists of more than physical placement in a general education setting. To be included, a student must be considered an integral part of the general education setting. Available research literature is full of reasons that students with disabilities should be included in classes with same-age peers without disabilities. In brief, inclusion benefits students by preparing them for a postschool transition to a life where they live and work in a community of people with and without disabilities. The idea is that friendships made in school will carry over outside of the school environment and to future environments, that students with disabilities will have role models (e.g., for social behavior, communication) who can support in both school and non-school environments, and that students with disabilities will have access to and participate in age-appropriate activities with same-age peers, which includes having access to the general curriculum taught to peers without disabilities (Westling et al., 2015). Studies have shown that students with disabilities who are in inclusive school settings can acquire academic content taught to their same-age peers without disabilities (e.g., Heinrich et al., 2016; Tekin-Iftar, Collins, Spooner, & Olcay-Gul, 2017).

However, despite these benefits of inclusion for all students, it is not the practice across all schools. While data reported from 1990–1991 through 2007–2008 found an increase in general education placements for students with disabilities, the degree of inclusion was related to the type of disability. Students with learning disabilities were included the most, whereas students with emotional and behavioral disorders and students with IDs were included the least (McLeskey, Landers, Williamson, & Hoppey, 2012). In addition, Ryndak et al. (2014) reported that, although there has been an increase in access to the general curriculum for students with severe disabilities, this has not resulted in more general education placements. Specifically, Kleinert et al. (2015) reported that, across a sample of 15 states, only 7% of students with significant IDs were served in regular education (3%) or resource room (4%) placements. Also, there is evidence that students with developmental disabilities in urban or suburban areas spend more time in segregated placements than their rural counterparts (Brock & Schaefer, 2015); the larger the school or the district, the less likely that inclusion is implemented.

In some studies, the school principal has been credited as being the driving force behind the successful implementation of inclusion within a school (Kozleski, Yu, Satter, Francis, & Haines, 2015). However, the principal cannot do this alone; teachers must be willing to work with the principal and have a similar philosophy to create a truly inclusive school culture. A principal in a case study of an effective inclusive school stated that he relied on "everyone on the faculty to be a leader as all have talents or something to offer to the school" (Hoppey & McLeskey, 2013, p. 253); in addition, the principal stated that "the leader's job is not to develop followers, but more leaders" (p. 253). In this case study, the school evolved to become a model wherein all teachers were responsible for creating and sustaining a collaborative school culture. In a second case study (McLeskey et al., 2014), a principal closed all special education classes, assigning special education teachers and paraprofessionals to work collaboratively with general education teachers in their classrooms. This principal stated a belief "in creating experts in your building and encouraging them to coach others. It's the same way with inclusion, if we've got some people who are leaders, they can share [effective practices] with other people" (McLeskey et al.,

What is your reaction to the idea that all teachers should be leaders or to the idea that leaders train leaders? Is there a point at which the line between special and general education begins to blur? If so, what is your reaction to this?

2014, p. 65). In a study of six inclusive schools, Shogren, McCart, Lyon, and Sailor (2015) found that special education teachers in segregated settings had become co-teachers in inclusive settings. While the principals of these schools exercised strong leadership, they also encouraged teachers to be leaders in the transformation: "Interventionists [special education teachers] are connected with grade level teams and their schedules allow them to be at planning times with [general educators] and help facilitate collaboration and planning" (Shogren, McCart et al., 2015, p. 183). They also noted that a school "leader must train and support a cadre of leaders who believe in inclusion" (p. 188).

Recall that, for students with disabilities to be truly included in the same environment as their peers, they must be an integral part of this environment—not just physically present, but fully present and involved. Successful implementation of this goal relies on successful collaboration between special and general education teachers (Watt, Therrien, Kaldenberg, & Taylor, 2013), wherein all teachers share the responsibility for all students. Friend and Cook (1992) defined **collaboration** as "a style of direct interaction between at least two co-equal parties voluntarily engaged in shared decision making as they work toward a common goal" (p. 5). Collaboration can include "co-teaching, peer coaching, collaborative consultation, and collaborative problem-solving" (Lingo, Barton-Arwood, & Jolivette, 2011, p. 6).

What has been your experience with inclusion? Have you observed or been a participant in a model that includes all students in all classroom activities? What has worked well and not so well?

One barrier to inclusion is that general educators may not feel prepared to serve students with disabilities (Able, Sreckovic, Schultz, Garwood, & Sherman, 2015; Klein & Hollingshead, 2015); yet the professional literature has numerous examples of effective inclusive programs. For example, Spaulding and Flanagan (2013), a general education teacher and a special education teacher, described their framework for conducting effective science instruction for students with and without disabilities through Project DIS$_2$ECT: 1) *design* (backwards) by getting to know all learners, 2) address *individualization* during planning, 3) use *scaffolding* to provide the level of needed support for students, 4) use effective teaching *strategies*, 5) engage students through *experiential learning*, 6) use *cooperative learning* groups so students can learn together, and 7) implement inclusive instruction using *teamwork*. In another example for science instruction, Rye et al. (2013) created an inclusive elementary program by having students learn together in a school garden. The following section offers strategies for special education teachers working to create more inclusive schoolwide environments.

Strategies for Creating Inclusive Environments

It bears repeating that simply placing students with disabilities in general education classrooms physically does not guarantee inclusion. A scenario in which a special education teacher or paraprofessional sits in the back of a general education classroom and provides individual instruction for a student with a disability, without that students being involved in whole-classroom instruction or with peers without disabilities, is not an example of inclusion. To be included, a student with a disability must be considered part of ongoing instruction delivered to all students in the classroom and must be engaged with same-age peers without disabilities. You can use the following strategies, discussed in the next sections, to facilitate an appropriate model of inclusion: find time to plan, model effective practices, use coaching, collaborate across shared personnel, practice co-teaching and co-assessing, and facilitate inclusion across school environments.

Find Time to Plan   The first strategy for creating an inclusive school environment is to ensure that teachers find time to plan together. In describing their effective framework for inclusive science instruction, Spaulding and Flanagan stated that inclusion "involves intentional planning to meet the varied and individualized needs of each student in the classroom" (2013, p. 14) and that "administrative support for inclusion is integral" (2013, p. 14). They noted that special education and general education teachers must have time allotted for planning and analyzing data together. This means that they need coordinated schedules. As a special education teacher, you can make an appointment with the school principal or other administrator to garner support for inclusion and create an overall matrix wherein schedules can be coordinated to allow for adequate planning time.

Model Effective Practices   The second strategy is to provide a way for general educators to feel more comfortable with including and providing instruction for all students; thus, you can and should be a model for working with students with disabilities within the general education setting. Unlike using a pull-out model to deliver individualized services, embedding services within the general education classroom allows general educators the opportunity to observe how to implement interventions or to benefit from the support or advice a special educator can provide (Able et al., 2015). For example, a review of the professional literature by Hudson, Browder, and Wood (2013) found that the constant time delay procedure, an EBP for teaching students with disabilities, has been effective in teaching academic content to students with moderate to severe IDs in inclusive settings; however, the constant time delay procedure may not be familiar to general educators, so it is beneficial to model it for them.

Use Coaching   As will be described in more detail in Chapters 3 and 4, you may need to go beyond sharing knowledge and modeling procedures to using a third strategy: coaching (Shogren, McCart, et al., 2015). **Coaching** allows you to provide support and feedback to general education teachers who work directly with students with disabilities. For example, Able and colleagues stated that general education teachers may find "suggestions from a skilled special education professional who understands autism [are] so important while he or she is working in the classroom with the target student" (2015, p. 51). It should be noted that you will also benefit from learning the strategies that general education teachers use to teach content. Scheeler, Congdon, and Stansberry (2010) found that when special and general education teachers provided coaching to each other via bug-in-the-ear technology (i.e., technology that allows one-way or two-way communication by wearing an electronic device [Bluetooth] in the ear), the practices they acquired increased, maintained, and generalized.

Collaborate Across School Personnel A fourth strategy for facilitating inclusion is to address it across all school personnel, not just those involved in delivering academic content. In addition to general education teachers, this may include collaboration with "therapists, nurses, social workers, psychologists and counselors, and rehabilitation specialists" (Ludlow, 2011, p. 4). For example, you may need to collaborate with school counselors and school psychologists in working with students with ASD (Able et al., 2015). Physical education teachers may benefit from information you can provide regarding medical and health information, safety, the role of paraprofessionals, IEP goals and objectives, modifications, and physical needs (Klein & Hollingshead, 2015).

Practice Co-Teaching and Co-Assessing A fifth strategy that has gained a lot of attention in recent years is **co-teaching** (e.g., Moorehead & Grillo, 2013; Morningstar, Shogren, Lee, & Born, 2015; Shogren, McCart, et al.; 2015). Co-teaching is a specific form of collaboration in which both the special education and general education teacher have an "active role in planning, delivering, and assessing instruction" (Fenty, McDuffie-Landrum, & Fisher, 2013, p. 29). According to Murawski, "the premise of co-teaching rests on the shared expertise that special educator and classroom teacher collaboration brings to the instruction, not merely on having two adults in the classroom" (2012, p. 8). Sileo noted that general education teachers may be considered "masters of content" whereas special education teachers may be considered "masters of access" (2011, p. 34), making the co-teaching model one in which each co-teacher has specific roles and areas of expertise. Sileo also compared the co-teaching relationship to dating and marriage, because teachers may need time to get to know each other and work out philosophical differences before embarking on a permanent relationship. Sileo suggested that co-teachers identify issues, develop alternative courses of actions, analyze associated risks and benefits before determining a course of action, and then analyze the results of the action once it has been implemented.

There are several models for engaging in co-teaching (Murawski, 2012; Spaulding & Flanagan, 2013). Murawski lists team teaching, parallel teaching, alternative teaching, and station teaching. These models can be described as follows:

- **Team teaching**—the general and special education teachers deliver content together

- **Parallel teaching**—the two teachers deliver content at the same time to two groups of students within the classroom

- **Alternative teaching**—one teacher leads a lesson while the other focuses on specific components of the lesson (e.g., vocabulary)

- **Station teaching**—both teachers develop and circulate among learning centers to provide support and facilitate learning

The type of co-teaching model selected may depend on the type of content being delivered. For example, station teaching may be the most effective model for co-teaching science and mathematics (Moorehead & Grillo, 2013) because it allows the opportunity for hands-on learning activities in which students can engage individually or in cooperative groups.

Murawski (2012) provided tips for co-teachers who are engaged in planning co-taught lessons. These include

- Establishing a regular planning time without disruptions

- Staying on topic using a premade agenda

- Determining individual roles and assignments that are equal but separate

- Maintaining a list of concerns

- Building time for assessment and feedback

- Using a what/how/who framework (i.e., *What* standards, objective, and ideas/questions will be addressed within a specific timeframe? *How* will co-teaching occur? *Who* will need individualized supports?)

Those teachers who engage in co-teaching also should remember that co-assessing is part of the process. Conderman and Hedin (2012) noted that co-teachers should discuss their assessment philosophies when they first begin working together and should continue to co-assess prior to instruction (e.g., prerequisite data), during instruction (formative data), and following instruction (summative data).

Voice of a Leader

Collaborating With General Education Teachers

Co-teaching and collaboration present new challenges but can be rewarding for everyone involved. Sara Stout Heinrich describes her own experiences collaborating with general education teachers.

Q: *You completed a research study in collaboration with general education teachers in a high school. Can you tell how you worked with these teachers? What kinds of supports did you facilitate for the students who were included in their classrooms?*

A: I met with each teacher prior to mainstreaming my students to their classes. We discussed their curriculum maps for the semester and how they corresponded to the alternate assessment standards for the students I wanted to include. I explained to the teachers that I would adapt all of the student work and that I would be sending a trained instructional assistant or peer tutor with the student. Each student who was included had a folder to take with them to the class. The folder included any adapted materials for classroom assignments that day, data sheets, and materials needed to instruct the student on two predetermined alternate assessment standards. I provided training for the instructional assistants and peer tutors on simultaneous prompting (the procedure they would be using to teach the alternate assessment standards). I also collected procedural fidelity data at least once per week on each assistant and peer tutor.

⟵——⟶

Facilitate Inclusion Across School Environments   The final strategy for facilitating inclusion is to remember that the school environment consists of more than classrooms. It is important that students with disabilities be included in the same types of activities in which their peers without disabilities engage. Traditionally, paraprofessionals have provided the primary support for students across school environments, but recent research has shown that this can have the unwanted side effect of less direct instruction from the general education teacher, physical separation within the classroom or school setting, and less interactions with peers without disabilities (Carter, Moss, et al., 2015). Robinson (2011) was successful in decreasing the "hovering" and uninvolved behavior of paraprofessionals by training them with a video package on how to use a pivotal response strategy with students with ASD, but research has consistently shown that peers without disabilities also can be trained to implement effective strategies with the added benefit of forming friendships (e.g., Collins, Branson, Hall, & Rankin, 2001). As illustrated in the following sections, the involvement of peers without disabilities across school environments can be beneficial for all students, allowing a less direct role for paraprofessionals in inclusive environments.

Provide Appropriate Supports   As a special education teacher, you likely often have the responsibility of identifying appropriate supports for students who are in inclusive environments. Some supports may be added by the teacher, such as visual aids (e.g., iPad) or auditory aids (e.g., iPod) that provide directions and prompts. For example, special education teachers who assist students with disabilities in designing daily schedules may note that transitions need attention. Leadership can include facilitating smooth transitions between classes and activities by identifying transitions that may be challenging, selecting supports (e.g., auditory, visual) to enable students with disabilities to negotiate those transitions, and collecting data to use in determining if the selected supports are effective (Hume, Sreckovic, Snyder, & Carnahan, 2014).

> What is the role of a paraprofessional in an inclusive school environment? What are the benefits of paraprofessional classroom support? What are the possible unintended barriers that can be created?

Supports may include **natural supports,** which are those that can be found in the natural environment for a student with a disability without being added. This can take the form of materials or people already present within the environment. Peers without disabilities can serve an important role as natural supports as all students learn together. To facilitate peer involvement, Carter, Moss, et al. (2015) recommended that the special education teacher work with the IEP team to develop a peer support plan and identify and meet with potential peer partners. Once peer partners are selected, the role and physical proximity of special education teachers and paraprofessionals can be systematically faded while they continue to monitor the peers, making adjustments as needed.

Engage Students in Activities Outside of the Traditional Classroom   One activity in which all students engage in the school setting is lunchtime, which is an ideal time to facilitate both communication and social interactions between students with and without disabilities. Hochman, Carter, Bottema-Ceite, Harvey, and Gustafson (2015) found that they could facilitate social interactions with students with ASD in a secondary school by recruiting and orienting peers without disabilities to be involved in a peer network during lunchtime. Special education teachers can develop a formal peer network for students with disabilities by offering academic credit for participating or by recruiting volunteers who are willing or who need to engage in service activities as part of an extracurricular club. During lunch (or other activities), peers can be assigned to support specific students or may rotate on a daily basis. Communication books used by peers without disabilities have been effective in increasing conversations between students with ASD or IDs and their peers without disabilities (Hughes, Bernstein, et al., 2013; Hughes et al., 2011) and can be easily used within a lunchtime setting as well as in other environments. Communication books may exist in hard copy or be available through technology (e.g., on an iPad) and can consist of words, symbols, or pictures that can be used as an impetus for having a conversation (e.g., school sports) or as a support in conversational turn-taking (e.g., prewritten or preprogrammed responses).

Another way to facilitate peer interactions across community environments is to involve students with and without disabilities in service learning (Carter, Swedeen, & Moss, 2012). Service learning can be a part of both academic and elective classes as well as a part of extracurricular clubs (Carter, Swedeen, & Moss, 2012). It is a strategy that allows instructional objectives to be addressed while students engage in community projects. This is especially valuable to students with disabilities, for several reasons. First, both functional (e.g., life skill) and academic objectives can be embedded in these projects. Second, students with disabilities are more likely to generalize skills when they are taught in settings where these skills will be needed. Third, students with and without disabilities may be more likely to form relationships when involved in fun activities. As a special education teacher, you can provide general education teachers with input on this type of learning as you plan together.

Elective classes and extracurricular activities provide still more opportunities for same-age peers with and without disabilities to interact. Even if students with disabilities are not included in academic classes, they often are included in elective classes. For example, Hughes, Harvey, et al. (2013) taught secondary peers without disabilities to interact with their peers with disabilities across elective classes that included guitar, art, and physical education.

In what way(s) can peers without disabilities serve a role in an inclusive environment? Are there ways to provide specific training or materials that might increase the effectiveness of the role they play?

Pence and Dymond (2015) noted that, due to challenges in communication and social skills, lack of support outside of the classroom, and lack of parent and teacher involvement, students with severe disabilities may have low levels of participation in extracurricular activities. Yet extracurricular activities, such as service learning, provide the opportunity for embedded learning in natural settings that may generalize to other settings. You can provide leadership in facilitating the inclusion of students with disabilities in extracurricular activities in several ways: by conducting an assessment of student interests and needs, by investigating and selecting appropriate extracurricular activities, and by collaborating to ensure that students receive the appropriate natural supports to participate. Once students with disabilities become involved, IEP objectives can be embedded in extracurricular activities (e.g., using a calculator during a bake sale).

Schoolwide Systems of Support

In addition to sharing your knowledge and skills to create inclusive school environments for all children, you and other special education teachers have the knowledge and skills to be valuable contributors to establishing other schoolwide initiatives. For example, **response to intervention** (RTI) is a general education initiative to provide specialized intervention for students at risk of being identified for special education services (Heward, 2013). While these students have yet to be identified for services from a special education teacher, the special education teacher can nonetheless be a valuable resource for sharing instructional and behavior management strategies that may be effective in a general education setting. The following sections list schoolwide initiatives in which you can play an important role.

Positive Behavior Support Systems Shogren, McCart, et al. (2015) found that a sample of effective inclusive schools also had an emphasis on multi-tiered systems of support (MTSS) and positive behavior interventions and supports (PBIS). Schools that use MTSS provide a wide tier of support for all students (e.g., stated expectations and consequences for all students within a given classroom), a small tier of support for specific groups of students (e.g., moderate interventions for students with behavior disorders), and individual supports for specific students, as needed (e.g., intense intervention to manage the most challenging behaviors). PBIS is a system that focuses on using positive proactive procedures that may decrease the likelihood that an inappropriate behavior will occur (Leach, 2010). In general, **schoolwide positive behavior support systems** (SWPBSs) provide a "proactive, system-level approach that provides tools and practices to help support students and staff and promote positive social and learning environments" (Good, McIntoch, & Gietz, 2012, p. 50). SWPBSs consist of three levels of support (Swain-Bradway, Pinkney, & Flannery, 2015):

> How involved should a special education teacher be in the implementation of initiatives such as RTI or PBIS? How involved should a special education teacher be in providing instruction or support to all students, regardless of ability? Why?

- **Primary support** for 80%–90% of the school population

- **Secondary support** for 10%–13% of the school population

- **Tertiary support** for 1%–5% of the school population

In other words, most students in a school can benefit from a basic support system, but a small percentage will need more intense, graduated levels of support.

Again, these are systems in which special education teachers can exercise leadership. Due to their background in behavior management, special education teachers can play a valuable role on school teams. For example, special education teachers have received training in how to assess the function of a behavior, how to identify appropriate reinforcers for behaviors, and how to implement strategies to increase or decrease behaviors. Thus, special education teachers can provide professional development, consultations, or coaching in addition to serving as members of school teams. It may take from 2 to 4 years to establish an SWPBS, and staff buy-in is crucial to sustained implementation (McIntosh et al., 2013).

Anti-Bullying Programs   In recent years, a good deal of attention has been devoted to establishing schoolwide programs focused on bullying. A schoolwide program to address bullying can be integrated into an SWPBS. For example, Good et al. described the Bully Prevention in Positive Behavior Support program, which was designed to 1) decrease bullying incidents and 2) teach potential victims how to respond to bullies using a "Stop, Walk, and Talk" strategy in which they are "to stop what they are doing, take a deep breath, count to three, and then go on with their day" in response to a stop signal (2012, p. 51) and, if necessary, seek assistance from an adult. Good et al. stated that "because of their specialized training and collaboration across the school faculty, special educators are in a strong position to guide SWPBS and bullying prevention efforts" (2012, p. 53).

In addition, it is important to note that data have shown that "children with disabilities are harassed by peers at higher rates than their peers without disabilities" (Raskauskas & Modell, 2012, p. 60). Special education teachers may be called on to show leadership in modifying schoolwide bullying programs for students with disabilities, especially those with moderate to severe ID (Raskauskas & Modell) or ASD (Chen & Schwartz, 2012). This may include adapting and individualizing materials to provide concrete examples for students with disabilities that they can comprehend, and then intentionally and systematically increasing their ability to respond to bullies in an appropriate way.

Voice of a Leader

Leading at the Schoolwide Level

Creating a truly inclusive environment for all students involves addressing every aspect of school life—not just academic classes but also elective classes, extracurricular activities, service learning, and day-to-day social interaction. Each of these areas provides opportunities for students with disabilities to connect to same-age peers who do not have disabilities. Each area also provides special education teachers with an opportunity to lead. Here, Sara Stout Heinrich discusses how working to effect schoolwide change helped her become a leader.

Q: *How did the collaboration you had within your school transform you into a teacher leader? What is your current position and how do you continue to work to influence positive schoolwide changes for students with disabilities?*

A: The collaboration within my school allowed the other teachers to see what I do every day and value my knowledge on disabilities and different learning styles. The summer following the end of my study, I was offered a position working as a low-incidence resource teacher for the entire district, providing programming support for students with moderate and severe disabilities enrolled in Jefferson County Public Schools. The first ARC [admission and release committee] meeting that I attended for a high school student in my new position gave me the opportunity to teach the school about inclusion of their students with moderate and severe disabilities. The school did not practice inclusion of students with disabilities at that time, other than for electives. I talked with the counselor and special education teachers about ways that I included my students into core content classes. They were resistant at first, but now inclusion is a regular part of their programming. I have been given the opportunity to provide professional development to staff across the district to support programming for our students with moderate and severe disabilities.

BE A LEADER: EFFECT SCHOOLWIDE CHANGE

There is much you can do as a special education teacher to effect schoolwide change and help to create a truly inclusive environment that benefits all students. You likely have experience and expertise in multiple areas: making academic content accessible, teaching nonacademic skills, managing behavior, fostering positive social interactions, collecting and analyzing academic and behavioral data, and more. This experience and expertise can be immensely helpful to other teachers, administrators, and support staff. The following guidelines are offered to special education teachers who want to expand their leadership skills at the schoolwide level:

1. Do not be shy in approaching school administrators or other school personnel to offer to share your expertise as a special educator.

2. Realize that planning with others is crucial to effective collaboration, and build time for this into your daily schedule.

3. Remember that assessment and data analysis are not only integral to effective classroom instruction but also to successful programming at the schoolwide level, and a special education teacher has the skills to assist with schoolwide data analysis and decision making across both behavioral and academic strategies.

4. Consider the role that peers without disabilities can play as natural supports in successful inclusion.

5. Note that schoolwide intervention is more than working with academic classes and should extend to elective classes, extracurricular activities, and free time (e.g., lunch, transitions).

6. Be open in discussing philosophical differences with others and recognize that all involved personnel have a valuable role to contribute.

FOLLOW-UP ACTIVITIES

In Chapter 2, you have learned about ways to be a leader outside of the boundaries of your own classroom. Special education teachers can be an invaluable resource to general education teachers, administrators, and students with and without disabilities. The connections you make with others and the guidance you provide can effect schoolwide changes and help to build a truly inclusive environment for all.

The suggested activities that follow are intended to help you build connections with other schools and with families and begin thinking about how to extend your leadership beyond the classroom. Time to take action!

1. **Explore inclusion in another school.** Either visit a school known to be fully inclusive or interview personnel who work in that school. How does the model differ from traditional models of service in the past? Do you note practices that could be improved or practices that should be changed? Note whether students with the most significant IDs, the most challenging behaviors, or the most intense health-related or physical needs are included and to what extent.

2. **Interview families of students in different phases of schooling.** First, interview the parent of a young child with disabilities about his or her attitude toward inclusion and the expectations of schools. Then, interview the parent of an older student with disabilities who is nearing transition from school about his or her attitude toward inclusion and experiences in schools. Are there notable differences in the two interviews? If so, how do they differ and to what do you attribute the difference?

3. **Explore SWPBS in another school.** Either visit a school that is known to have an SWPBS or interview personnel who work in that school. What do you note about the school atmosphere or the attitudes of personnel and students? Find out what role the special educators in the school have played in the development of the model or what roles they currently play. How are the roles of special educators perceived?

4. **Research anti-bullying programs.** Do an Internet search for incidents of school bullying and programs that address school bullying. Note whether you find any references to students with disabilities. If you do, are the students with disabilities identified as the instigators or victims of bullying? Are the programs adapted in any way to meet their needs, and if so, how?

3 Mentor Others

Learning Objectives

After reading this chapter, readers will be able to

- Explain why teacher attrition is a problem in the field of special education

- Identify mutually beneficial aspects of the mentor–mentee relationship

- Explain the reasons why both preservice and in-service special education teachers, paraprofessionals, and general education teachers may need mentoring from an experienced special education teacher

- Know and apply strategies that can be used to effectively mentor novice special education teachers both face to face and at a distance

Terms to Know

Apprentice teaching

Asynchronous mentoring

eCoaching

Side-by-side coaching

Supervisory coaching

Synchronous mentoring

INTRODUCTION

Most special education teachers can recall their initial year of teaching students with disabilities. No matter how well prepared you are, teaching special education can be a challenging profession. The rate of special education teachers who leave the classroom during the first 3 years of teaching can be as high as 40%, a higher rate than is found in general education (Kaufman & Ring, 2011), with first-year special education teachers 2.5 times more likely to leave the classroom than first-year general education teachers (Jones, Youngs, & Frank, 2013).

Attrition is one of the factors cited in explaining a national shortage of special education teachers (Jones et al., 2013), and those who enter the profession before being fully licensed (approximately one third of new special education teachers) may be more at risk (Kaufman & Ring, 2011), especially if they are teaching in a rural area (Berry, Petrin, Gravelle, & Farmer, 2012). For example, Robertson and Singleton (2010) reported that 4.5% of special education teachers who were working on waivers and permits in Tennessee were teaching 16.1% of the state's special education students, and 14% left after 5 years, many for other professions.

Factors that may cause special education teachers to leave the profession include a high case load, hiring dates after the school year has begun, job burnout, the nature of job responsibilities, lack of school support (especially in high-poverty schools), little curricular guidance, low salary, poor benefits, poor working conditions, and a lack of proper mentoring (Berry et al., 2012; Kaufman & Ring, 2011; Robertson & Singleton, 2010). In a survey, Berry et al. found that administrators most often point to retirement and personal reasons (e.g., paperwork, salary and benefits, geographic isolation) as contributing to special education teacher attrition, but 42% of teachers planning to leave within a 5-year timeframe cited retirement as the reason or mentioned the option of taking a leadership or related position. Berry et al. also found that special education teachers may want to change schools or work with different age groups, and they often ask to transfer from positions teaching students with high-incidence disabilities to positions teaching students with low-incidence disabilities. One third of the special education teachers Berry et al. surveyed stated that they had to provide services for which they were unprepared, as evidenced by the comment of one teacher who was expected to provide services for students with learning disabilities, behavior disorders, IDs, and ASD in a single classroom.

One explanation for the lack of teacher preparation for working with students across specific types of disabilities is the variance in teacher preparation from one state to another (Robertson & Singleton, 2010), with some states preparing teachers to work under licensure for specific or general categorical special education labels and others under a general education licensure for unified programs. Conderman, Johnston-Rodriguez, Harman, and Walker (2012) stated that there may be a disconnect between a teacher's preparation program and the reality of the teaching assignment that causes teachers to go into "survival mode."

What is clear is that the need for special education teachers continues to grow (Robertson & Singleton, 2010), and the problem of special education teacher attrition must be addressed. A number of factors can be associated with deciding to remain in teaching positions within special education; these include favorable principal leadership, school climate, and working conditions (Jones et al., 2013), as well as the manageability of the number and type of disabilities the teacher is expected to serve and the quality of the teacher's preparation program (Conderman et al., 2012).

Mentoring also may play a significant role in the retention of special education teachers, for two primary reasons. First, it is important that future teachers receive adequate mentoring in clinical sites during their preservice programs to prepare them for the realities of a career in special education. Second, because it is impossible to address all of the realities of potential job requirements, it is important that in-service teachers receive sufficient support through mentoring during their initial years of teaching; this is even more critical for new teachers who are hired and working in classrooms before they obtain licensure. Thus, if you are an experienced special education teacher, you have the opportunity to exercise leadership with both preservice and in-service teachers. You might serve as a mentor for preservice teachers during the clinical experiences in their preparation programs, or for in-service teachers who are new to the profession and need support from school-based or district-based special education teachers who can orient them to their profession. This chapter focuses on how you can demonstrate leadership if you have the opportunity to serve as a mentor to preservice and in-service special education teachers.

CONNECTION TO PROFESSIONAL STANDARDS

The teacher's role as a mentor is supported by several professional standards listed under the Teacher Leader Model Standards (TLEC, 2012) and the CEC Standards for Professional Practice and Advanced Preparation Standards (CEC, 2015).

Teacher Leader Model Standards

Although not specific to special education, the Teacher Leader Model Standards (TLEC, 2012) address the need to serve as a model across domains. These include "model[ing] effective skills" for others, listed under *Domain 1: Fostering a Collaborative Culture to Support Educator Development and Student Learning*, and modeling a professional attitude, listed under *Domain 4: Facilitating Improvements in Instruction and Student Learning*.

Council for Exceptional Children Program Standards

All of the Special Education Professional Practice Standards developed by CEC (2015) list ways in which special education teachers can serve as models, but the CEC Special Education Advanced Preparation Standards specifically state that special education teachers should serve as models of ethical practice (5.1) under Standard 5 (Leadership and Policy) and as models of high professional expectations and ethical practice (6.2, 6.3) under Standard 6 (Professional and Ethical Practice). Standard 6 also states that special education teachers should participate in the mentoring (i.e., preparation and induction) of prospective special educators (6.6).

Dr. Ann Katherine Griffen is an example of a special education teacher leader with outstanding skills as a special education teacher mentor. She has had a long and varied career that has included mentoring students and paraeducators in her own classroom as well as working as a practicum supervisor for a university. Her exceptional teaching and analytical skills made her a valued collaborator on applied research investigations conducted in her classroom (e.g., Collins & Griffen,

1996; Griffen, Schuster, & Morse, 1998). For a period of time, she left the classroom to work at a university on a number of federally funded personnel preparation, research (Bottge et al., 2015), and technical assistance grants, while also completing her doctoral studies. In 2014, she returned to the classroom as a special education teacher and continues to mentor teachers. Her impact on the field as a special education teacher mentor has been astounding, considering the large number of special education teachers working across the state whom she has supervised during her career and the number of students with a disability and their families that those teachers continue to serve. Throughout this chapter, she discusses her work as a teacher and mentor.

Voice of a Leader

Providing Clear Expectations and Feedback

Certified in MSD (moderate to severe disabilities) K–12 and elementary education 1–8, Dr. Ann Katherine Griffen has many years of teaching experience working with diverse student populations in a variety of school settings and with students with a range of abilities and needs. She has worked in self-contained MSD classrooms, in an LBD (Learning and Behavior Disorders) classroom following an emergency certification, in schools where most students were from upper-income families, and in schools where most students were from far less privileged backgrounds. She has taught alone and as part of a teacher team. Not only does Dr. Griffen have a diverse range of teaching experiences, she has also had experience supervising clinical practices of students as a university supervisor and mentoring preservice and in-service teachers.

Mentoring a beginning teacher, in particular, provides you with a unique opportunity to shape that teacher's philosophy and practice. Below, Dr. Griffen describes her own experiences mentoring teachers just beginning their careers in special education.

Q: Describe a typical mentoring session with a student teacher. What were your expectations of the student? How did you make those clear? What were the expectations that student teachers had of you?

A: A typical mentoring session begins [with] some conversation in general, leading to conversation about questions about teaching and coursework, and then transitions to a specific discussion about the observation feedback. Expectations are spelled out in a very detailed manner via the syllabus and through the observation document. I think the expectations that the student teachers had were that I would be honest and straightforward about the feedback and that I would help them in any way possible to learn the skills they needed to learn.

Q: Special education teachers can be an influence on beginning teachers. How have you worked to help shape beginning teachers in your own classroom?

A: How one works with any beginning teacher depends on where that person currently is in their knowledge level and experiences to date. In many ways, it is just like determining a student's current level of skills (any student, including those with and without disabilities) and then prioritizing which skills to address first, all the while keeping a focus on what is immediately useful and meaningful. I think a lot about the model I am presenting, in part because I know how closely I watched the teachers I worked with, both as a university student and as a beginning teacher in my own classroom. I try to be positive and encouraging and to see the humor in what we do. I also model respect for my students and for all students and all types of families. Students are individuals, as are their families, and how [families] want to interact with and be involved in their child's school experiences is a very individually determined thing. I communicate these things indirectly through my actions and overtly in what I specifically say and how I say it. I also try to be very clear about what I think a good MSD teacher needs to know and do. I feel very strongly that we need only the best teachers for our students, and the best teachers continue to learn and grow and improve over time.

YOUR ROLE AS A MENTOR

As a seasoned special education teacher, you have a wealth of experience to share and use in shaping preservice and in-service teachers. You have the opportunity to model best practices and to shape attitudes. If you are selected as an official mentor, regard this as an honor, because your abilities have been recognized as exemplary by teacher preparation programs that search for positive clinical experiences, and also by school- or district-level personnel who seek to provide nurturing models versed in best practices for novice teachers. Even if you do not have an official mentoring role, you can demonstrate leadership by taking on the role of unofficial mentor to new special education teachers who are overwhelmed or struggling in their teaching assignments. Even a novice special education teacher who appears to be proficient in teaching will appreciate a supportive atmosphere while adapting to a new school's culture and learning new rules and regulations, which can be daunting. As a mentor, you may find that working with preservice and in-service special education teachers is a rewarding experience, in that you may be forced to reflect on your own skills and attitudes. You will also have the opportunity to learn new practices in which the mentee has been prepared and with which you may be unfamiliar (e.g., updates to assistive technology and instructional strategies).

Mentoring Preservice and In-service Special Education Teachers

The clinical experiences of preservice special education teachers influence how prepared they will be as they begin their teaching careers. When Conderman et al. (2012) surveyed 64 special education teachers, they found that student teaching and other clinical experiences had a great impact on the success of their first year of teaching. For example, one survey participant stated, "Student teaching helped me understand the expectations and workload of a special education teacher as well as responsibilities and time management skills" (Conderman et al., p. 70).

If you wish to become a leader through mentoring the clinical experiences of preservice special education teachers, contact local teacher preparation programs to see what is required—for example, how many years of teaching experience or graduate courses completed. Institutions of higher education (IHEs) that use technology to prepare teachers at a distance may be willing to use special education mentors in remote regions where they are preparing special education teachers, even if the teacher preparation program is not near the school. Some clinical supervision experiences, such as initial practica, may not be compensated, whereas others may include minimal monetary compensation or other incentives, such as a tuition stipend for graduate courses in exchange for more time-intensive supervision (e.g., supervision of student teachers). Regardless of compensation, mentoring student teachers for an IHE has the added benefit of providing you with access to experienced faculty who are versed in the latest research. By serving as a mentor to student teachers, you may find you can learn more about current best practices as you provide guidance based on your own years of experience.

Mentoring Newly Licensed Teachers

No matter how strong their teacher preparation programs were, new special education teachers in their first years of teaching will encounter challenges that include the following (Billingsley, Israel, & Smith, 2011; Conderman et al., 2012):

- Adjusting to the expectations of administrators, families, and general educators

- Attending parent conferences

- Collaborating with general educators

- Completing paperwork (e.g., IEPs)

- Conducting assessments and collecting data

- Implementing mandates (e.g., alternate assessment)

- Learning and using a new curriculum

- Managing challenging behavior

- Managing diverse caseloads

- Selecting and implementing instructional strategies

Kaufman and Ring noted that, although newly licensed special education teachers may begin their first jobs with a great deal of enthusiasm, they can experience burnout in a short period if they do not receive support and guidance that provides "pathways to leadership and professional development" (2011, p. 52). Likewise, Jones et al. stated that newly licensed special education teachers "face a double jeopardy for attrition" (2013, p. 366) because special education and general education are often separated, resulting in less access to colleagues.

Some of the challenges that newly licensed teachers face—such as adapting to the school culture and procedures, honing instructional and behavior management skills, and learning new curricula—are common to both general and special education teachers, but the latter may be faced with added responsibilities such as locating resources, adapting materials, generating IEPs, and complying with special education laws and procedures, which can consume as much as 12% of their time (Jones et al., 2013). In addition, it is difficult for preservice programs to prepare special education teachers for all of the challenges that they may face in their first year of teaching (Sindelar, Brownell, & Billingsley, 2010). Even a diversity of preservice clinical placements cannot fully prepare a new special education teacher, due to the diversity of disabilities that students on the teacher's caseload may have and the fact that not all types of disabilities will occur in all classrooms or schools. For example, a new special education teacher may have no prior experience managing specific types of behaviors, such as physical aggression or pica, or implementing specific types of health-related procedures, such as seizure management or tube feeding. A capable, caring, and experienced mentor can be a critical resource for a new special education teacher. According to Jones et al., "there is some evidence that informal support from mentors and colleagues is associated with increased commitment among novice teachers" (p. 367).

Some states have required induction programs for new teachers, a practice that has been recommended as helpful to novice teachers (Sindelar et al., 2010). For example, all new teachers in Kentucky (i.e., those with fewer than 3 years of experience) are enrolled in the Kentucky Teacher Internship Program (KTIP; Whetstone, Abell, Collins, & Kleinert, 2012). Most induction programs have a mentoring component to provide "career support and psychosocial support" (Israel, Kamman, McCray, & Sindelar, 2014, p. 47) and to provide a means to evaluate whether new teachers have the necessary skills to succeed in a teaching career.

Israel et al. (2014) described a formal teacher induction program based on the Danielson (1996) framework. The induction program required that assigned mentors conduct both formal and informal observations of new teachers. Comments from the mentees were positive, describing the benefits of mentor access, support, feedback, and sharing of resources. Although the mentees sometimes found observation and evaluation to be intimidating, they realized that the feedback was meant to help.

In states that have a formal induction program for new teachers, you can exercise leadership by investigating the process for becoming an official mentor—for example, a resource teacher. This role may or may not be compensated, but the dividends are great. Mentoring can be a personally gratifying experience while also ensuring that the next generation of special education teachers remain in their teaching positions and acquire the skills to make a difference in the lives of the students with disabilities who are assigned to them. To become an official mentor in an induction program, some additional training may be required (i.e., professional development on how to complete forms and conduct effective observations), but this should only serve to strengthen your mentoring skills.

Mentoring Teachers Without Licensure

Perhaps one of the most important opportunities you can have to serve as a mentor and a leader is to work with a special education teacher who is hired without licensure. Some of these teachers may not even have a degree in teaching or a related field. Due to the national need for special education teachers, especially in those geographic areas where it is difficult to recruit teachers or for those positions that serve students with the most challenging disabilities, many districts are forced to hire individuals who are willing to work on licensure while being employed under a waiver or temporary licensure; thus, a number of states provide alternate routes to certification that may include enrollment in an alternate licensure program. For example, Childre (2014) stated that the state of Georgia experienced special education teacher attrition rates that exceeded the national average, causing a situation in which the least qualified teachers were serving the most disadvantaged students. These teachers entered alternate route certification programs in which they completed their internships in the classrooms where they were employed.

Sindelar et al. (2012) found that most alternate certification programs take 2 years to complete and that the teachers who enter these programs (85% female) often had prior work experience outside the field of education, with some taking salary cuts to enter this field. Although these special education teachers had little, if any, preparation unless they had previous experience as a paraprofessional, the positive finding is that most intended to continue to work in the same school in the same position once they received licensure; thus, if special education teachers prepared through alternate certification programs receive the support needed to make it through the initial years in their positions, hiring them may be a cost-effective investment for school districts. Robertson and Singleton (2010) provided evidence to back up this outcome when they stated that more than half of the special education teachers who completed the University of Memphis's alternate certification program remained in their teaching positions, compared to one third who remained after completing an undergraduate special education preparation program.

If you are an experienced special education teacher employed in a district that hires special education teachers before they complete a licensure program, your value cannot be overstated. As much as special education teachers who have completed traditional teacher preparation programs can benefit from mentoring, this is even more true for those who have not. Special education teachers in alternate certification programs may be more likely to remain in their teaching positions for a number of reasons; for instance, they may be less likely to relocate because they already are settled in the area where they are needed. As a teacher leader, you can serve an important role by mentoring and supporting those teachers until they acquire the skills needed to feel comfortable in and even excel at their jobs.

Mentoring Other Colleagues

In addition to mentoring preservice and in-service special education teachers, you may also have the opportunity to mentor other colleagues in your school who work with students with disabilities. These colleagues include paraprofessionals and general education teachers.

Paraprofessionals   It is common for special education teachers to have classroom assistants assigned to work with the students with disabilities on their caseloads. It cannot, however, be assumed that paraprofessionals will have prior experience in working with students with disabilities or knowledge of best practices. Thus, these paraprofessionals may need mentoring.

Stockall (2014) suggested that paraprofessionals can benefit from side-by-side coaching, direct instruction, and feedback—some of the same strategies that experienced special education mentors use with preservice and in-service special education teachers. As an example, Britton, Collins, Ault, and Bausch (2015) used systematic instruction (i.e., constant time delay procedure) to teach an experienced paraprofessional how to use systematic instruction (i.e., simultaneous prompting procedure). As with all mentoring relationships, it is important that your mentoring relationship with a paraprofessional consist of two-way communication, with both you and the paraprofessional acknowledging what you each have to offer and sharing from your experiences.

In addition, once you have some experience mentoring paraprofessionals, you may find yourself providing guidance to another group of colleagues: less experienced special education teachers who are not yet confident about how to mentor paraprofessionals in their own classrooms. It can be intimidating for new special education teachers to provide mentoring to paraprofessionals who are older than they are or who have been employed in the school setting longer than they have; thus, Stockall (2014) observed that new special education teachers may not be prepared to provide mentoring to paraprofessionals. If you have experience in doing so, you can be a valuable resource in teaching new teachers how to mentor classroom staff.

General Education Teachers   You may also serve as a mentor to a general education teacher. This mentoring relationship has more potential challenges but can also benefit both teachers and students. General education teachers have strong backgrounds in EBPs for working with students without disabilities but may lack preparation in EBPs for working with the students in their classes with disabilities.

Because general and special education teachers may have differing philosophical preparation foundations (e.g., constructivist versus behavioral), the chasm sometimes can seem difficult to span. However, "difficult" does not mean "impossible." Tekin-Iftar et al. (2017) found that general education teachers who received coaching were able to implement systematic instruction that resulted in students with ASD learning core content in their classes. Jones et al. (2013) stated that a "collective responsibility" for all students is needed when special and general education teachers work together. In addressing curricular issues and instructional procedures, common planning periods can provide the opportunity to discuss differences and share expertise, creating a mutual mentoring experience.

> In addition to preservice and in-service special education teachers, who else might benefit from mentoring? Why?

Voice of a Leader

Building Rapport With Your Mentee

The mentor–mentee relationship is a professional one—but its success depends in part on establishing a personal connection, as is described in subsequent sections of this chapter. Below, Dr. Ann Katherine Griffen discusses the importance of establishing rapport with a mentee and describes some strategies for doing so.

Q: *What advice would you give to a special education teacher who is involved in mentoring clinical practices for a university? What advice would you give to a special education teacher who has the opportunity to mentor beginning teachers in his or her school or district?*

A: My advice would be to think about ways to begin establishing a rapport with the beginning teacher. There are all kinds of ways to do this: asking about the student's interests and life outside school, sharing some of your own interests, telling them (briefly) about your family and your family origins. Sharing my family origins was a piece of information that served me well when seeing students who lived in Appalachia and making a connection with them. Be sure to greet and say goodbye to the paraeducators in the classroom and talk with the students, too.

←——→

Ask the teacher about his or her concerns about teaching; ask about the students and classroom; ask about any questions about course content; encourage the teacher to speak up and ask questions in class, particularly if the student is a distance learning (DL) student. Talk with the teacher about the resources available at the university library (do this for all students, both on-campus and DL). Take examples of data sheets and graphs and easy materials to use for all of the different instructional procedures and ways to graph. Take blank copies so you can go through all of the steps together. Talk about the observation instrument you will be using with the teacher and explain all of the sections and behaviors listed and what each means. Give examples. After observing, go over the feedback. Ask the student what went well and what he or she needs to do better. Then, start with the feedback. Prioritize what to focus on first. Tell the student specific behaviors to change, and make it clear that you will be looking for those changes in the next observation and that the score will be contingent on seeing those changes. Give the student ways to make contact (e.g., e-mail, cell, text, iMessage), and encourage the student to contact you with questions. Emphasize that the student is not to wait until you are walking in the door for the next observation to ask a question, particularly if it's about the changes the student is supposed to be making.

Strategies for Mentoring

It is clear that mentoring is a mutually beneficial experience for all involved and that mentoring others is an area in which some special education teacher leaders provide a valuable service for teacher preparation programs, for their school districts, and, indirectly, for students with disabilities. Based on a mentoring model at Georgia College and State University, Childre and Van Rie (2015) asserted that special education mentors should be prepared to model best practices, provide guidance and feedback, and share resources. The following sections provide strategies that special education teacher leaders can use to become effective mentors: sharing resources, giving personal advice, coaching, using technology, and participating in apprentice teaching experiences.

Sharing Resources   The first strategy you can use in mentoring a new special education teacher is to be a resource and share resources. No matter how well trained a new teacher is, there are forms and protocol to learn in a new teaching position, as well as schedules and navigation within the school facility. All new teachers need to be mentored on policies that dictate where forms and materials are kept and how to find them; who can supply needed information at the school, district, and state levels; what curricula are to be followed; and how related assessment is to be conducted. A new special education teacher has even more to learn in regard to school, state, and federal policies. Even though the teacher's preparation program should have addressed legal issues and methods for conducting instruction and managing behavior, the issues specific to a new classroom's composition that arise can leave a new special education teacher grasping for resources. Additional health-related or cultural issues may arise as well. Even though most new teachers can search the Internet for basic information, you can share information and guide new special education teachers to additional resources you have found helpful in your experience. For example, Billingsley et al. (2011) listed the following organizational web sites and other online materials as electronic resources that may be helpful to new special education teachers: the IRIS modules and case studies provided by the IRIS Center of Peabody College at Vanderbilt University, LD OnLine, the Special Connections site developed by the University of Kansas, CAST, 4Teachers.org, the Center on Response to Intervention at American Institutes for Research, Intervention Central, Beach Center on Disability, and CEC. In addition, Billingsley et al. noted that, if an experienced special education teacher is not in the same school as the new teacher in need of mentoring, this mentoring can occur at a distance through web conferencing (e.g., Skype, iChat), wikis (e.g., Wikispaces, Google Docs, PBworks), virtual technologies, and online communities of practice (e.g., LeadScape). (More information on electronic mentoring is provided at the end of this section.)

Giving Personal Advice   If you become a special education mentor, professional resources are not all you will need to provide. You must also be prepared to advise new special education teachers on techniques that will help them find balance in life and avoid teacher burnout. Through experience, you most likely will have developed coping skills that will provide a good model for a new special education teacher to emulate. These skills can include paying attention to health and vitality through eating a balanced diet and setting aside time for exercise, investing time in personal supportive relationships, and becoming involved in extracurricular activities outside of the teaching profession (Kaufman & Ring, 2011). Although it is important to encourage professional reading to keep up with best practices in the field, as a special education mentor you may also share inspirational fiction and nonfiction (Kaufman & Ring).

The most important aspect of providing emotional support for a new special education teacher, however, may be developing good listening skills. The importance of this aspect of mentoring is illustrated by the comments of a new special education teacher, as reported by Israel et al.: "At times, I think I may panic about something with my lessons and she'll say, 'No. Calm down. You can do it like this.' And she'll walk and talk me through it to help me be a little calm" (2014, p. 58). The mentor's remarks show that she hears her mentee's concerns and feelings of anxiety, and her response focuses on helping the new teacher regulate her emotions as well as helping her deliver effective instruction.

Coaching   Coaching goes beyond providing resources and emotional support; coaching is a way to provide individualized support to special education teachers. When coaching, you can provide a model for best practices, observe the novice pre-service or in-service teacher using the practices, and provide feedback on performance. Based on a review of the professional literature, Kretlow and Bartholomew (2010) identified two types of coaching: 1) **supervisory coaching,** in which feedback is provided following observation of a teacher, and 2) **side-by-side coaching,** in which feedback is provided as a teacher is attempting to use a procedure.

The professional literature provides numerous examples of successful coaching. Horrocks and Morgan (2011) reported the coaching of seven teachers on effective response prompting strategies (i.e., time delay, system of least prompts, most-to-least prompting, graduated guidance) for working with students with a profound ID; coaching included modeling (live and video), role play, and feedback. Simonsen, Myers, and DeLuca (2010) used coaching to increase the behavior management skills of three special education teachers; coaching consisted of the PORT protocol: 1) **p**rompt (provide prompting for specific behaviors), 2) **o**ccasion (find opportunities to respond), and 3) **r**einforce **t**raining (provide specific praise).

Some evidence indicates that coaching can increase fidelity to procedures following initial training (Kretlow & Bartholomew, 2010). For example, Bethune and Wood (2013) followed up a 6-hour in-service session on the assessment of problem behavior, conducted for six special education teachers, with coaching, and they found that the coaching (not the in-service training) resulted in 100% fidelity in implementing the procedure. Likewise, Brown, Stephenson, and Carter (2014) followed a presentation on the simultaneous prompting procedure with modeling, role play, and feedback on performance and found that teachers acquired and maintained the ability to use the procedure. In addition, Barton and Wolery (2010) and Barton, Chen, Pribble, Pomes, and Kim (2013) taught teachers to use a system of least prompts procedure, contingent imitation, and praise to increase play skills in young children with disabilities. Coaching consisted of an initial training session, a video, role play, and feedback and praise during practice. As a result, the teachers could use the procedures with fidelity. More specifically, Suhrheinrich (2011) followed up a 6-hour workshop with coaching to teach 20 teachers to use pivotal response training. Although 15% of the teachers could use the procedure after the workshop alone, coaching resulted in an increase to 80% of the teachers using the procedure with fidelity.

> Some mentors like to interrupt mentees to provide immediate feedback as they observe, whereas others prefer to wait until an observation session ends and then provide feedback. What are the advantages and disadvantages of each type of mentoring?

Israel et al. (2014) reported positive comments from teachers that alluded to the coaching they had received in several areas (e.g., instructional strategies, co-teaching, challenging behaviors). One teacher stated, "She [her mentor] would come in and work with the kids with me. She came in and watched in different settings. She watched science, math, pullout. She pretty much hit every area" (2014, p. 57); another stated, "She gave me tons of model lesson plans . . . and she modeled a lesson for me" (pp. 57–58). According to Israel et al., explicit feedback from a mentor was critical in addressing areas of weakness.

Using Technology   The Internet provides an effective way to deliver content in preparing special education teachers at a distance (e.g., McDonnell et al., 2011). In addition, the professional literature provides several models for mentoring using technology. For example, web conferencing, wikis, wireless headphones, and online communities of practice (Billingsley et al., 2011) can be used to mentor teachers at a distance. Online options for mentoring can be asynchronous (i.e., with mentoring video or materials placed on the Internet for future reference) or synchronous (i.e., with mentoring occurring in real time).

Asynchronous Mentoring   **Asynchronous mentoring** can be an effective way to mentor both preservice and in-service teachers at a distance. As an example of mentoring preservice teachers, Capizzi, Wehby, and Sandmel (2010) found that providing virtual feedback on recorded video for three student teachers increased the rate of targeted skills the teachers displayed (e.g., using behavior-specific praise, increasing opportunities to respond).

Asynchronous mentoring may be even more important for in-service teachers. According to Hunt, Powell, Little, and Mike, "the need for induction-level mentoring is critical" (2015, p. 288) because "a novice special education teacher is expected to complete the same expectations as a veteran teacher from day one" (p. 287). Hunt et al. also noted that it may be difficult to locate experienced special education mentors within the same school, or even the same geographic region, in which novice special education teachers are employed.

If you are interested in providing asynchonous mentoring, the Internet can serve as the means for providing mentoring materials to you and your mentee so that these materials are readily accessible for mentoring sessions. For example, members of the Low Incidence Consortium in Kentucky aligned the Kentucky New Teacher Standards with the CEC Standards and then adapted the required lesson plan format used in the state's induction program (KTIP) to reflect best practices for working with students with MSD. They placed the final support tool (the MSD Strategic Addendum or MSDSA) online so it could be used by assigned mentors (i.e., resource teachers) and their mentees across the state. In addition, they provided a link to video of experienced special education teachers using the practices listed in the lesson plan. The need for this online resource stemmed from the fact that many new MSD teachers in the state were, out of necessity, assigned mentors who were experienced in working with a different age level or who did not have a background in special education (e.g., a secondary chemistry teacher assigned to mentor an elementary low incidence teacher). A follow-up survey found that the MSDSA was useful to the special education mentors and mentees who used it (Abell, Collins, Kleiner, & Pennington; 2014).

In another example, Hunt et al. (2015) employed a model of asynchronous mentoring during the induction process when they organized online discussions on pertinent topics—for example, behavior management, co-teaching, and conflict resolution—in which both mentors and mentees engaged. Data showed that the mentoring project contributed to knowledge of professional standards and law in the 22 novice special education teachers who participated.

Synchronous Mentoring **Synchronous mentoring** through distance education technology provides a means for real-time observation and virtual coaching. This is a useful practice for mentors in special education teacher preparation programs who would otherwise have to spend a great deal of time traveling to rural sites (Schmidt, Gage, Gage, Cox, & McLeskey, 2015) and may be necessary when novice preservice and in-service teachers experience a lack of proximity to a skilled mentor (Hunt et al., 2015).

The professional literature provides a number of examples of synchronous virtual mentoring. One example is **eCoaching,** which Rock et al. have described as "a relationship in which one or more persons' effective teaching skills are intentionally and potentially enhanced through online interactions with another person" (2014, p. 162). Ploessl and Rock (2015) used bug-in-the-ear technology and a webcam for eCoaching novice teachers in co-teaching practices. Acting as mentor, the coach provided real-time feedback from a remote office to three dyads of co-teachers as they delivered a cooperative lesson, and all found the practice to be helpful. An advantage to bug-in-the-ear technology is that mentees can correct errors and adjust teaching practices immediately, rather than repeating errors as they wait on delayed feedback (Scheeler, McKinnon, & Stout, 2012). Research by Rock et al. has found that teachers who received eCoaching maintained the skills they acquired, such as instructional strategies, when assessed after 2 years.

Although virtual mentoring and eCoaching can be efficient and effective practices for personnel who work in teacher preparation programs, they also can facilitate mentoring between experienced and novice teachers who work at a distance from each other. Hager, Baird, and Spriggs (2012) described a project in which a graduate special education program at the University of Kentucky paired advanced special education teachers working on a master's degree with beginning special education teachers working on licensure through an alternate certification program. Because the mentees worked at a great geographic distance from the university, in rural schools where they did not have access to adequate mentoring, the advanced special education teachers could provide mentoring using remote observation technology.

> Technology can be used for mentoring within the classroom setting or for mentoring at a distance. What types of technology can be useful during the mentoring process? In what ways?

> Describe several strategies that special education teacher mentors can employ to ensure that mentoring is effective.

Apprentice Teaching   As described in the previous chapter, co-teaching is the practice of special and general education teachers providing instruction together to all students within an inclusive classroom. However, experts in education also have used this term to refer to the practice of advanced and novice teachers providing instruction together. According to Friend, Embury, and Clarke (2015), co-teaching is better described as **apprentice teaching** when it is an alternate approach to a traditional student teaching experience. In a traditional model of student teaching, the novice teacher provides instruction while being observed by an experienced teacher. In an apprentice teaching experience, a master special education teacher (the mentor) delivers instruction alongside a beginning special education teacher, and both are accountable for teaching and learning. Although the master teacher or mentor has the ultimate responsibility for all student outcomes, an apprentice teaching model has the advantage of building skills in collaboration and planning while also providing the opportunity for side-by-side coaching as instruction is delivered.

Voice of a Leader

Leading by Modeling Lifelong Learning

Dr. Ann Katherine Griffen was a leader in the classroom long before she began to serve as a mentor to other teachers. She has found that her work supervising other teachers has strengthened her own awareness that being an effective teacher— and mentor—means being committed to lifelong learning and growth. Here, she discusses the leadership qualities she brings to her role as a mentor teacher.

Q: *How did mentoring clinical practices transform you into a teacher leader? What is your current position, and how do you continue to be a mentor?*

A: I believe that I was a teacher leader when I was a classroom teacher before I became a supervisor of students' clinical practices at the university. . . . [As a mentor], I had the support of a close relationship with university professors who placed their practicum students and student teachers in my classroom and who worked with me in doing research (theirs and my own). There are many ways in which they provided support to me. One way was my being able to watch them and model their skills in supervising university students. Again, this sampled the range of experiences, skills, and behaviors. My very first student teacher failed student teaching. A great job was done in the classroom, but the university course assignments were simply not submitted. I still think about that experience (the student's, the university supervisor's, and my own) and am reminded of how difficult it can be to be a successful student at any level. This student successfully completed a subsequent student teaching placement. I watched the university professors interact with and support their students in many ways while, at the same time, they always pushed the students to learn and develop the next set of skills. . . .

I returned to the classroom a year and a half ago as a middle school MSD teacher. I am halfway through my second year back in the classroom. . . . This upcoming spring semester will be the first time that I will have a student teacher this time around as a classroom teacher. . . .

I think my strengths as a mentor are based on a balance of several things: 1) having high expectations for what a good teacher knows and does; 2) a firm belief in the specific knowledge, skills, and behaviors a good teacher must learn; 3) a vivid recollection of my own thoughts and feelings as a young teacher who did not yet know many things and was finding my way; and 4) a recognition that good classroom teachers become good over time with much support and encouragement. I think that mentoring is a two-way process and it is a way of interacting with all others. There is much to learn from others, and I have many things to share. The focus we place on students being lifelong learners should also apply to ourselves as teachers, and I hope to be a model in showing how one puts that belief into practice. The mentoring process has begun with [my newest] student teacher, who will begin in a few short weeks, and will continue throughout her time in my classroom. It may be possible for that relationship to continue into the future as well.

During this time back in the classroom and prior to working directly again with university students, my focus has primarily been on developing a relationship with the paraeducators assigned to my classroom and working to unify us as a team. However, I continue to be in contact with some of the student teachers from long ago and with some of the practicum students I worked with while at the university. I highly value the support and camaraderie that is possible with collaboration. Having someone to talk with and laugh with is simply invaluable. It has been a former master's student/classroom paraeducator who has been my biggest resource during this last year and a half back in the classroom. She is now a therapist, and we share a student. I cannot adequately express the difference having her support has made in this transition back to the classroom. I think, while these relationships could be described as a shared back-and-forth mentoring, a better way to describe them would be as colleagues.

BE A LEADER: BECOME A SPECIAL EDUCATION MENTOR

If you are a seasoned special education teacher with years of accumulated knowledge and experience, you can be an invaluable resource to many of your colleagues: preservice and in-service special education teachers just beginning their careers, general education teachers who will benefit from your expertise in working with students with disabilities, and paraprofessionals working in your classroom. Mentoring typically involves sharing resources, giving personal advice, coaching, using technology, and participating in apprentice teaching experiences. It is a relationship built upon shared standards of professional excellence, strong connections between mentor and mentee, clear expectations and feedback laced with encouragement and support, and mutual commitment to lifelong learning as teachers. The following guidelines are offered to help you expand your leadership skills in mentoring:

> What are some of the benefits that a special education teacher mentor can take away from the process?

1. Keep a file of EBPs and a journal of effective practices that have worked within your classroom.

2. Compile a list of practical information that a new teacher in your school or district would need to know to be successful.

3. Be familiar with web sites that can be helpful to new special education teachers.

4. Let administrative personnel in your school and district know if you are interested in being assigned as a mentor to new special education teachers, in addition to contacting faculty in a teacher preparation program who place student teachers. (Administrative personnel to contact at your school might include your principal, special education director, and/or field experience coordinator.)

5. Make the first move to be a resource to new special education teachers in your school and district.

6. When mentoring, listen, observe, and establish rapport before providing advice.

7. If you cannot work with a special education teacher in a face-to-face format, consider using asynchronous and synchronous technologies to interact across a distance or after school hours.

8. Always begin a mentoring session by providing positive feedback before discussing areas where support is needed; then, make expectations for improvement clear.

9. For clarity and future discussions, always document mentoring sessions and provide a copy for the mentee; then, follow up.

FOLLOW-UP ACTIVITIES

Chapter 3 has discussed ways you can be a leader by mentoring colleagues—beginning special education teachers in particular. This one-to-one relationship is uniquely rewarding. It gives you a chance to support other teachers and to be a lasting influence upon their teaching philosophy and practices. It also serves to build your awareness of your own skills and strengths.

The suggested activities that follow are intended to help you think about the mentor–mentee relationship in connection with your own teaching career. As you complete them, consider whether mentoring is a leadership path you want to pursue—and if so, how you will act on this.

1. **Recall the mentoring you received as a beginning teacher.** In her interview, Dr. Ann Katherine Griffen recalls her own initial years of being a special education teacher and how those experiences shaped her mentoring style. Recall your own experiences as a new special education teacher. Who were your mentors and how were they helpful or unhelpful to you? In what areas did you think that you needed the most support? Did you receive this? Are there changes you would have made to the mentoring process that you received?

2. **Compile valuable resources.** What resources have you found to be most helpful in your career that you might share with others? Consider books that have shaped your teaching philosophy or practice, articles that you may have kept for future reference, or web sites to which you turn when you need inspiration and technical assistance. Compile a list that you could share.

3. **Evaluate the culture of the school where you teach.** Are experienced teachers and staff welcoming and collegial to new teachers? If so, in what ways? Are there resources that help new teachers negotiate the logistics of the physical facility or the daily schedule? What could you do to make your school's culture more navigable for a teacher who has just joined the faculty?

4. **Record, review, and reflect upon your own teaching.** Video has become an accessible and inexpensive component of the mentoring process. Make a video of yourself as you teach and review it in private. In what areas do you believe you are a good role model? Are there areas in which you think you could improve?

5. **Determine what qualities an effective mentor teacher should have.** If you are not already serving as a clinical experience supervisor, contact a teacher preparation program to ask about their expectations for special education teacher mentors. Request a copy of the forms that are used to evaluate students in clinical experiences. Do you think that the forms adequately reflect the skills that a special education teacher needs, or are they more generic so they can be used across age levels and subject areas? If you could design your own observation and evaluation form, what skills would you list as most important and how would you assess them? If your state has an official induction program for new teachers, repeat this exercise with information about that program.

4 Conduct Professional Development and Consultations

Learning Objectives

After reading this chapter, readers will be able to

- Distinguish among professional development, consultation, mentoring, and coaching

- Advocate for the special education teacher's role in the delivery of professional development and consultations

- Use knowledge of current models, practices, and issues to develop a working method for effectively delivering professional development and conducting consultations

- Integrate technology in the delivery of professional development and consultations

Terms to Know

Conceptual model

Logic model

INTRODUCTION

As discussed in Chapter 3, teaching is a profession that requires lifelong learning. No matter how effective a teacher preparation program may be, teachers in the field need to stay abreast of new teaching practices that are supported by research and emerging technologies that can increase and facilitate learning. This is especially true in instructional and assistive technology, where advances seem to be made on a daily basis. Even if you attempt to stay current through reviewing published research, the amount of information available about a single topic can be overwhelming.

If you have expertise in a specific topic, you can be a valuable resource by sharing your expertise with other teachers through organized professional development or one-to-one consultations. For example, you may be skilled in using research-based behavior management strategies, systematic instructional procedures, new types of technology, or communication strategies such as sign language. Your expertise may have come from advanced coursework, involvement in a research project, or years of classroom experience. As a special education teacher who is involved in the classroom daily, you may be more convincing to peers than an outside expert who is removed from daily classroom experience and paid to deliver information in a single quick overview. Special education teachers like you have an advantage: You can share experiences and information with teachers who are striving to improve, while also relating to the realities of their daily schedules and heavy workloads.

Sometimes a train-the-trainer model (i.e., a modified pyramidal training model) can be employed in professional development (Kunnavatana et al., 2013); in this model, people receive professional development on a topic and subsequently train others. Thus, if you have received high-quality professional development, you may get to take on the leadership role of providing it for others. This model is a good alternative to large-scale professional development sessions and may be more effective because its small-group format can allow time for role-play and guided practice with feedback.

The need for professional development in special education can be illustrated by data from researchers addressing two specific questions: how to work most effectively with individuals with ASD and how to counteract the "school-to-prison pipeline" phenomenon for students who are at risk.

In the area of ASD, Kelly and Tincani (2013) reported a possible gap between behavior analysts' responsibilities and the professional development they had received; although the majority of applied behavior analysts responding to a survey reported that they collaborated with others on supporting individuals with ASD, 45% reported that they had received no professional development on collaboration. In another study, Able et al. (2015) reported that general education teachers who included students with ASD wanted professional development that focused on academic and social skills and noted that this should be collaborative across general and special education. To put it another way, they wanted access to the same professional development a special educator would have so that they could work more effectively with special educators in serving this student population. In a large-scale study conducted with 456 participants, Brock et al. (2014) surveyed special education teachers and their administrators who took part in the Treatment and Research Institute for Autism Spectrum Disorders at Vanderbilt University's medical center and found that special education teachers of students with ASD were interested in learning more about self-management strategies, computer-assisted instruction, and social skill groups, whereas special education administrators perceived the need for teachers to learn more about FBA, self-management, and response interruption strategies, making clear that some professional development topics selected by administrators may not match teacher needs. Brock et al. concluded that professional development should be tailored to the needs of the participants—what teachers state that they need—and not on what administrators think the participants need.

Counteracting the school-to-prison pipeline is another area in which teachers may lack access to the professional development they need. The "pipeline" refers to the sociological phenomenon in which stringent disciplinary policies (e.g., zero-tolerance policies) lead to at-risk students being suspended from school, expelled, or even arrested, sometimes for minor rule infractions. These students, who are already at risk for poor school and career outcomes, are subsequently more likely to become involved with the juvenile or adult justice systems and more likely to be incarcerated. In addition, a larger percentage of students who are incarcerated have disabilities (most often emotional and behavioral disorders or learning disabilities) than the percentage found in the typical school population, thus making this a special education issue (Houchins & Shippen, 2012). The need to provide professional development to address the school-to-prison pipeline outcome for students who are at risk has been considered great enough that *Teacher Education and Special Education* devoted an entire issue to this topic in 2012. In this issue, Houchins, Shippen, and Murphy (2012) stated that the billions of dollars spent annually for professional development on this topic by federal, state, and local governments, as well as private foundations, have been ineffective—that is, no research data exist to support the effectiveness of this spending. Shippen, Patterson, Green, and Smitherman (2012) proposed that continuing professional development for educators and school staff at the building level may be a more effective way to solve this problem than working through agencies, because teachers can be taught to implement preventive academic and behavioral interventions before students are referred to the juvenile system. In addition, Gagnon, Houchins, and Murphy (2012) asserted that sustained collaborative, cross-disciplinary professional development of teaching and correctional staff in juvenile correction schools on both special and general education instructional content, effective instructional approaches, and how to address behavioral and mental health needs such as drug addiction may have a more lasting effect than simply offering the same generic professional development that teachers in traditional school receive.

> Are there reasons that special education teachers can be particularly effective in providing professional development or consultations for others? Who might be the recipients of expertise in these activities?

Since traditional professional development is geared toward providing general information on a topic to a group of participants, individualized sharing of knowledge may be needed to address specific issues that teachers and staff encounter. In that case, you can be valuable in the role of consultant. Again, a local consultant who understands the school's culture and the teacher's specific needs and who is available on a continuing basis may be more effective than an external consultant retained by a district for a single day of observation and recommendations. This chapter focuses on the involvement of special education teachers in professional development and consultations, based on the assumption that experienced special education teachers can be effective and valued in these leadership roles within their own schools and districts.

CONNECTION TO PROFESSIONAL STANDARDS

The teacher's role in sharing information through professional development and consultation is supported by several professional standards listed under the Teacher Leader Model Standards (TLEC, 2012) and the CEC Standards for Professional Practice and Advanced Preparation Standards (CEC, 2015).

Teacher Leader Model Standards

Although not specific to special education, the Teacher Leader Model Standards (TLEC, 2012) address the need to serve as a model across domains. Specific standards address facilitating the professional learning of colleagues, with attention to the diverse learning needs of adults and the use of technology, listed under *Domain 1: Fostering a Collaborative Culture to Support Educator Development and Student Learning;* facilitating content knowledge through coaching, listed under *Domain 4: Facilitating Improvements in Instruction and Student Learning;* and "shar[ing] information within and/or beyond the school district . . . [on] trends and policies," listed under *Domain 7: Advocating for Student Learning and the Profession.*

Council for Exceptional Children Program Standards

The Special Education Standards for Professional Practice developed by CEC (2015) address professional development for teachers, noting that special education teachers should promote continuous improvement in performance (3.3) and advocate for schoolwide and personal professional development (3.4). The Advanced Preparation Standards state that, in addition to facilitating their own professional growth (6.4), special education teachers should participate in the planning, presentation, and evaluation of professional development for others (6.5) under Standard 6 (Professional and Ethical Practice). One example of a special education teacher leader who fulfills these standards is Sally Miracle, introduced in the following feature.

Voice of a Leader

Giving Dynamic, Informative Presentations

Sally Miracle is a regional special education consultant for special education teachers who work with students with moderate to severe disabilities. As a special education teacher in a secondary school, she built her expertise by developing a peer-tutoring program that she shared through professional presentations, by developing an effective model for community-based instruction, by mentoring preservice teachers, and by participating in classroom-based research (e.g., Miracle, Collins, Schuster, &

←———→

Grisham-Brown, 2001). She has found that working as a special education consultant has caused her to pull from her own experience as a special education teacher while developing her skills as a presenter. Here, she describes her work providing professional development and the role that research plays in this work.

Q: Describe your experiences offering professional development and in-service for special education teachers.

A: During the first couple of professional developments I provided, I was scared to death and did a horrible job. I went to training on how to be a successful presenter. It taught me how to keep my participants engaged and learning. It taught me how to present and use materials to present. It taught me different learning activities to use with my participants. Now, when I attend classes, meetings, and trainings, I evaluate how others present. I am someone who cannot sit still and learn, so I use that when I present to others. I always have an evaluation with more than just the "feel good" questions. I try to change my presentation based on the feedback. I always make sure to end with a summary or closing activity to make sure that participants acknowledge what they learned. There are times I have to present on topics that are not my areas of interest or areas that I feel extremely comfortable in, so I am nervous. I try to use videos to help.

Q: How does research play a role in the information that you provide for others?

A: I make sure that I share evidence-based practices with teachers. I share data and research on what I want others to implement so that they understand why and how it works. I want them to see that others are using it and it is not just me saying, "Hey, let's try this." I send staff to sites where they can see videos and get user-friendly information on the evidence-based practices I ask them to try. I try not to overwhelm staff with research articles but instead provide user-friendly things to read or practical videos to watch. I often develop cheat sheets for understanding.

YOUR ROLE IN CONDUCTING PROFESSIONAL DEVELOPMENT

Professional development on special education topics can be conducted in a variety of ways. Unfortunately, much of the professional literature on this subject is anecdotal rather than research-based, and many teachers do not believe that they receive appropriate professional development (Brock et al., 2014; Gagnon et al., 2012). The professional literature, however, has documented examples of effective professional development (e.g., Bottge et al., 2015) that are highlighted in the following sections. If you have the opportunity to facilitate professional development for others, consider these strategies.

Planning for Professional Development

Adequate planning for professional development is essential to its effectiveness. A solid conceptual model and the use of a logic model can provide the foundation for this planning; both models are discussed in the following sections.

Conceptual Model   A **conceptual model** simply is the theoretical framework that provides the underpinnings for a project. A well-conceived conceptual model can provide the framework or underpinnings for designing professional development. Houchins et al. (2012) described a conceptual model with several components that facilitators of professional development should consider: collective participation, common content foci, ecological systems, coherence and continuums, implementation stages, implementation fidelity, and data-based decision making. Although their research focused on the school-to-prison pipeline, the components the authors identified can be used to address a variety of professional development topics:

1. *Collective participation:* Which disciplines should be involved in professional development on a specific topic? For example, it may need to involve general educators, special educators, and related service personnel to ensure vested parties are working together on a single topic.

2. *Common content foci:* What does each participant have to share on the topic? Recognize that participants may bring expertise and experience to a session that should be shared with others.

3. *Ecological systems:* Does the topic extend across environments? For example, for some topics, professionals should examine settings outside the school, such as the home or community, and have input from individuals in these settings.

4. *Coherence and continuums:* How are policy and practice connected? It is helpful to examine services provided longitudinally across disciplines to clarify how and when a topic currently is being addressed.

5. *Implementation stages:* How can professional development become an active process? Rather than being a one-shot affair, it may be viewed as a plan that will be implemented in stages.

6. *Implementation fidelity:* Will data be collected to ensure that practices are implemented as planned? Once information is shared, data can show whether professional development is effective in obtaining desired outcomes.

7. *Data-based decision making:* How will the data collected on the effectiveness of professional development be used? An analysis of follow-up data will determine the need for additional professional development and tweaking of practices that have been addressed.

One topic teachers have identified as an area in which they need professional development is inclusion (Able et al., 2015). We can apply the components identified by Houchins et al. (2012) to develop a conceptual framework for professional development on this current topic:

1. *Collective participation:* Professional development on the topic of inclusion should include both general and special education (Able et al., 2015; Bottge et al., 2015) because it is difficult to implement if both groups of teachers do not share the same background and philosophical approach. It also may be advantageous to include others who are involved, such as administrators, related service personnel, paraprofessionals, and families.

2. *Common content foci:* Once the group comes together, recognize that each participant will bring experiences to the table that should be shared, respected, and discussed. For example, participation in previous professional development

or years of experience may affect teachers' perceptions of the need for professional development (Brock et al., 2014).

3. *Ecological systems:* Inclusion within school settings can be extended to address inclusion in extracurricular activities that involve the community (e.g., organized youth groups such as scouting or recreational activities such as sports leagues).

4. *Coherence and continuums:* Policies toward inclusion need to be examined within school districts and across other settings and groups, including past and future environments (e.g., elementary through high school), bearing in mind that professional development needs can vary across schools and districts (Brock et al., 2014).

5–7. *Implementation stages; implementation fidelity; data-based decision making:* The professional development session(s) can highlight strategies, discuss how these can be implemented over time with fidelity, and include a plan for follow-up to analyze what is and is not working.

An example of a conceptual model for inclusion addressing points 1–4 in the preceding list can be found in Figure 4.1.

Logic Model   Whereas a conceptual model provides the underpinnings for an approach to professional development, a **logic model** is another framework that can be helpful during the planning process. It focuses on the resources or inputs that will go into professional development, the activities that will be part of its implementation, the outputs that emerge from these activities, and what the desired results and outcomes will ultimately be (i.e., the ultimate impact of the professional

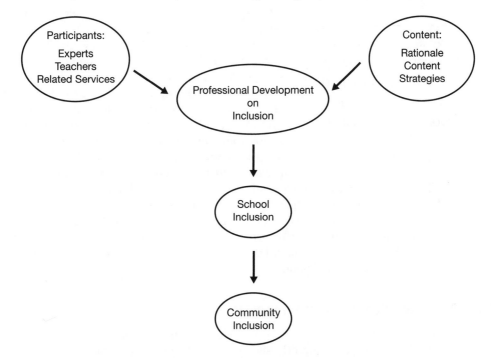

Figure 4.1.   Example of a conceptual framework for professional development on inclusion.

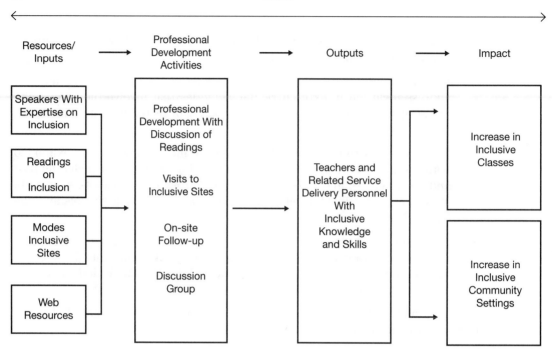

Figure 4.2.   Example of a logic model for professional development on inclusion.

development). Thus, a logic model can provide a tool for evaluating the effectiveness of professional development: Did those inputs result in the desired outputs? A simple Internet image search can yield numerous graphic examples of logic models used for a variety of purposes that can serve as templates. (These examples vary slightly in what specific components they include in addition to the basic components listed previously.)

> What is the difference between a conceptual model and a logic model? How are each useful to anyone who is designing professional development?

As an example, Bellini, Henry, and Pratt (2011) described a logic model they developed for the Indiana Resource Center for Autism school team training program. The *resources/inputs* consisted of the funding and the staff designated for the professional development to be provided, the implementation *activities* included workshops they conducted, the *outputs* consisted of workshop participants and the action plans they developed, the *outcomes* included the evaluation of the professional development and the implementation of the action plans, and the *impact* was the quality of the resulting programming and student performance. The logic model drove the evaluation process rather than making it an afterthought, which often may be the case when planning professional development. Figure 4.2 shows a logic model for implementing professional development based on the previously described conceptual model for inclusion.

Effective Strategies for Professional Development

Effective professional development should consist of more than a lecture. It should involve participants directly and actively. The delivery format should allow them to engage in activities that will provide practice and feedback.

The professional literature contains several examples of the delivery components used by other special education practitioners that include 1) information conveyed through presentations and materials, 2) the opportunity for teachers to observe and experience using strategies, and 3) feedback on performance. For example, Bottge et al. (2015) provided effective professional development on anchored instruction for math teachers and special education teachers that consisted of hands-on activities, modeling of strategies, in-depth explanations, and role-play. In another example, Courtade, Browder, Spooner, and DeBiase (2010) provided professional development for special education teachers of students with MSD that included how to use a system of least prompts procedure as a part of inquiry-based science. The training package included a video with guided notes, a verbal presentation of a manual, role-play with feedback, and coaching; the authors found the professional development to be effective with high teacher satisfaction. Finally, Horrocks and Morgan (2011) addressed assessment and instruction for students with significant intellectual and multiple disabilities through a package that included face-to-face training, video modeling, role-playing, and feedback.

Based on the What Works Clearinghouse, Browder et al. (2012) developed a specific "tell-show-try-apply" package for providing professional development to teachers of students with severe disabilities that contained the following components: 1) *tell*–provide information based on a professional research base, 2) *show*–model the presented strategies for the participants, 3) *try*–provide time for role-playing and planning for instruction, and 4) *apply*–follow up with assignments for teachers to use the newly acquired strategies with the students they teach. The authors conducted the professional development package across language arts, science, and math for 3 full days (7 hours each day, including training to fidelity) and found it to be effective.

Kunnavatana et al. (2013) also found a train-the-trainer model to be effective in preparing teachers to use functional analysis. The professional development they provided consisted of a 60-minute presentation on conducting an FBA to identify the function of challenging behaviors. Afterward, participants had the opportunity to practice with hypothetical data and then engage in role-play in small groups; participants then replicated the professional development for others.

Determining Length and Frequency and Providing Follow-Up

Professional development should be more than just a one-shot affair at which information is shared. When Shippen et al. (2012) discussed interventions for reducing delinquent behavior, they noted that professional development for teachers and administrators should be a continuing process to be effective. In fact, the No Child Left Behind Act of 2001 (PL 107-110) required that teachers receive high-quality professional development to improve student achievement that uses scientifically based strategies, is longer than 1 day, and is shown to have a lasting effect through regularly collected evaluation data (Gagnon et al., 2012).

The scope and specificity of the professional development may influence session length and frequency and the amount of follow-up provided. For example, when Bottge et al. (2015) conducted professional development on enhanced anchored instruction in inclusive math, they brought teams of special education and math education teachers together for 14 hours across 2 days in the summer, when they were free from teaching responsibilities and could plan together for the upcoming year. Noting that professional development "must be intense, focused, and supported by assessment of the effectiveness of implementation and support" (2012, p. 317), Gonsoulin, Zablocki, and Leone proposed a three-tiered approach providing

- *Quarterly universal staff development*–broad regular meetings that focus on sharing and communication

- *Monthly targeted staff development*–problem-solving and training sessions for those who have daily contact with students

- *Weekly intensive staff development*–meetings to ensure that issues are addressed with consistency

Follow-up coaching and mentoring are two ways to ensure that professional development is effective.

Voice of a Leader

Engaging Your Audience and Following Up

So far in this chapter, you have learned about effective techniques for planning and conducting professional development and the importance of providing follow-up. The most effective professional development consists of more than a "one-shot" workshop; reconnecting with workshop participants and following up over time helps to ensure that they understand and implement what they have learned. Below, Sally Miracle discusses her techniques for engaging her audience and incorporating follow-up.

Q: **What tips do you have for special education teachers who may be asked to provide professional development or in-service for other teachers?**

A: Some tips I have learned and recommend are as follows:
- Always start out with an activity to do a prelearning assessment.
- Never read your slides.
- Never give your entire PowerPoint presentation to others. Why do they need you?
- Never talk for more than 30 minutes without an activity.
- Always end with Pluses and Deltas. Follow up with your group on the Deltas. (A Plus is what you take away that you can use. A Delta refers to what a participant would recommend be adapted or changed prior to the next meeting or presentation. A Delta provides feedback to a presenter as to what would have made the meeting or presentation perfect.)
- Never have more than 20 words on a slide.
- Send items ahead of time to prepare for the topic.
- Provide guided notes.
- Always use personal stories—even [stories about times] when you failed or were not successful.
- Use humor.
- Do not use a lot of animation. Research shows it turns people off.

- Allow time for self-reflection for participants to apply what they are learning to their own situations.
- Limit, but allow, soapboxes and "gripe sessions."
- Acknowledge frustration.
- If one participant hogs the floor, call on others.
- Always provide an agenda, just like research says to have schedules in the classroom.
- Do not lecture. Talk with–share with–participants. They can find information from the Internet and books. What do you have to offer as a presenter that they cannot get from a book?

Q: *Do you ever conduct follow-up or monitor performance after you have worked with special education teachers? If so, how often?*

A: Follow-up is very important to successful and continuous change/growth. Face-to-face follow-up is not always easy in my position. I would prefer every other week follow-up with teachers, but working with 23 [school] districts, that is not always easy. At all trainings I do, I have participants set goals and develop an action plan. Sometimes, follow-up consists of me sending e-mails or having teachers check in with each other for accountability. I have some cadres come together on a monthly or every-other-month schedule for follow-up. Sometimes, I provide monthly follow-up face-to-face. Follow-up depends on the staff, situation, and availability. I wish I was able to do more.

   Immediate follow-up/feedback, however, is important. Make it positive. Ask the teacher how they think something went. Include questions/comments like these:

- Here are some research-based strategies I saw you use today. . .
- Here is something I learned from you today. . .
- I saw you. . . This is a sound practice because. . .
- I enjoyed being in your classroom today because. . .

Coaching   As described in Chapter 3, coaching (e.g., Courtade et al., 2010) is an EBP you can employ as a follow-up component to make professional development even more effective. For example, Kretlow, Wood, and Cooke (2011) found that, although 3 hours of professional development were effective in increasing kindergarten teachers' ability to use direct instruction, the teachers showed even more growth after they participated in side-by-side coaching. Suhrheinrich (2011) found similar results when providing professional development on pivotal response training for students with ASD; although participants increased their skill following a 6-hour workshop that included instruction, video modeling, practice with feedback, and discussion, follow-up classroom coaching resulted in even higher increases in performance. In yet another example, Brock and Carter (2015) found coaching to be more effective than video modeling in teaching paraprofessionals to use a constant time delay instructional procedure. The professional development package (i.e., video modeling plus abbreviated coaching) consisted of an initial workshop with a description and demonstration of the procedure followed by role-play. A video modeling component then allowed participants to compare their performance to a model, and subsequent coaching allowed participants to receive an hour of feedback, modeling, and practice in a natural setting. The paraprofessionals rated the workshop as helpful, the video modeling as very helpful, and the coaching as extremely helpful.

Mentoring   Short-term coaching can provide feedback until a professional development participant exhibits skills at a specified criterion level, but long-term mentoring support also can increase the workshops' effectiveness. Even if you do not facilitate the initial workshop, by getting involved in follow-up mentoring, you can help the teacher(s) make lasting changes, as described in Chapter 3.

As an example, Maddox and Marvin (2012) described how the STEPS project (Strategies and Techniques for Effective Practices in Schools Educating Children with Autism) set up regional teams that included special education teacher leaders. Using a train-the-trainer approach, the teams received professional development in strategies for students with ASD, such as instruction, social skills, and applied behavior analysis, until they could use these strategies with fidelity; they then served as mentors and consultants to teachers in local districts for 8–10 days over time. The mentoring approach provided a way for rural and isolated teachers to receive quality professional development.

Use of Technology

Professional development workshops are typically provided in a central location to a single group of participants. Bringing teachers together in the same room, however, may sometimes be difficult. For example, rural teachers may find it inconvenient to travel long distances to attend face-to-face meetings, and school districts may not find this to be an efficient or cost-effective use of time and funds. Brock et al. (2014) found that rural teachers did not express interest in web-based professional development. However, technology can be used to convey information on a specific topic to a large group of participants in a way that breaks down the barriers of travel and cost (Odom, Cox, Brock, & National Professional Development Center on ASD, 2013; Rakap, Jones, & Emery, 2015). Videos can also be an effective component when used to provide models during face-to-face training (e.g., Browder et al., 2012; Courtade et al., 2010; Horrocks & Morgan, 2011; Suhrheinrich, 2011); when used to archive content online for participants' future reference (Bottge et al., 2015); and when used to provide immediate feedback during follow-up coaching through teleconferencing (Machalicek et al., 2010).

> Why is follow-up an important component of professional development and consultation? Given that it may be difficult for special education teachers to provide face-to-face follow-up, what are some ways in which technology can be used to solve this problem?

Odom et al. (2013) implemented a large-scale model of professional development that involved providing an online course on ASD for local teams followed by local summer workshops in EBPs. As an example, they described how a middle school established a team that included three special education teachers in addition to an administrator, a speech/language pathologist, a parent, and general education teachers. After the team completed the online course and workshop and subsequently received a year of coaching, they shared practices with other teachers in the school and became a model site for training teachers in other schools. Through this model, special education teachers who received online professional development served as leaders to share information with others in their school.

YOUR ROLE IN CONDUCTING CONSULTATIONS

Not all special education teachers have the opportunity to deliver professional development. However, another way to provide leadership is to conduct consultations. You may be asked to consult with another teacher on a specific student with a disability—for example, consulting about how to complete an FBA of a specific challenging behavior. You might be consulted on strategies for working with students with disabilities in general, such as ways to adapt and modify materials. The consultation process differs from the process typically used for professional development. Instead of sharing a broad category of information with others, you must provide a professional with information on a specific issue so you can work together to share expertise and generate solutions.

Like professional development, consultations are more likely to be effective when they involve providing feedback on implementation over time, instead of delivering recommendations once with no follow-up. For example, in one study, consultants worked with parents on providing positive behavior support (PBS) for their children, following the parents' participation in a workshop on PBS (Erbas, 2010). All of the parents participated in four consultation meetings lasting 15–20 minutes each and structured as follows: 1) discussion of problem behaviors and how to use a behavioral assessment form, 2) observation of the child in the home, 3) generation of acceptable behavior statement with more observation, and 4) creation of a PBS plan. Erbas found the consultation protocol to be more effective for parents who received additional feedback sessions as they implemented the plan; these 10- to 15-minute sessions consisted of feedback (e.g., correction, praise) as the consultant and the parent watched videotapes of the plan being implemented. In another example (Stephenson, Carter, & Arthur-Kelly, 2011), consultants worked with teachers on tailoring communication strategies for students with severe disabilities. After completing observations (live or on video), the consultants met with the teachers to discuss potential communication strategies and then followed up with visits to discuss progress.

Voice of a Leader

Combining Authority with Support

Being an effective consultant is a delicate balancing act. As Sally Miracle explains, consultants typically use an authoritative, take-charge approach. At the same time, being respectful and supportive toward colleagues is paramount. Below, Ms. Miracle discusses her consulting work and the tips she typically provides classroom teachers. These tips hinge on one crucial idea: Create an environment in which every adult is respected and valued just as much as students are.

Q: Describe your experiences as a consultant for special education teachers.

A: I have learned over the past couple of years that there is a difference between being a consultant and a coach. I view a consultant as someone who tells what to do, how to do it, and what needs to be changed. In consultation, the consultant does most of the talking. I view coaching [as parties working] together as partners where both are learning and growing together. Coaches interact with the students and get involved in the lessons. The coach influences rather than dominates. When coaching, both partners work together to analyze data, plan solutions, develop lessons, and work past barriers. In coaching, both partners are seen as equal contributors. In business, coaches are seen as a positive support, but, in education, coaches are seen as a negative because teaching is personal. I try to work past this to let teachers know that I am not evaluative, but rather a support, and I want to learn from them, too.

Q: What are some of the tips that you provide for special education teachers when you are consulting with them?

A: Tips I provide for teachers to be successful in their room include the following:

- Make sure that all adults are treated as equals.
- Write a positive note of praise to each staff person at least once a week. Be specific. We naturally reinforce the students, but we need to reinforce the adults, too.
- Never have others do a job or task that you would not do.
- Give each adult a responsibility/job to be in charge of.
- If you need another adult to change, become a coach and ask them to sit down and brainstorm ways to change something in their classroom because "something" is not working—not because they are doing it wrong.
- Be willing to be flexible. Teachers are natural leaders and directors. Allow all staff and students in your room to have input on how things work. This allows buy-in to new things. We have to model how we are willing to change and adapt if we want others to change.
- Get things organized from Day 1, but every other week have a 10-minute meeting with all staff in your room to discuss what is and is not working. It took 2 years to get things running smoothly in my classroom. We made continuous changes on what we felt was not going smoothly. I had to be flexible to allow the other staff to have a say in how things should go.

On many days, I was more of a manager than a teacher with all the different things going on in my room, but it ran smoothly. My staff [were] just as in charge of teaching, discipline, lesson development, data collection, and classroom management as I was. I referred to my paraprofessionals as teachers. They were just without the training and piece of paper.

BE A LEADER: PROVIDE PROFESSIONAL DEVELOPMENT AND CONSULTATION

Great teachers are committed to lifelong learning, and that learning process will likely involve participating in professional development workshops; working with a consultant, mentor, or coach; or some combination of these activities. Professional development and consulting work offers you an opportunity to demonstrate leadership. As a special education teacher, you have acquired expertise on specific topics that you can impart to colleagues in both general and special education. In addition, you can relate to teachers' day-to-day classroom experiences and provide professional development and advice that is grounded in mutual respect and desire to learn and improve. The following guidelines are offered to special education teachers who want to expand their leadership skills in professional development and consultation:

1. Look for opportunities to share your expertise with others and volunteer. Collaborating with an experienced presenter or consultant in the beginning will help you observe techniques that work and help alleviate any anxiety that you may have.

2. Identify presentation techniques that engage you—or don't. When you attend professional development sessions or conferences, observe and take notes on what the presenter does that is effective and ineffective.

3. Before sharing strategies with others, make sure that the strategies you suggest, model, and recommend are evidence-based. Offer to share the evidence with others. (See Chapter 1 on identifying best practices.)

4. Know your audience and make sure that you build in time to listen to the experiences of others. Doing some homework on those who will be participating in a professional development or consultation can pay off.

5. If using technology, take advantage of any available training and make sure that you complete a practice run ahead of time. If technology fails, have a back-up plan. This might include having a handout for a face-to-face event or having a call-in number for an online event.

6. When possible, find ways to provide follow-up. This may consist of face-to-face discussions or observations, phone calls, e-mails, discussion boards, online video chats, or review of videos.

7. Consult experts for tips for preparing effective slide presentations, quality videos, and engaging activities. Also consult experts on techniques for providing engaging presentations (note that face-to-face and online presentations may differ) and for developing trust while providing consultations.

8. Be careful about talking above the heads of others (e.g., using too much jargon or unfamiliar terms), but also be careful about talking down to others (e.g., oversimplifying statements or assuming a lack of background/experience).

9. Practice professional presentations in front of others and take their feedback. Be sure to time how long each segment (e.g., lecture, activities, discussion) takes.

10. When providing consultations, get as much information as possible (e.g., interviews of involved parties, personal observation of classroom issue, available data) before providing any recommendations.

FOLLOW-UP ACTIVITIES

Chapter 4 has discussed ways you can be a leader by conducting professional development or consultations. This work allows you to integrate your teaching and presentation skills, classroom experiences, and expertise in special education topics in ways that inform, guide, and support your peers.

The suggested activities that follow are intended to help you consider professional development and consultation from the perspective of the audience or recipient as well as from the perspective of the presenter or consultant. These activities will also help you link what you have learned in this chapter to what you learned in Chapter 3. In the course of completing these activities, think about whether your path to leadership might include conducting professional development and/or consultations.

1. **Critique the most recent professional development that you attended.** Was the topic beneficial? Was it presented in a manner that engaged you? Did the presenter inspire you? Did the materials and activities used during the presentation contribute to your learning? Were you given useful materials or resources to use following the presentation? Did the presenter make efficient use of the time, stay on topic, and handle discussions, questions, and comments effectively? What aspects of the presentation would you use or not use in planning your own professional development presentation?

2. **Interview an experienced presenter.** This may be someone who works in your school or at the district level or someone from an unrelated field. What tips does your interviewee provide?

3. **If you ever have interacted with a consultant on a specific classroom issue, critique the consultation.** If not, interview someone who has been the recipient of consultation. What types of information did the consultant request? Before making recommendations, did the consultant observe the problem or discuss it with you? Were the recommendations presented verbally or in writing, and was the feedback immediate or delayed? Did the consultant provide any modeling, coaching, or feedback based on the recommendations? Were follow-up observations conducted or follow-up data reviewed?

4. **Interview an experienced consultant.** This may be someone who works in your school or at the district level or someone from an unrelated field. What tips does your interviewee provide?

5. **Reflect upon the roles of consultants, coaches, and mentors.** In her interview, Sally Miracle presented her viewpoint that consultation is more about providing information and coaching is more about sharing information. Based on the information presented in this chapter and in previous chapters on mentoring and coaching, what is your personal viewpoint on the roles of the consultant, the coach, and the mentor? What do these roles have in common? How do they differ?

5 Work Effectively With Families

Learning Objectives

After reading this chapter, readers will be able to

- Describe issues that uniquely affect families of children with disabilities

- Communicate effectively with families by using multiple modes of communication and taking into account important considerations for communication

- Identify and apply strategies to improve the process of setting educational goals with families

- Explain why families should be involved in home intervention in collaboration with school intervention

- Identify and put into practice ways of providing family support and facilitating equal partnerships

Terms to Know

Facilitator

Generalization

Graphic facilitator

Maintenance

Partnerships

Process facilitator

← ——— →

INTRODUCTION

All special education teachers can be leaders in their work with the families of their students with disabilities. The IEP and transition processes provide established opportunities to meet and talk with families; during these meetings, you may be the designated **facilitator**—that is, the person who, because of your skills and experience, is tasked with leading the group toward consensus. However, your involvement with families goes much further than this; family contact should be sustained throughout the year, not limited to a single annual event. Involvement with families has been linked to academic achievement for students with disabilities (Sawyer, 2015). This makes sense given that teachers have access to children only a few hours each week for part of the year, but families are with their children every day almost throughout their lives (Ludlow, 2012). Therefore, the more you can work with families to provide support and resources, the greater the likelihood that these families' children will benefit.

Although it is important for all teachers to view families as equal partners in their children's education, this can be even more important for families of children with disabilities. Family stress can be exacerbated in families of children with disabilities, and the type of disability can make a difference. Miranda, Tarraga, Fernandez, Colomer, and Pastor (2015) found stress to be higher in families of children with ASD and attention-deficit/hyperactivity disorder (ADHD) than in a control group. In addition, Meadan, Halle, and Eata (2010) reported that the stress of having a child with ASD may have a negative impact on the parents' marriage and that mothers may carry more day-to-day responsibility for the child and be more affected by any challenging behaviors the child displays. They also noted that stress associated with ASD may be due to the permanence of the disability, lack of acceptance by others, low levels of support, economic burden, concerns for the future, and challenging behaviors. An analysis of special education complaints filed by parents of children with ASD in a single state showed parental dissatisfaction with the content and implementation of IEPs, amount of parental participation, evaluation and conferencing procedures, staff qualifications, and behavioral procedures (White, 2014).

Family issues such as heightened stress are also associated with disabilities besides ASD, and other family characteristics (e.g., parental age, socioeconomic status) are also linked with the degree of stress families of children with disabilities might experience. De Boer and Munde (2015) found that parents of children with motor disabilities typically have more positive attitudes than parents of children with significant intellectual disabilities, that mothers are likely to be more positive than fathers, and that younger parents are likely to be more positive than older parents. Research also has shown that stress can increase as children with disabilities age or have more health concerns, and it can be greater in families that are Hispanic or non–English-speaking (Marshall, Kirby, & Gorski, 2016). When families live in poverty, their children are more at risk for achieving academic success, child care and transportation can be issues, and the need for support and resources is crucial (Parish, Rose, & Andrews, 2010). In addition, families in poverty may have access to less information and fewer resources than others (Meadan, Halle et al., 2010).

Both socioeconomic status (SES) and geography can play a role in working with families of children with disabilities. For example, researchers have linked specific issues associated with poverty to rural special education services. Thurston and Navarrete (2010) found that rural mothers at poverty level who had children with disabilities sometimes felt discomfort around teachers. As one mother stated,

"I'm trying as hard as I can. I just can't do any more" (Thurston & Navarrete, 2010, p. 45). The authors suggested that teachers should consider these mothers' material hardships and lack of education, and the fact that some parents may themselves have been served in special education when they were in school. Mallory (2010) also asserted that rural mothers may be under more stress than other caregivers due to a culture of dependence on the mother, sometimes to the exclusion of support from outsiders. Mallory pointed out the need for respectful intervention that takes into consideration the political and economic conditions of rural families. On the other hand, Williams-Diehm, Brandes, Chesnut, and Haring (2014) found that rural districts had higher levels of student involvement in the IEP process and suggested that this may be due to rural parents being more likely to be involved in their school districts. Likewise, Murphy, McCormick, and Rous (2013) concluded from national data that rural teachers use more transition practices than urban teachers and that they report fewer barriers.

Parents of children with disabilities may also be affected by the presence of challenging behaviors. Some parents have reported feeling like they live in a "war zone" when continually dealing with the most challenging behaviors and have voiced a belief that professionals may not appreciate how much their lives are affected on a daily basis (Hodgetts, Nicholas, & Zwaigenbaum, 2013). In spite of the need for behavioral intervention, parents may have concerns about the types of interventions used with their children, and research has shown that parents appreciate professionals who listen to their concerns on behavioral issues as well as academic issues (Haines, Gross, Blue-Banning, Francis, & Turnbull, 2015). Other research, however, has found that parents may have limited knowledge of how to provide appropriate intervention for challenging behaviors (Hodgetts et al.). Brown and Traniello (2010) examined mothers' perceptions of the use of aversive interventions by schools in reaction to their children's challenging behaviors (e.g., throwing, hitting, scratching, threatening, screaming, running, crying). The study found that the mothers believed that they were discouraged from being involved in IEP meetings and in identifying behavioral supports and that they received little support, even though parent input as part of an FBA could have been helpful. As one mother stated, "The school didn't call for a meeting, just called me at work and said she needed to leave" (Brown & Traniello, 2010, p. 131). Special education teachers need to realize that what may come across as hostility in parents can be related to the challenging behaviors of their children (Bader, Barry, & Hann, 2015).

Another area in which parents of children with disabilities may believe that their preferences are not addressed is inclusion (Carter, Swedeen, Cooney, Walter, & Moss, 2012). Inclusive services have been linked to families having a stronger sense of belonging and trust and to school and staff having higher expectations (Haines et al., 2015). Families' SES, however, can affect parent advocacy for inclusive services. Lalvani (2012) found that higher-SES parents were more likely to

- Be aware of inclusive practices and that inclusion was an option for their children

- Invest a lot of time and effort in negotiating the educational system

- Educate themselves on best practices

- Participate in national organizations and parent groups

- Feel equipped to question professional recommendations

- Take the lead in educating teachers about their children's needs

On the other hand, Lalvani found that parents from a lower SES category had very different beliefs about, and ways of managing, the education of their children with disabilities. Often they did not think inclusion was an option for their children. They had schedule and financial limitations that interfered with advocating for their children. They were less connected with parent resources and groups. Often these parents did not believe their advocacy made a difference, and they were more likely to follow the recommendations of professionals without question.

On the positive side, research has shown that several factors can result in a higher degree of resilience in families of children with disabilities: a higher SES, social support, open and predictable communication, a supportive family environment, hardiness, coping strategies, a positive outlook, and a belief system (Greeff & van der Wah, 2010). Rieger and McGrail (2015) reported that families who used humor as a coping strategy were better able to cope with stress and recommended that teachers be aware that the types of humor used can be a sign of the family's ability to function. For example, some types of humor are used to entertain, some to demean or manipulate, and some to gain acceptance. In addition, Meadan, Halle, et al. (2010) reported that families of children with ASD may develop strategies to cope with related stress, with some strategies (e.g., being proactive and taking actions) being more effective than others (e.g., escape and avoidance).

> Reflect on some of the assumptions that you or others have made about families of children with disabilities (e.g., assuming that parents do not care about academic achievement when they do not participate in school activities, assuming that parents cannot manage behavior when a child acts in an inappropriate way in public). What is the least dangerous assumption in each of the scenarios that you recall?

As a special education teacher, you understand many of the issues that confront the families of children with disabilities. This understanding provides an opportunity to demonstrate leadership as you work with families, providing an example for your colleagues. You probably have noticed what kind of professional demeanor helps the families you work with feel comfortable, respected, and valued. In conducting interviews with families, Hebert concluded that, in addition to having their children served in inclusive settings, parents want them to have teachers who are "warm, invested, and dedicated" (2014, p. 118), who are available and willing to address their concerns, and who can provide information on appropriate interventions. In a similar vein, Haines et al. concluded that, in addition to their children having access to differentiated instruction, parents want professionals to be "approachable, available, responsive, and caring" (2015, p. 229), and they also want to be treated as equals in the educational process and have leadership opportunities within the school (e.g., assisting teachers, volunteering for events).

Taking all of these factors into consideration, this chapter addresses ways you can be a school leader in working with families to

- Establish open channels of communication

- Set their children's educational goals (e.g., by developing IEPs and transition plans)

- Share strategies so parents can be home interventionists

- Provide support and resources

- Establish equal partnerships in the educational process

Although much of the chapter's content stems from research on working with parents, recognize that it is important to think in a broader sense, including caregivers, siblings, and extended family members as well.

In 1984, Donnellan and Miranda proposed that a *criterion of least dangerous assumption* be applied when professionals work with families. This concept states that, "in the absence of conclusive data, decisions should be based on the assumption which, if incorrect, will have the least dangerous effect on the student [and his/her family]" (Donnellan & Miranda, 1984, p. 22). This is an important concept to keep in mind in your work with students and families.

CONNECTION TO PROFESSIONAL STANDARDS

Your role in working with families of students is supported by a number of professional standards listed under the Teacher Leader Model Standards (TLEC, 2012) and the CEC Standards for Professional Practice and Advanced Preparation Standards (CEC, 2015).

Teacher Leader Model Standards

Although not specific to special education, the Teacher Leader Model Standards (TLEC, 2012) address the need to serve as a model across domains. These include a focus on "promot[ing] a sense of partnership" with families and other groups in the community, listed under *Domain 6: Improving Outreach and Collaboration with Families and Community*. Doing so involves understanding the students' backgrounds and issues pertaining to diversity, demonstrating "effective communication and collaboration skills with families," "develop[ing] culturally responsive strategies," working with colleagues to develop a "shared understanding . . . of the diverse needs of families," and "develop[ing] comprehensive strategies to address the diverse educational needs of families and the community."

Council for Exceptional Children Program Standards

The Special Education Standards for Professional Practice developed by CEC (2015) address special educators' work with parents and families (6.0) through the need to use culturally appropriate and respectful communication that will be understood with accuracy (6.1); to seek and use the knowledge of parents in planning, conducting, and evaluating special education services while empowering parents as partners (6.2); to maintain parent communication with attention to privacy, confidentiality, and cultural diversity (6.3); to promote parent education opportunities (6.4); to inform parents of their rights (6.5); to practice respect for cultural diversity (6.6); and to engage in professional and appropriate relationships with parents (6.7). The Advanced Preparation Standards state that teachers should use the professional literature to improve practices with families (4.2); create a supportive environment for individuals with exceptionalities and their families with attention to high expectations and ethical practices (6.2); and collaborate to improve programs, services, and outcomes for individuals with exceptionalities and their families (7.0). One teacher who exemplifies such practices in her work with families is Abby Evans McCormick, introduced in the section that follows.

Voice of a Leader

Maintaining Communication in Periods of Transition

Abby Evans McCormick is a special education teacher who has been involved in classroom research in special education (e.g., Collins et al., 2007). She recently took on a leadership role in her current school, where she works with parents and teachers as a facilitator for IEP and transition plan development. As her interview responses imply, she is an experienced teacher who is still learning how to be a leader with the families of the students she serves and how to be a liaison between school and home. Currently, Ms. McCormick works with seventh and eighth graders. Here, she comments on how important it is to establish good communication with families during this transitional period in an adolescent's life.

Q: *Describe your experiences as a facilitator for IEP development. What tips do you have for special education teachers as they work with the families of their students with disabilities? What are the best ways for special education teachers to communicate with families?*

A: What I have learned is how difficult it is for parents to [make the] transition to a new school as well [as students]. We are departmentalized, so the special education teacher does not travel with the same students all day. I have observed the extreme importance [of our communicating] weekly, either through e-mail or newsletter, both [about] what is going on in our school academically and [about] extra activities. Teachers (case managers) are more of a support to parents than I think teachers realize. Parents need that extra support; even though their students are in the seventh grade, they still need the reassurance that their child's needs are being met. I think this is an age in which children typically are changing, and parents are unsure if this is because of their disability or just developmental. Possibly, they still have not accepted their child has a disability, whether it is a specific learning disability or a low incidence disability.

YOUR ROLE IN WORKING WITH FAMILIES

Professionals do not always communicate well with families, leading to the perception that families are uninformed or untrained in working with children with disabilities (Sansosti, Lavik, & Sansosti, 2012). Before relationships and partnerships can develop with families, lines of communication between school and home must be open. When that happens, you have a better chance of working with families on setting mutual goals for their children with disabilities, sharing strategies they can use at home to increase the amount of instruction their children receive in natural environments, opening channels of support, and developing partnerships in the education process, as outlined in the following sections.

←——→

Communicating With Parents

Rodrigues, Blatz, and Elbaum (2014) found that parents of children with disabilities who communicate frequently with their children's teachers tend to feel more positive about their experiences with their children's schools and to view their children's teachers as competent and trained; on the other hand, parents who have communication issues with their children's teachers feel more negative toward their children's schools and perceive a lack of sufficient support. Communicating effectively with families is crucial to developing a good working relationship with them.

The first rule to remember is that communication can take place through many different available modes, including telephone calls, letters, e-mail, and face-to-face meetings. If one mode is not working well, try another. As one parent with a positive communication experience with a teacher stated, "She was one of the best. She would e-mail, she would call you up, she would send notes; she would make sure you were involved" (Rodrigues et al., 2014, p. 90). On the other hand, parents have voiced dissatisfaction when they considered communication about their children to be inadequate: As one parent said, "I mean, I would love to get like, a summary every night of what he does, and what's going on every day. It's just like this little paragraph. I want more" (Podvey, Hinojosa, & Koenig, 2013, p. 216). As a teacher, you need to determine which modes are effective for communicating with families and how often they should be used. Regular communication through a variety of methods is ideal.

These modes can include spoken or written communication and face-to-face communication in group or individual contexts. Noting the need for parents to be involved in RTI as a strategy before their children are identified for special education services, Byrd (2011) suggested setting meetings, making telephone calls, recruiting parents to lead and be part of support groups, using Parent Teacher Association (PTA) meetings to share information, and providing written and online materials, with attention to cultural diversity and the possible need to provide information in multiple languages. To facilitate family literacy (and, thus, child literacy), Valerie and Foss-Swanson (2012) suggested the use of family journals in which the child writes to the family about his or her school day and members of the family reply. When face-to-face meetings with families occur, they can be as informal as talking to a parent who is dropping off or picking up the child at school, or as formal as holding a required IEP meeting (Conroy, 2012). Helpful materials that facilitate or supplement communication include frequent progress reports, fill-in-the-blank notes, an agenda or planner to keep up with assignments, a cheat sheet of definitions of special education jargon, and examples of student work (Diliberto & Brewer, 2014).

Regarding communication with families with cultural and linguistic diversity (CLD), Conroy (2012) cautioned that establishing trust can be an issue. For example, families from some cultures may consider it respectful to have the teacher come to their home. When meetings occur in the family home, it is important that teachers return that respect by maintaining a professional demeanor and speaking in the family's native language, even if this requires an interpreter who understands the cultural issues involved and does not simply act as a translator. Meetings should be about building relationships, not just addressing problems.

Keep in mind that, due to communication and cultural issues, it is not uncommon for families with CLD to have difficulty grasping concepts that special educators may value. In interviewing parents from four distinct cultures (i.e., African American, Asian American, European American, and Hispanic American), Zhang,

Landmark, Grenwelge, and Montoya (2010) found different perspectives on self-determination that affected understanding of the concepts of goal-setting and decision making and the ability to do so. For example, some of the interviewed parents did not believe in talking to their children about the future. A parent interviewed by Shogren (2012) had this caution about working with Hispanic families: "Don't assume that the Spanish speaking families all reach out the same way that Anglo families do. Stop sending those newsletters and surveys. It's an American Model. If you're really interested in knowing valuable information, you have to establish that trust" (2012, p. 180). Please also note that issues related to working with families with CLD can be exacerbated in rural areas by long distances, lack of child care, and lack of transportation (Conroy, 2012).

In summary, the first step to working with families is to establish strong, viable modes of communication and to communicate on a frequent basis, taking into account differences in perceptions that may be due to CLD issues. Once communication is established and a bond of mutual respect and trust is developed, you can be more effective in working with parents for the benefit of their children with disabilities.

Setting Goals With Parents

One area in which parents have stated that they feel like "outsiders" is in the development of their children's educational plans during two critical transition periods: from preschool to elementary school (Podvey et al., 2013) and from school to adulthood (Hetherington et al., 2010). Once lines of communication are open, it's easier to establish a process for working with parents to set goals for their children with disabilities. As all special education teachers should know, legally mandated meetings to establish goals for IEPs or transition plans rely on the sharing of information by both professionals and families; as a special education teacher, however, you can do much to set a positive tone for these meetings. In some cases, a skilled special education teacher, hired by the school as a full-time facilitator, may be the designated facilitator for meetings; in others, the responsibility may fall to the student's special education teacher. (In my experience, larger and more urban schools are more likely to hire facilitators, whereas smaller, more rural schools are more likely to rely on the special education teacher to facilitate.) Whoever assumes this role, the facilitator must "be committed to a student-centered philosophy, be an aware and conscious listener, and be able to communicate clearly" (Espiner & Guild, 2012, p. 62), as well as "be able to guide the group towards a common understanding while encouraging the student and other participants to share information, learn from one another, remain focused, solve problems, make decisions, and plan work" (pp. 62–63).

Researchers and professionals have generated numerous tips for running successful IEP meetings. Although many school personnel such as teachers, administrators, and service delivery personnel will be involved, the most important individuals present are the child's parents or other appropriate family representatives. As noted by Diliberto and Brewer (2014), parents should serve an important role from the beginning as you work with them to develop a draft form of an IEP. The authors also noted other ways to involve parents, including making early contacts from the beginning of the school year on, encouraging school visits and participation in school activities, providing multiple forms of school–home communication, taking into account parents' native language and ability to read legal materials, walking parents step-by-step through the IEP process (especially when it is the first IEP meeting), and making parents aware that they can bring an advocate to meetings and including this person in all discussions. Other tips from Diliberto and Brewer include sharing ideas at a premeeting; having the facilitator stick to an agenda with items from everyone present; setting respectful communication ground rules, such as being open to others' ideas and focusing on the future instead of the past; recognizing the family's knowledge of their child's strengths and weaknesses; and providing a one-page reference guide to the jargon that will be used.

A chart can be an effective tool during educational meetings. For example, as part of the process for creating an upcoming-year "vision" for a student with a disability, Espiner and Guild (2012) recommended the completion of a chart designed by an educational planning group. The advantage of creating a chart was that copies could be placed on walls at school and at home as visual reminders. The authors noted that this process involved two facilitators: 1) a **process facilitator** to oversee the meeting's steps and content and 2) a **graphic facilitator** to capture the discussion on the chart. Wells and Sheehey (2012) noted that charts can be used in planning person-centered transitions from birth through adulthood. To make the process more comfortable for families, they suggested that meetings with a facilitator occur in a comfortable place suggested by parents (with refreshments provided)—and at a round table so all participants are considered equal.

Cultural issues often come into play during educational planning meetings. For example, Shogren (2012) found that some Hispanic parents interviewed wanted to participate in IEP meetings whereas others did not; however, all stated that the family's values should be respected and voiced frustration when what the family valued at home was not addressed at school. Noting that families can differ within a culture, Shogren stressed that teachers should get to know families and not make generalizations because they are from a specific culture, as illustrated by this quote from a parent: "Schools need to understand that families are going to be different and may value different things. . . . I just wish we could find a way to understand each other better and accept both ways to doing things and teach our children about both traditions" (Shogren, 2012, p. 180). When families are from a different culture, Lo (2012) suggested assisting the IEP process with a few simple steps that include providing advance information through means such as face-to-face conversation, written materials, or video; making sure parents are greeted at the door and escorted to the meeting room; making introductions and indicating the meeting's anticipated length; using an interpreter familiar with the family's dialect who has been given an advance copy of terms that will be used; paying attention to body language that may be cultural so that this will not be misinterpreted; and providing a summary of the meeting, translated into the family's home language if necessary.

Several components come together to create a successful educational planning meeting; however, it can be just as helpful to consider what should *not* occur. Cheatham, Hart, Malian, and McDonald (2012) suggested that 1) goals and objectives should never be selected in advance to save time, 2) a presumption should never be made that a special education setting is needed over a general education setting, 3) a meeting should never take place without everyone present, 4) practices that do not work should not be continued in place of trying other data-based options, 5) parents should never be blamed when their child does not learn, and 6) a child should never be moved to a more restrictive setting simply because that is what has occurred in the past. A quote from a qualitative study of parents whose children were making a transition from preschool illustrates how parents feel when best practices are not used in developing the IEP: "They trampled on all of our rights, and none of the process got handled in a timely manner . . . we were presented with a draft IEP for a signature, with 15 minutes worth of discussion before we needed to be ushered out for the next ones to come in" (Podvey et al., 2013, p. 215).

The ultimate outcome of an educational planning meeting is that special education teachers and families listen to each other as they set goals for children with disabilities. Be aware of ways in which communication can break down. An example is safety skill instruction—a concern for many parents as their children with disabilities approach the transition from school to adulthood (Griffen, McMillan, & Hodapp, 2010). When Agran and Krupp (2010) surveyed 121 parents of students with disabilities, they found that 93% considered safety skills to be the most important skills that should be taught to their children, yet safety skills were not included on their children's IEPs, nor had they been discussed with their children's teachers.

Open communication is key to setting goals with families, but additional skills also need to be developed to ensure that the outcomes of educational planning will be both appropriate and effective. Once you have developed effective leadership skills in working with families, you can provide further leadership by coaching new teachers in those skills. For example, Votava and Chiasson (2015) suggested that experienced early interventionists trained in family assessment serve as coaches to new early interventionists involved in family assessment for the first time.

Preparing Parents as Interventionists

After effective communication has been established and educational goals have been set, the next opportunity to show leadership is to empower parents to serve as interventionists in the home. The home is the natural setting where children with disabilities need to use many of the skills identified during the IEP or transition plan meeting, and preparing parents as interventionists has the potential for reducing family stress (Suppo & Floyd, 2012).

Chapter 1 discussed the importance of using EBPs with fidelity, and this is just as important for parents. When you share EBPs with parents and teach them to use the procedures with fidelity, the effectiveness of instruction can be maximized (Cook, Shepherd, Cook, & Cook, 2012; McDonnall, Cavenaugh, & Giesen, 2012; Suppo & Floyd, 2012). When parents, as well as grandparents and siblings, are involved in home intervention, students learning skills are more likely to reach both **maintenance** (the continued use of skills over time) and **generalization** (the use of skills across a variety of people, settings, and materials, beyond those used when the student initially learned the skill; Park, Alber-Morgan, & Fleming, 2011). To quote a professional, "When you model an activity and show [the family] a couple of varieties, and when the next time you see them they've incorporated that into functional routine and generalized it to different settings you are like, wow!" (Bezdek, Summers, & Turnbull, 2010, p. 361).

Several examples from available research literature serve to illustrate the importance of parent training. For instance, Valimarsdottir, Halldorsdottir, and Sigurdardotter (2010) increased the variety of foods eaten by a 5-year-old boy with ASD who previously had screamed and thrown food at mealtime after they involved his parents in implementing the same procedures at home that were used at school (e.g., reinforcing bites of nonpreferred foods with bites of preferred foods while slowly increasing the amount of nonpreferred foods consumed over time). In another example, Olcay-Gul and Tekin-Iftar (2016) taught family members (i.e., one sister and two mothers) to use social stories to increase specific social skills in youth with ASD: greeting others, responding to others, and asking permission. Six hours of training resulted in the youth acquiring, maintaining, and generalizing the targeted social skills. The research shows that, in addition to implementing procedures with high fidelity in the home, parents can collect data with a high degree of reliability (Witmer, Nasamran, Parikh, Schmitt, & Clinton, 2015a).

You can work with families in several ways to prepare them to provide intervention in the home, including the use of manuals, lectures, face-to-face and video modeling, and Internet delivery of guidance (Suppo & Floyd, 2012). Most special education teachers, however, do not have the time or budget to invest in training families to use EBPs in the home setting. The use of technology shows promise as a way that all special education teachers can provide training without having to travel to families' homes after school hours. One possible use is to help parents locate existing online materials that demonstrate best practices. For example, Suppo and Mayton (2014) found that parents who reviewed modules on the Ohio Department of Education Center for

> The professional literature contains a number of studies on teaching parents and siblings to provide both academic and behavioral interventions for children with disabilities. Given what you read in the previous chapters, how might you provide professional development or coaching for families?

Autism and Low Incidence (OCALI) web site could correctly apply the acquired information to create visual schedules for their children with ASD. They noted that Internet modules also have the advantage of saving parents the cost, time, and travel potentially associated with face-to-face training. In another example, professionals used phone and video conferencing to coach rural parents of children with developmental delays to use naturalistic teaching strategies through the Internet-based Parent-Implemented Communication Strategies (i-PICS) program (Meadan, Meyer, Snodgrass, & Halle, 2013). The training protocol included sharing online materials, providing instruction through Skype, and coaching parents to criterion. (More detail about directing families to Internet resources is provided in the next section, "Providing Support for Parents.")

When students with disabilities enroll in online classes, the family's role becomes even more important because families must provide the support for completing daily classwork, making modifications as needed. A teacher who is at a distance can find it helpful to establish family lines of communication through e-mail, phone, or videoconferencing and to provide an initial introductory letter that spells out responsibilities (Currie-Rubin & Smith, 2010).

Voice of a Leader

Following Up on Shared Decisions

Some families will be immediately able to implement home-based interventions to help their child meet the goals established during an IEP meeting or to carry out other shared educational decisions. Others may need more support and follow-up to ensure they can effectively use available resources and apply helpful strategies. Below, Abby Evans McCormick reflects on how follow-up might be incorporated into her work with families.

Q: Do you ever conduct follow-up with families after the IEP meeting? If so, why? How often?

A: At this time, I do not; however, after reading this question and answering the previous questions, I need to maybe do my own newsletter. This may include information regarding Community Work Transition, upcoming tests, opportunities for students with disabilities, and so forth.

Providing Support for Parents

In addition to teaching parents to be home interventionists, you can show leadership in providing several different kinds of support for families of children with disabilities. These include social support, respite care, and information from professionals (Meadan, Halle, et al., 2010). Parents who have children with challenging behaviors and feel isolated due to safety issues may need respite care and professional support (Hodgetts et al., 2013). Also, during certain times, such as times of transition, you can anticipate that families may need more intense support and act accordingly (Meadan, Halle, et al., 2010).

There are times when educators can predict that the family of a child with a disability may experience added stress (e.g., when the child is making the transition from school to adulthood). Generate a list of some of these times. What kind of added support might be available that you could recommend?

Many online resources are available to parents, and special education teachers can take the lead in directing parents to legitimate web sites that contain EBPs. For example, the Kentucky Autism Training Center (KATC) web site provides a service directory, library, listserv, and family guide while also maintaining a Facebook page (Pennington et al., 2013). When Parette, Meadan, Doubet, and Hess (2010) surveyed 148 parents of children with a variety of disabilities, they found that most had access to the Internet and used it to get information, such as details about treatment and intervention, and support, such as opportunities to communicate with other parents and professionals. The parents were satisfied with the sources they used and wanted more; they also stated that they preferred web sites and e-mail to other sources of support.

Since there is a plethora of legal information that is relevant to the processes involved in special education, Turnbull et al. (2010) suggested that family partnerships can be supported by providing parents with a written guide on how to turn knowledge into action. Noting that parents are likely to be overwhelmed by all the information available on the Internet and are not likely to consult professional journals that are written in technical terms, Turnbull proposed that a family-friendly guide can serve as a useful resource on research, knowledge, and policy.

Establishing Partnerships With Parents

When effective two-way communication is in place, it is easier for teachers to establish partnerships with parents that lead to success in setting goals, providing training, and facilitating support. In defining and describing partnerships with parents, deFur (2012) noted that **partnerships** should be intentional relationships with both partners serving a distinct function; a partnership implies joint interest in a common goal, with shared decision making and shared responsibility for success or failure. In a partnership, teachers and families have common goals and a shared vision, culturally responsive and proactive communication takes place, and problems are solved creatively and evaluated for effectiveness with shared ownership.

The professional literature contains several frameworks for involving families in partnerships. Edwards and Da Fonte (2012) provided a five-point plan for fostering successful partnerships with parents that included the following components:

- Being positive, proactive, and solution-oriented (e.g., engaging in frequent and positive communication)

- Respecting families' roles and cultural backgrounds (e.g., gathering information and engaging in activities to better understand the family and their child)

- Communicating consistently, listening to families' concerns, and working together (e.g., keeping families informed of their children's progress in both general and special education)

- Considering simple, natural supports to meet student needs (e.g., using family input and feedback on needed supports)

- Empowering families with knowledge and opportunities for involvement in regard to their child's needs (e.g., providing sufficient information on services and supports)

Sawyer (2015) described a BRIDGES framework for involving parents: 1) **b**uild (e.g., create a foundation), 2) **r**ecruit (e.g., get input from parents), 3) **i**ndividualize (e.g., use personalized strategies), 4) **d**ialogue (e.g., have frequent contact that includes listening), 5) **g**enerate (e.g., teach parents to use EBPs at home), 6) **e**mpower (e.g., share knowledge and resources), and 7) **s**trengthen (e.g., participate in school events and activities).

In forming partnerships, one crucial decision is how much should be expected of families. Bezdek et al. (2010) used the phrase "The Goldilocks Perception" to describe the dilemma of determining how much involvement is not enough, too much, or just right; they noted that not enough involvement can cause frustration, too much can overstep into the roles of professionals, and just the right amount should consist of a two-way relationship with follow-through. (Note that, although it can be tempting to blame parents who do not want to engage in a partnership, it is important to recognize and respect the decision of parents who choose not to participate.)

Voice of a Leader

Leading by Cultivating Empathy

As a special educator, you will work with families who are diverse in many respects: life experiences, cultural background, familiarity with various educational practices, need for support, personal values, and more. It is important always to keep each family's unique characteristics in mind to inform your work with that family. Abby Evans McCormick describes the empathetic approach she uses: putting herself in a parent's shoes so she can determine the best way to communicate and build a strong partnership.

Q: *Do you have any advice for a special education teacher who is trying to take a leadership role in working with families?*

A: Before you [go] into a professional meeting, get to know the family prior to the meeting so you can relate to them and approach them in the best way. For example, one of my students has two parents who are attorneys, so I need to speak more at their level. When I have a family that is less educated about special education, it's different. I want to sit by them and make them feel more equal and comfortable. I try to have a short summary of the meeting for them and make clear they can bring a family member or a friend to the meeting. This is more important than anything else. I have a background in hospitality, and that taught me that you want to know the customer's background. Realizing this helps me decide the amount of jargon and type of wording that I need to use. I think about this: What did I learn in my very first course in special education that I can use with parents when they are as overwhelmed as I was then?

In my new job, we have a family of an older student that still has not accepted their child's disability. I try to think about how they feel about issues, and I try not to be offended by some of the inappropriate language they use in discussing their child and the other students their child may encounter during the day. I have to put myself in that family's shoes and try to figure out where they are coming from. I try to be compassionate but also help parents still be accountable. I have discovered that it can be more difficult as students grow older. There is always more to the story, and we need to try to put ourselves in the parents' shoes and not be too quick to judge.

Given that a teacher may be limited in the capacity to work with families by factors such as cost and time, what are some ways that technology can be applied to assist in the process?

Involving Siblings

As mentioned at the beginning of this chapter, it is important to consider siblings when working with families of children with disabilities. Just as you might train peer tutors to work with students with disabilities at school, you also can include siblings when training family members to be interventionists (e.g., Olcay-Gul & Tekin-Iftar, 2016). Research has shown that siblings can have a large impact on children with ASD (e.g., Banda, 2015). In addition to addressing skill generalization, the advantage to working with siblings is that they will have a lifelong relationship with your student and can be a long-term source of support. In cases in which siblings are negatively affected by the child with a disability, you can pay attention to including them as you search for sources of support for their families (Moyson & Roeyers, 2011).

BE A LEADER: WORK EFFECTIVELY WITH FAMILIES

Chapter 5 has discussed ways you can demonstrate leadership in how you work with families of students with disabilities. Skillful communication is paramount; this includes communicating regularly and informatively through multiple modes; using the modes a family prefers; and being mindful of a family's unique characteristics, including CLD and the ways SES can affect advocacy. Additional ways to work well with families include involving parents and families in goal-setting, including IEP meetings; preparing them to use intervention strategies at home; providing additional social supports and resources; working with parents (or other guardians) as partners; and involving siblings in these processes. The following guidelines are offered to help you expand your leadership skills in working with families of students who have disabilities:

1. Be aware of the issues at play in the lives of families of children with disabilities, and develop empathy toward families who are dealing with these issues, recognizing that each family is unique, even within a culture. Instead of making assumptions, use family data to guide you in your work. Respect the position of families who cannot or choose not to be involved in their child's school.

2. Communicate often with families and in a mode that they prefer.

3. Go out of your way to make planning meetings positive experiences for families. Instead of simply following the parameters set by the law in conducting meetings for developing IEPs and transition plans, exercise leadership by going one step further to ensure that the experience will be positive for families. This can involve 1) providing a simple summary of the procedures that will be followed or an agenda ahead of time; 2) creating a draft that includes goals that the family values; 3) creating a welcoming atmosphere by greeting the family on arrival; 4) meeting in a setting that is comfortable for the family; 5) arranging seating so that all parties have equal status; 6) providing an interpreter, if necessary, who is familiar with the family's culture as well as the language and is aware of jargon that will be used in advance; 7) considering helpful supplementary materials (e.g., a chart to summarize the discussion, a "cheat sheet" of terms); and 8) following up afterward to see if the family has additional thoughts or questions.

4. Explain to families the importance of using EBPs with their children and ask if they would like you to share these with them. Without pressuring families, explain that consistently using the same strategies at home that are used at school can result in a quicker rate of learning and ensure that children will be able to apply learned skills in environments where they are needed.

5. Listen. Get into the practice of listening as much as you speak when engaging in interactions with families. Show that you respect the knowledge about their child that they have to offer.

6. Lead by modeling leadership skills and mentoring others: teachers, staff, and families. Set an example in your school in the way you interact with and speak about families. Find ways that families who want to be involved can become leaders within the school (e.g., PTA, volunteer activities, family councils).

7. Guide families toward high-quality resources. Recognize that some of the resources that families locate may not reflect best practices. Guide families to legitimate web sites and other resources that present EBPs.

8. Remember that families consist of more than the parents. Offer to include siblings, extended family members, and other caregivers when developing family partnerships.

FOLLOW-UP ACTIVITIES

Chapter 5 has discussed important factors to consider in working with the families of your students with disabilities, including the amount and type of involvement family members want to have in their child's education, issues of SES and CLD, family stress, and ways to communicate effectively. The activities that follow are designed to help you explore these factors in greater depth, so as to help you work more effectively with families to set goals, implement interventions at home, and gain access to needed supports.

1. **Reflect on how involved your own parents were when you were a student.** Were there school activities in which your parents were active? Were there activities in which they chose not to participate? If possible, interview your parents or other family members to determine what was going on in their lives at that time (e.g., stressful job, illness of a family member, loss of income, divorce or remarriage). How might these factors affect the lives of families that have a child with a disability?

2. **Either reflect on the last educational planning meeting that you attended as a teacher or request to be present at a scheduled meeting with a family.** What do you think went right in the meeting? In what ways could it have been improved?

3. **Interview the family of a child with a disability.** How do family members feel about the educational process for their child? Do they view their relationship with the special education teacher as a true partnership? Why or why not?

4. **Examine the diversity of your community or state, using the Internet to find available data.** Have the demographics and degree of diversity changed in the past 10 years? If so, how? Do a follow-up interview with a special education teacher to learn how the school addresses diversity and whether or not this has changed in recent years. This may be more evident in terms of CLD, but recognize that there are other types of diversity that may be addressed (e.g., religious diversity, gender diversity).

5. **Explore the ways poverty may affect families in your community or state.** Do an Internet search to find data on the prevalence of poverty and demographics about who is affected. Have the prevalence and/or demographics changed in the past 10 years? If so, how? Do a follow-up interview with a special education teacher to learn how poverty appears to affect the performance of students with disabilities and the educational participation of their families.

6. **Research interventions for a specific type of disability using the Internet.** Evaluate the sources that you find. Do they reflect evidence-based or

research-based practices? What evidence do they provide to promote interventions (e.g., peer-reviewed research, personal testimony)? Make a list of valid Internet web sites or other resources to share with families.

7. **Research available support groups for families.** Use the Internet to find professional organizations (e.g., The Arc, Autism Society, Down Syndrome Society, TASH) that offer support groups for families. Are support groups affiliated with these organizations offered in your community? Is support offered online (e.g., through discussion groups)? Make a list of valid support group networks to share with families.

6 Support Students During Transitions

Learning Objectives

After reading this chapter, readers will be able to

- Apply leadership skills during the development and implementation of a transition plan

- Conduct transition meetings that address crucial topics in a way that helps students with disabilities lead a more independent adulthood

- Explain the rationale for teaching self-determination skills to students with disabilities

- Use their understanding of different types of postsecondary educational programs (including strengths and limitations) to assist students in choosing the most appropriate postsecondary program available to them

- Plan how to increase the likelihood of future employment for students with disabilities

Terms to Know

Cultural competence

Family partnerships

Guardianship

Partial guardianship

Person-centered planning

Plenary guardianship

Self-determination

Supported decision making

Temporary guardianship

Transition

Triangulated goal

Triangulation

INTRODUCTION

To become a special education teacher leader in the area of transition, it is first important to recognize that **transition** is a lifelong process. It does not begin when students prepare to leave school and end when they enter adulthood; rather, it is a process that continues across the lifespan, from cradle to grave, whenever a person progresses from one stage of life to another. All students participate in certain transitions as they enter preschool services; make the transition to school-based services; begin elementary, middle, and secondary education; and exit secondary school for adult living that may include postsecondary education and, ideally, employment. Other life transitions include changes in living environment (where one lives and with whom); changes in activities, such as recreational groups and faith communities; changes in sources of support, such as family members, friends, or agency personnel; and changes in types of support, such as health services, finances, and technology. As a special education teacher, you are likely to find that the role of facilitating many of these transitions often falls on you. In this role, you will collaborate with the student, his or her family, support personnel, and relevant agencies to help create and implement transitions that will reflect the student's wishes and desires.

Ryndak, Ward, Alper, Montgomery, and Storch (2010) illustrated the importance of adequate transition services when they compared the life outcomes of a young woman and young man, both with significant disabilities, who had been classmates in a segregated classroom when they were young. The young woman, considered the lowest functioning student in the class, progressed through inclusive settings in middle and secondary school, made the transition to a college program with support, obtained employment (ultimately with benefits) in the community, and settled into her own apartment with community support. The young man, considered the highest functioning student in the class, struggled first in school and then in a sheltered workshop while continuing to live at home, lacking friends in the community to provide support. Only when the young man married the young woman did he begin to live a more supported and inclusive life. It is clear that transition plans and their implementation made a difference in both their lives, before and after they became a couple.

National data have shown that students who spend the least time in inclusive settings are less likely to participate in their transition meetings, whereas students who are white or higher functioning are more likely to be involved (Griffen, Taylor, Urbano, & Hodapp, 2014). Although ensuring that students participate in their own transition meetings is considered a best practice, teachers who lack training may be unaware of best practices. This is one barrier to successful transition. Morningstar and Benitez (2013) found that a random sample of middle and secondary teachers surveyed had completed an average of only 1.07 courses on transition and 28 hours of professional development on the topic, with 14% having had no professional development. These teachers rated themselves as "somewhat prepared" to "somewhat unprepared," with transition specialists and teachers of students with IDs having received the most preparation. The greater the degree of preparation, the greater was the teacher's ability to engage in transition services. Plotner, Mazzotti, Rose, and Carlson-Britting (2013) corroborated these data when they reported the results from a survey of middle and high school teachers that revealed that 1) 50% of direct service providers and 68% of educators never or seldom received training on EBPs for transition, 2) 45% of direct service providers and 50% of educators never received resources for transition, and 3) 53% of direct service providers and 62% of educators did not receive professional development on EBPs. Although 78% of those surveyed failed to receive information on transition from their higher education programs, 60% of direct service providers and 48% of educators indicated that they got transition information from professional journals, leading the researchers to recommend that educators join professional organizations to gain more information and that local school districts provide journals on transition for teachers. It is interesting to note that lack of transition knowledge is not just a national issue, but a global issue as well. For example, Alnahdi (2013) noted that special education teachers in Saudi Arabia are just beginning to focus on transition for students with disabilities, and the majority surveyed thought they were unprepared to plan for transition or conduct programs with this focus.

The law has mandated transition plans for students with disabilities (Stodden & Mruzek, 2010), but you and other special education teachers may be perplexed and confused by some of the issues and contradictions affecting transition. For example, a successful transition plan should take a holistic view of the life outcomes for students with disabilities that includes postsecondary education and employment as well as the skills needed for independent living and community inclusion, yet most educational programs for students with mild ID do not focus upon functional skills (Bouck & Joshi, 2012). Likewise, educational programs for students with MSDs may not focus on higher education as an option (Hart, Grigal, & Weir, 2010). In a national survey, Murphy et al. (2013) found possible differences in transition practices across rural and urban districts. For example, rural teachers may devise more strategies for communicating with parents but provide less information on how to enhance transition. Across states, the age at which transition plans are mandated can vary from 14 to 16 years, and data show that students with a range of disabilities were more likely to be employed following school in states with early transition plans (Cimera, Burgess, & Bedesem, 2014). Finally, in studying outcomes for students with ASD and ID, Carter, Boehm, et al. noted that positive traits of people with disabilities, such as "happy, dedicated, resilient, positive, self-determined, and having a sense of humor" (2015, p. 112) can influence positive outcomes (e.g., inclusion, employment). This raises the question of how special education teachers can influence students to develop these traits.

This chapter will focus on ways you can provide leadership in the area of transition, including implementing strategies for developing effective individualized transition plans, facilitating self-determination in students with disabilities, and increasing awareness of postsecondary options.

CONNECTION TO PROFESSIONAL STANDARDS

The teacher's role in providing support for the transition of students with disabilities is supported by a number of professional standards listed under the Teacher Leader Model Standards (TLEC, 2012) and the CEC Standards for Professional Practice and Advanced Preparation Standards (CEC, 2015).

Teacher Leader Model Standards

Although not specific to special education, the Teacher Leader Model Standards (TLEC, 2012) address the need to serve as a model across domains. These include a focus on "promot[ing] a sense of partnership" with families and other groups in the community, listed under *Domain 6: Improving Outreach and Collaboration with Families and Community;* developing these partnerships is an essential part of helping students and families navigate transitions, especially the transition from school to adulthood. This process involves understanding the different backgrounds of students and issues related to diversity, using "culturally responsive strategies," understanding the "diverse educational needs of families and the community," and "collaborat[ing] with families, communities, and colleagues to develop comprehensive strategies" to address these needs.

Council for Exceptional Children Program Standards

The Special Education Standards for Professional Practice developed by CEC (2015) address transition through teaching and assessment (1.0), systematic individualization of learning outcomes (1.1), and the use of effective and culturally responsive instructional materials (1.5). The Advanced Preparation Standards apply to transition in that teachers should design and implement assessments that evaluate effectiveness of the practices and programs that they use (1.2) and should align standards with the curriculum to meet the needs of students with disabilities (2.1). In addition, teachers need to address programs, supports, and services for students with disabilities through design, implementation, and improvement (3.1); understanding of cultural, social, and economic diversity (3.2); evaluation of progress toward vision, mission, and goals (3.5); and collaboration to promote understanding and build consensus (7.3). One teacher leader who fulfills these standards in her work with students in transition is Renee Hollinger Scott, who describes her work in the interview that follows.

Voice of a Leader

Helping Young Adults With Disabilities Join a College Community

Renee Hollinger Scott is a special education teacher who has been involved in applied research with secondary students with disabilities who are making the transition from school to adulthood (Scott, Collins, Knight, & Kleinert, 2013). She first gained experience working in a postsecondary program for secondary students ages 18 to 21 years, which was housed on a college campus when she was a student teacher. She now works in a similar program that she helped establish in another school district, the

Providing Access to Community Transition (PACT) Program. Here, she describes the goals of her program and what a typical day is like for her and her students.

Q: **Describe your current position in working with students who are making the transition from school to adulthood. How is your program unique? What led you to this job?**

A: I am currently working in the PACT program. This program is a public-school program for ten 18- to 21-year-old students with moderate to severe intellectual disabilities located on the University of Louisville campus. This job is unique because I work in a single FMD classroom on a college campus. [Note: FMD stands for functional mental disability, the state of Kentucky's designation for students with moderate and severe disabilities and complex support needs.] These are students who are working toward an alternative high school diploma, and they would not otherwise get to experience college. I did my student teaching at a similar program at Asbury College in Jessamine County, KY. A job opening was advertised, and I applied because I loved my experience at Asbury.

Q: **What is the typical day like for you and the students in your program?**

A: Typically, students attend one university course in the morning. Courses students informally attend include Public Speaking, History of Rock and Roll, Acting for Non-majors, Creativity and the Arts, Flag Football, Pilates, Aerobics, Ultimate Frisbee, Soccer, Weight Training, Basketball, and many more. They spend time in the PACT classroom working on IEP goals and other academic skills. Students eat lunch at the Student Activities Center. Students participate in any special campus activities and events open to students during the school day. One afternoon a week, our class delivers the university newspaper to buildings on campus. They are paid for the job. Students spend one afternoon a week in a campus computer lab working on basic computer skills. We have whole-group instructional lessons focusing on social skills or vocational skills. We go off campus one day a week to work on other community skills, such as grocery shopping and community travel. Some students have volunteer jobs on campus during the week.

YOUR ROLE IN PROVIDING SUPPORT FOR TRANSITIONS

Regardless of the age level of the students with whom you work, you can be involved in the transition of students with disabilities. Although early involvement is important, involvement becomes more crucial as a student progresses through school, and it is mandated by the time a student is in secondary school. As a special education teacher, you will be involved in the development and implementation of transition plans with a team that includes the family, service providers, and, as much as possible, the student. This chapter explains how to develop strong transition plans and how to use effective strategies to implement these plans, including building family partnerships, fostering self-determination, helping students find opportunities through peer relationships and service learning opportunities, and helping them form connections with adults with disabilities.

Your leadership can set the stage for optimal outcomes. When you work with a student and his or her family during transition, you have the opportunity to influence that student's future outcomes in adulthood through sharing knowledge on topics such as guardianship, postsecondary educational programs, and employment. Each of these topics is one variable that can affect the student's future outcomes, and some students and families may not know about or clearly understand these variables.

The sections that follow address each of these topics from a leadership perspective. However, you will want to do further research to make sure you have the most current knowledge and information about services and policies within your community and state.

Developing Transition Plans

Transition plans should be more than a few lines on an IEP. They should consist of short-term and long-term goals based on input from the student and the student's family as well as activities (with specific timelines) to be completed toward achieving those goals. Regardless of the student's age and the type of transition that is occurring, it is crucial to communicate clearly and respectfully with the student and with his or her family and to involve both student and family in the planning process as actively as possible.

As noted earlier, teachers can address transition issues and develop transition plans for students of any age. Chapter 5 discussed how parents who were sending a child to preschool for the first time reported they had the impression that they were going from "insider" to "outsider" status: "We were presented with a draft IEP for a signature, with 15 minutes worth of discussion before we needed to be ushered out for the next ones to come in" (Podvey et al., 2013, p. 215). A clear transition process with adequate communication can address issues such as this. Teachers who work in preschool programs may help develop transition plans for students who are moving on to kindergarten as part of the individualized family service plan, with teachers and family working together to identify services and supports in the new setting. Transition activities can include sending written communications to the family, making home visits, going over records, and making visits to the new setting prior to registration or enrollment (Murphy et al., 2013).

Similar goals and activities can be identified during IEP meetings when students make the transition from elementary or middle school or at any time the school environment changes. When a student is in elementary school, transition can be facilitated by activities that build self-determination, including having the student get involved in the IEP meeting, participate in career awareness activities, and create responsibility charts (Papay, Unger, Williams-Diehm, & Mitchell, 2015). Involving the student and the family in the transition process is crucial, and it is desirable to involve them earlier rather than later. In fact, the official transition process for preparing to exit school can begin before the legally mandated age if the IEP team believes that the challenges of the student's disability justify this (Wells, Sheehey, & Moore, 2012).

When surveyed about the components of transition from school to adulthood (Collet-Klingenberg & Kolb, 2011), special education teachers identified the following components in order of importance:

1. Timing of the transition process (e.g., beginning early)

2. Curriculum (e.g., inclusion of self-advocacy)

3. Employment (e.g., instruction in community settings)

4. Leisure and recreation (e.g., choice, access)

5. Independent living (e.g., guardianship and alternatives)

6. Instruction (e.g., skills that replace problem behavior)

7. Transportation (e.g., instruction on problem-solving issues that arise)

8. Postsecondary education (e.g., setting options)

As discussed earlier, beginning the process early is crucial for managing any educational transition well. The remainder of this section discusses this component and other components specific to making the transition from school to adulthood.

When a student with a disability reaches the age at which transition plans are mandated by law in his or her state (14–16 years), the development of a transition plan becomes a formal process in which the transition team works with the student and the family to identify long-term outcomes for the student's life following exit from secondary school. Research has shown that some parents feel like outsiders during this process; they may not recall being actively engaged in a discussion on specific transition goals within the context of an IEP meeting or may believe that the process began too late to make a difference (Hetherington et al., 2010). You can increase productive participation in a transition meeting by holding a premeeting to identify those who should be included, determining whether accommodations need to be made for language, selecting a comfortable setting for meetings in a location suggested by the family (or using technology if they cannot attend in person), having participants sit at a round table where all are equal, and providing food as an icebreaker (Wells & Sheehy, 2012).

Knowing the student's skills and strengths, short- and long-term goals, and potential limitations is important for planning that student's transition to adulthood. Thus, assessment data are crucial to developing a transition plan. To gather assessment data and use it for this purpose, you will need to know what is to be assessed (e.g., interests, skills, behavior), have access to appropriate assessments, know how to conduct the assessment, know how to analyze the results, and know how to use the data to develop the plan (Rowe, Mazzotti, Hirano, & Alverson, 2015). For example, you could select valid and reliable transition assessments (e.g., academic achievement test, career interest inventory, a self-determination instrument, life skills rating scale) to identify student interests, desires, and options for the future and conduct these assessments over time. You would then work with the transition team (including the student, the family, related discipline personnel, future employers) to develop goals together based on assessment data that take into consideration postsecondary education, employment, and living options. The transition plan for one student may focus on college preparation with support prior to employment, whereas the transition for another student may focus on teaching independent living skills while identifying options for supported employment.

The **person-centered planning** approach can be used in assessment and development of transition plans for students with all types of disabilities. Person-centered planning focuses on creating a long-term vision (i.e., 3–5 years) for a student with disabilities based on the student's history, likes and dislikes, strengths and needs, dreams and fears, the role of supportive people and resources, the team's awareness of what works and does not work, the vision for the future, and fears and concerns (Hagner et al., 2012; Meadan, Shelden, Appel, & DeGrazia, 2010; Wells &

Sheehey, 2012). In sum, the vision of desired outcomes is based on student input. Also, as noted in Chapter 5, charts can be a useful tool when developing a transition plan (Espiner & Guild, 2012; Hagner et al.; Wells & Sheehey). Using charts creates a visual representation for the family during person-centered assessment that remains a visual reminder once transition goals are identified and monitored. A number of person-centered tools and approaches are available to facilitate the transition discussion, such as Choosing Outcomes and Accommodations for Children (COACH; Giangreco, Cloninger, & Iverson, 2011) and Making Action Plans (MAPS; Falvey, Forest, Pearpoint, & Rosenberg, 1997). With input from family and peers, you can facilitate the assessment by helping everyone share thoughts, develop an action plan, and then set a date to assess the implementation of the action plan (e.g., in 4–6 months). (Note that the COACH tool is appropriate for students ages 3–21, so it can also be used with younger students making transitions throughout their years in school; when used with students who have mild disabilities, this tool should be adapted.)

In interviewing families, be sensitive to where and when interviews take place, who should attend, how involved the student is, and whether questions should be provided in advance (Meadan, Shelden, et al., 2010). Although the student's presence and input are central to the process, some disabilities may present challenges for the student's active participation, providing the opportunity for you to show leadership by brainstorming ways to be inclusive. For example, Wells et al. (2012) found that a student with ASD had communication, social, and behavioral challenges that made it difficult to participate in specific settings or to respond to questions. Thus, the transition team used adaptations that included providing questions in advance and typing responses on PowerPoint slides. In addition, Hagner et al. (2012) found that helpful accommodations for students with ASD included holding informal meetings to build rapport, scheduling breaks during meetings, allowing the student to listen and participate from another room, using a communication device or system, and attending the meeting via videoconferencing (e.g., Skype).

Another consideration in developing a transition plan is **cultural competence** (Povenmire-Kirk, Bethune, Alverson, & Kahn, 2015). This means that those on a transition team work together to have a nonjudgmental awareness of, and sensitivity toward, the culture of the student and family. This may involve understanding nuances of communication, such as cultural norms for eye contact and social touching, and typical aspects of family participation in students' education, such as participation in school meetings and assistance with homework. Developing cultural competence requires that you develop an awareness of diversity and biases, be open-minded when conflicts arise, talk with families about differences on issues, and treat the student and family with respect for their culture.

In selecting transition goals, it is important that the transition team focus on postsecondary outcomes while still addressing IEP goals related to core content (Szidon, Ruppar, & Smith, 2015). When Anderson, McDonald, Edsall, Smith, and Taylor (2014) interviewed students with ASD, they found that only 42% planned to leave home when they exited school services, leading them to conclude that transition plans should include skills needed in adulthood, such as daily living skills. Likewise, when Miller-Warren (2016) interviewed the parents of students with disabilities, she found that, even though transition plans had been written for all of their children, 58.3% reported that their children were still living at home and 50% reported that their children were unemployed, making a case for teaching vocational skills as well as daily living skills. It is important, however, to recognize that as a teacher, you may have a different perspective than parents have concerning the skills that are important for students with disabilities to acquire for transition. For example, Carter, Brock, and Trainor (2014) reported that, although both parents and teachers rated leisure skills as important, parents noted more areas of strength in their children than their teachers did.

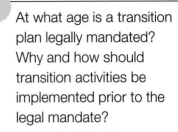

At what age is a transition plan legally mandated? Why and how should transition activities be implemented prior to the legal mandate?

It can be frustrating to develop transition plans for the skills that your students will need in adulthood while also addressing the core content you are required to teach, yet it is possible to address both. Core content can be linked to transition skills in two ways (Bartholomew, Papay, McConnell, & Cease-Cook, 2015):

1. By embedding a transition skill in academic instruction (e.g., embed instruction on conflict resolution when teaching *Of Mice and Men*; Steinbeck, 1937)

2. By embedding an academic skill in transition skill instruction (e.g., embed instruction on irrational numbers when teaching food preparation)

Table 6.1 provides examples of research studies that have combined academic and functional transition skill instruction within the same lesson.

A more formal way to combine academic and transition skills is to use triangulation. **Triangulation** is an approach for writing transition goals that include both academic and functional transition skills (Gothberg, Peterson, Peak, & Sedaghat, 2015; Peterson et al., 2010). Triangulation takes three variables into consideration: a student's postsecondary goal (e.g., riding a city bus), industry standards (e.g., behavioral skills needed for community travel), and the state educational standards

Table 6.1. Examples of core content linked to transition goals

Academic focus	Core content	Transition goal	Reference
Literacy	Identify meanings of words and phrases	Define political words in the newspaper (e.g., *president, governor*)	Collins, Hager, and Galloway (2011)
Literacy	Interpret specialized vocabulary	Follow written cooking directions	Karl, Collins, Hager, Schuster, and Ault (2013)
Math	Use order of operations	Compute sales tax on advertised items	Collins et al. (2011)
Math	Use the Pythagorean theorem to solve a problem	Calculate amount of fringe needed in trimming a quilt	Creech-Galloway, Collins, Knight, and Bausch (2014)
Math	Determine percentage of increase and decrease	Create a shopping budget with sales tax and sales prices	Karl et al. (2013)
Science	Identify and categorize chemical properties of elements	Identify changes in properties while cooking (e.g., liquid, gas, solid)	Collins et al. (2011)
Science	Describe laws of motion	Describe force needed during cooking (e.g., crack eggs)	Karl et al. (2013)
Science	Explain transmission of genetic information	Develop healthy lifestyle (e.g., exercise, diet) in response to inherited disease (e.g., heart disease, diabetes)	Riggs, Collins, Kleinert, and Knight (2013)

(e.g., literacy), to be addressed in an annual **triangulated goal** (e.g., orientation and mobility). For example, a triangulated goal may be as follows:

> When riding public transportation to preidentified destinations, the student will demonstrate appropriate behavior while selecting the correct bus route from a printed bus schedule. Preidentified destinations will include addresses for home, education, recreation, and employment. Appropriate behavior is defined as having respect for the space of others by keeping hands to self and using a moderate tone of voice in conversation.

Voice of a Leader

Assessing and Teaching Adult Skills

Every student has a unique combination of interests, skills, needs, and available systems of support. When assessing and instructing students in the skills they will need for adulthood, it is important to balance awareness of students as individuals with attention to skills that most adults will need to develop in order to lead a life they find rich and fulfilling. Below, Renee Hollinger Scott describes how she balances these concerns during goal-setting and instruction.

Q: How do you determine the skills that your students need? Do you have tips for working with the students and their families on transition goals?

A: I determine the skills students need by parent interview and survey, student interview and survey, and informal and formal assessments. I think it is important to consider the parents' goals for their son/daughter, the student's personal goals, and the student's present levels to determine and identify priority areas of instruction.

Q: What types of skills do you teach? Does research play a role in the way you teach? If so, how?

A: I teach functional skills related to money handling, social skills, vocational skills, pedestrian safety and community travel, shopping skills, reading, writing, and health and nutrition. Research definitely plays more of a role in how I teach these skills. I use a lot of research-based instructional and behavioral strategies to teach these skills (e.g., systematic instructional strategies, social stories, role play, modeling, fading prompts). I try to teach skills in the environment where they will be used as much as possible.

Strategies to Facilitate Transitions

Once the team has developed the transition plan, it must be implemented. The sections that follow outline numerous ways you can facilitate successful implementation of the transition plan. Recommended strategies are grouped in four broad categories:

1. Ways to build a partnership with the family

2. Ways to foster students' self-determination

3. Ways to connect students with opportunities available through peers and through service learning

4. Ways to involve adults with disabilities who have navigated the challenges your students now face

Family Partnerships   Family partnerships are central to successful transitions, and developing these partnerships must be intentional. By definition, **family partnerships** involve sharing a vision and working to implement it through shared decision making and problem solving (deFur, 2012). Engaging in a family partnership requires you to be

- Culturally responsive to the family, showing respect for their traditions

- Proactive and effective in communicating with the family

- Caring and committed, refraining from placing blame on the family when issues arise

- A good listener, building trust so families will share information

- Creative in brainstorming with the family (deFur, 2012)

A lack of parent involvement may be due to negative past experiences, cultural differences, and communication issues (Sawyer, 2015). To establish a family partnership, communication is essential. In addition to phone calls, this communication can take many forms that include sending written communications (e.g., letters, e-mails) and making home visits (Murphy et al., 2013), taking into consideration the way in which families want to communicate.

As you work with families, recognize that transition periods can be a time of stress that may call for targeted interventions and supports. As noted in Chapter 5, parents of children with ASD may experience stress related to the permanence of the disability, lack of acceptance by others, financial burden, challenging behaviors, and concerns for the future, with mothers carrying more of the burden (Meadan, Halle, et al., 2010). If you recognize the family's potential to experience stress during transition times, you may be able to identify resources such as respite care that can help a family cope.

Some families may be less willing or less able to get involved in the transition process, and ultimately, you must respect the family's choices. Nevertheless, parent involvement can signal to their child that the process is important, so effort should be made to involve families if possible. The BRIDGES framework for involving families in their children's education (Sawyer, 2015), introduced in Chapter 5, applies to transitions as well: build trust, recruit, individualize, keep dialogue going, generate solutions by helping families implement EBPs, empower families, and strengthen successes by celebrating them.

One way you can provide and demonstrate leadership during transition is to develop and present family workshops. Just as you might provide professional development workshops to other teachers, as described in Chapter 4, you can also provide workshops to families as part of the transition process. When students with disabilities approach transition periods, families will need access to information, which can provide you the impetus to deliver it to them. An example of the kind of information you can provide in a family workshop is to address future employment with parents as goals are developed. For example, Francis, Gross, Turnbull, and Parent-Johnson (2013) found that a 2-day family workshop on employment awareness was effective in raising families' expectations during the transition process.

When face-to-face workshops are not possible, consider using technology to give families the information they need about transition. For example, Rowe and Test (2010) provided four computer-based lessons on the transition process for parents that used a model–lead–test format: listen to the model, say it with the model, say it on your own. This format increased parents' knowledge of the process, and that knowledge was maintained over time. For others who are preparing similar lessons, Rowe and Test suggested that the material be simple, jargon be avoided, sessions be brief, lessons be limited to one topic, parent knowledge be assessed, and information be provided to parents early (e.g., when the child is 13 years old) so they can be active in the transition process. Even if you do not have the opportunity to provide formal family workshops, you can share information in other ways, such as providing brochures or tip sheets about the transition process or informing parents of agency-created presentations that provide information about planning for the future (Kellems & Morningstar, 2010).

Self-Determination   Perhaps one of the strongest and most researched strategies for facilitating successful transitions is to teach **self-determination** skills—a set of competencies that provide students with disabilities with a degree of control over their own lives and enable them to exercise more independence when they transition to adulthood. These skills include, but are not limited to, choice making, decision making, problem solving, goal setting and attainment, self-observation, self-evaluation, self-reinforcement, self-awareness, self-advocacy, and self-knowledge (Westling et al., 2015). Self-determination skills can be taught to students with various types of disabilities, for example, ID and learning disabilities (Shogren, Plotner, Palmer, Wehmeyer, & Pack, 2014). These skills can be taught at all age levels, including preschool (Zheng et al., 2015), elementary school (Mazzotti, Wood, & Test, 2012), middle school (Lee et al., 2011), and secondary school (Wehmeyer, Palmer, Shogren, Williams-Diehm, & Soukup, 2013). For example, the Kentucky Youth Advocacy Project (Kleinert, Harrison, Mills, Dueppen, & Trailor, 2014) facilitated self-determination for students ages 7–21 years who had labels that included ASD, MODs, and multiple disabilities. The students received instruction during "I Can Day" activities; set goals in areas that included academic, communication, daily living, leisure, and social skills, and monitored them weekly; then celebrated during an "I Did It Day" in which 205 (71.2%) of the goals were reached.

Despite the importance of self-determination, it may not always be emphasized in the education of students with disabilities. Administrators consider self-determination skills important but are not always certain that their staff teach these (Carter, Lane, et al., 2011). Hughes, Cosgriff, Agran, and Washington (2013) found that students with severe disabilities who spend the majority of their time in segregated classrooms or attend high-poverty schools have less opportunity to learn self-determination skills, even though research has shown that they can.

A number of curricula are available to help you foster students' self-determination (e.g., Lee et al., 2011; Lee, Wehmeyer, & Shogren, 2015; Shogren, Wehmeyer et al., 2015; Test et al., 2004). For a list of curricula that have been field-tested, see resources listed by Bremer, Kachgal, and Schoeller (2003) at http://www.ncset .org/publications/viewdesc.asp?id=962.

There is also evidence that, in lieu of face-to-face instruction, online instruction on self-determination skills can have a positive influence (Lee et al., 2011; Mazzotti et al., 2012). In developing IEPs and transition plans, recognize that self-determination skills can be taught within the context of Common Core State Standards. For example, Bartholomew, Test, Cooke, and Cease-Cook (2015) taught self-determination skills to secondary school students with ID within the context of the standards for speaking, listening, and delivering a presentation, and these skills generalized to the students' transition plan meetings.

Research also has shown that a self-determined model of instruction has been effective in the United States and beyond (e.g., Lee et al., 2015; Zheng et al., 2015), although cultural differences can affect its implementation. For example, the individualist culture that fosters independence in the United States is different from the collectivist culture that fosters dependence in some Asian countries (e.g., China [Zheng et al.], Korea [Seo, 2014]). Special education teachers who work with students from different cultures need to remember that these differences exist and be sensitive to them.

When Shogren (2012) interviewed Hispanic mothers of children with severe disabilities, the mothers thought that self-determination was important but were confused about what it meant for their children, as demonstrated by the following quote:

> When I go to the IEP meetings they get scary, you know. I say "What do you mean she's going to be on her own? No, she's going to stay with the family." Being from Mexico, it takes longer to consider someone an adult. You really don't move out at 18. (Shogren, 2012, p. 173)

Another parent stated the following:

> For us, and many of our Hispanic friends, the expectation is that you will always be with family in some way. When we buy houses, we think about if it will go well with the extended family. . . . It's like they [schools] have to have it their way and impose values or systems on us rather than thinking about how different approaches can enrich us. (Shogren, 2012, p. 177)

Overall, the mothers had negative perceptions of transition meetings, believing that the meetings wasted their time by focusing more on paperwork than on meaningful goals; this ultimately strained their relationship with school personnel. As noted earlier in this chapter, it is imperative to build your cultural competence so you can understand values systems when working with families of different cultures, and cultural values may determine how much they value self-determination.

Peer Involvement and Service Learning   Establishing relationships with same-age peers can help students with disabilities to build a strong source of support during transition. Peers can help them to negotiate new school environments and learn new skills. If the relationships are established with forethought as to proximity or common interests, peers can provide ongoing support into adulthood that may extend to such areas as employment, leisure skills, and transportation. (For example, if a high school student without a disability plans to take a job in the local community or attend the local community college, that student may be a support to the student with a disability who plans to work at the same place or attend the same school—providing a daily ride to work or school or supporting the peer in other ways.) You can implement several strategies to enhance peer involvement and lead to potential friendships. For example, you can conduct "opportunity mapping"

(Swedeen, Carter, & Molfenter, 2010) to identify settings where students with disabilities can interact with peers based on common interests (e.g., academic classes, extracurricular activities) by talking with students and staff, reviewing the school web site, meeting with athletic coaches and club sponsors, and attending to weekly school announcements and letters. You can also involve students with disabilities in service learning projects (see Chapter 2) in which they engage with peers in the community to complete activities that also promote learning. Examples include building benches and signs in parks, hosting events to discourage the use of discriminating language, hosting meals at a homeless shelter, and preparing care kits for children in the foster care system (Carter, Swedeen, et al., 2012). You also can organize peer-mentoring programs (Kellems & Morningstar, 2010) as an effective way for students with disabilities and their peers to get to know each other.

Involving Adults With Disabilities Sometimes the most supportive person during the transition process is a person with a disability similar to your student's who already has learned to negotiate the challenges and barriers of a new environment. An adult with a disability can be a powerful mentor, and you can facilitate this process by identifying potential mentors and setting up activities during which mentoring can take place. For example, Bell (2012) described a mentoring program in which transition-age youth with blindness received weekly mentoring from adults with blindness through in-person activities such as attending sports events and eating meals at restaurants, in addition to phone calls, e-mails, and messaging. If you cannot locate adult role models who have the time to be mentors, you may, instead, try to consult with adults with disabilities to learn about their experiences during their school years. For example, Angell, Stoner, and Fulk (2010) interviewed 12 adults with physical disabilities and found that teachers could learn ways to foster self-determination in their students with physical disabilities from those who had first-hand experience (e.g., teaching students to set goals, self-assess, and self-reflect; creating an action plan and providing opportunities to practice self-determination skills).

> What are some transition goals that should be considered for students with disabilities besides education and employment to ensure that they have a full life? How can these goals be met?

PLANNING FOR THE FUTURE

To prepare students with disabilities and their families for transition, it is necessary to have a good working knowledge of the issues that arise as students come of age and the options that are available when students exit the school system. It is never too early to begin to address the future with parents; however, it becomes crucial once students reach adolescence. If you are teaching high-school–age students, you will need to be knowledgeable about areas such as guardianship, postsecondary education, employment, and basic rights. Some parents may have little information, little awareness, or low expectations about these different variables that can affect a student's long-term outcomes.

←——→

Guardianship

Guardianship is a legal process wherein a court appoints an adult (or an agency) to make decisions on a person's behalf when that person is incapable of making his or her own decisions (Jameson et al., 2012; Millar, 2014b; Rood, Kanter, & Causton, 2015). Until the process of transitioning to adulthood begins in secondary school, families of students with disabilities may not realize that a decision about their child's guardianship (or conservatorship) must be made when the child reaches the legal age of majority (18–21 years, depending on the state in which they live). Families may assume the only option is to transfer a child's rights to a guardian, not realizing that some students with disabilities are able to assume the same legal status as their nondisabled peers upon reaching the age of majority. Guardianship is appropriate for some adults with disabilities, but not all.

Plenary (i.e., full) **guardianship** is considered restrictive because the guardian has the right to make all decisions for the ward (e.g., where to live, type of education or vocation, how leisure time is spent, type of health care, how finances are spent; Millar, 2011; 2014b). On the other hand, the granting of **partial** (i.e., limited) **guardianship** allows the guardian to make decisions only in the areas in which the person is not capable (e.g., finances; Jameson et al., 2012). Under certain circumstances, **temporary guardianship** can be appointed for a limited period (e.g., during a time of emergency; Millar, 2011). As part of the IEP planning process, you can share information with families about guardianship and help them to pursue the choices most appropriate for their child's needs.

According to the Individuals with Disabilities Education Improvement Act (IDEA) of 2004 (PL 108-446), 1 year before a student reaches the age of majority the IEP must include a statement that the student has been informed of his or her rights, and the student subsequently becomes the decision maker in the educational process. IDEA of 2004 also states that a parent or other person can be appointed as the student's guardian. It is at this point that parents must make the difficult decision about guardianship, and it is an opportune time to discuss the topic of guardianship with parents, with the conversation focusing on what the student can do with and without support and recognizing that the decision should be up to families and not the school or other agencies (Rood et al., 2015).

When a judge appoints a person as guardian, the child becomes a ward of the guardian, who has the authority to make some or all decisions for the child, depending on the type of guardianship that is awarded. Thus, guardianship is a practice that can be in opposition to self-determination, where a person makes his or her own decisions. For a parent to become a guardian of his or her child, the parent must petition the court with a claim that the child does not have the capacity to make decisions. An investigation takes place and is followed by a hearing in which the judge decides and signs a decree (Millar, 2011; Rood et al., 2015). In some states, the decision is made based on the child's diagnosis or label (Rood et al.), with a label of ID considered sufficient to mandate guardianship (Jameson et al., 2012). A guardian must be a competent adult; if the guardian fails to make decisions that are in the best interest of the ward, guardianship can be revoked (Millar).

Given an expected lifespan of 50–70 years (Millar, 2014b), parents need to be aware that, if they become the appointed guardians and predecease their child, a new guardian will be appointed after their deaths, and this could be a person unknown to them (Jameson et al., 2012). A study supported by TASH (Jameson et al.)

How is guardianship in conflict with self-determination? What alternatives to full guardianship could be considered?

revealed that people with disabilities are more likely to have a court-appointed guardian than their peers without disabilities, that parents receive little training on guardianship and may be under the impression that full guardianship is their only option, and that school personnel are not usually involved in training on guardianship issues.

As you facilitate the transition process, be aware that there are alternatives to full guardianship and discuss these with parents as you provide support. For example, deciding on a model of **supported decision making** allows a student with disabilities to retain legal rights and be active in the process of making legal decisions (Jameson et al., 2012). Other alternatives to full guardianship (Millar, 2014b; Rood et al., 2015) include the following:

- Setting up support through family members, friends, or professionals to assist the child in supported decision making

- Preparing legal documents with advance directives tailored to specific needs or a living will

- Assigning someone durable power of attorney to act on the child's behalf in areas of need

- Establishing a trust to provide for financial needs

- Approving a co-signer for banking transactions

- Securing case management services (e.g., in-home care or home visits) tailored to the child's needs

Millar (2014b) suggested the use of a Guardian Alternative Model that puts the student at the center of the guardianship decision. This model consists of the following components:

- *Self-determination*, such as advocating for the least restrictive environment

- *Assessment and planning*, such as exploring legal guardianship alternatives

- *Education and instruction*, such as developing and implementing a plan of action

- *Coordination and collaboration*, such as establishing supports without guardianship

- *Policy and process evaluation*, such as continuously evaluating those considered at risk for having a guardian appointed

In addition, Millar (2014a) suggested the use of a Guardianship Alternative Assessment Template (GAAT) to facilitate discussion on alternative guardianship that considers the student and family's vision and values, the student's ability to perform daily living skills, the student's cognitive functioning, and any risks and concerns.

The discussion regarding guardianship needs to address the basic rights that a person with disabilities has and to ensure that these rights will not be taken away in adulthood. For example, 44 states prohibit people with ID from voting, and those who can vote seldom receive instruction on the process (Agran & Hughes, 2013).

Basic rights that may be prohibited under restrictive guardianship, such as voting, forming romantic relationships, and becoming parents, need to be part of the conversation as the transition process prepares students for a full adult life.

Postsecondary Educational Programs

The availability of postsecondary educational programs is another topic on which families may need information. Parents may not realize their children with disabilities have postsecondary educational options, because higher education has exclusive admission requirements (Hart et al., 2010), yet participation in a postsecondary educational setting can enhance a student's independence regardless of whether a degree is earned. There are additional reasons to consider making a transition from high school to a postsecondary educational setting, including the normative experience of being college students, the potential for better employment outcomes, and the positive impact that students with disabilities can have on their peers without disabilities (Hart et al.; Kleinert, Jones, Sheppard-Jones, Harp, & Harrison, 2012). A survey of parents of students with disabilities revealed that, although they were most concerned with safety, parents considered postsecondary education to be important (Griffen et al., 2010).

Students who enroll in IHEs have several options that include taking classes for credit, auditing classes, and participating in continuing education classes, with supports and accommodations (e.g., notetakers, recorded lectures) provided as needed (Hart et al., 2010). Some college programs for students with disabilities (ages 18–21 years) are conducted with dual enrollment in secondary school, and others are college-initiated and open to students (ages 18–24 years) who have exited secondary school (Hart et al.).

In 2010, Hart et al. reported that there were more than 250 programs on IHE campuses specifically designed for students with ID and ASD. Typically, these programs take place in natural environments, are person-centered, operate across agencies, employ universal design, use peer mentoring, provide educational coaching, have employment-focused outcomes, include a focus on communication skills, provide opportunities for self-determination and self-advocacy, and include evaluation to ensure that the programs are appropriate and working. One way in which special education teachers can assist students and their families in the transition process is to advocate for dual enrollment partnerships with local colleges.

When Griffin et al. (2010) surveyed parents of students with ID, they found that parents valued postsecondary education for their children but did not think that special education teachers encouraged this or that they received enough information and guidance on the availability of programs. In considering postsecondary education programs for their children with ID, parents worried about safety due to their children's vulnerability and wanted a focus on employment as an outcome.

Several models of postsecondary education transition programs are available for students with ID. A survey of 64% of these programs (Papay & Bambera, 2011) revealed that the majority are operated by school systems and most have few students enrolled (with a median of 12); the low enrollment number indicates that only some of the students in school districts are selected for the programs. Some IHE programs for students with ID are stand-alone programs housed on the campus, some are inclusive programs in which students with ID take part in classes that exist for all students, and some are mixed programs in which students with ID take special courses but are included in extracurricular activities on campus (Kleinert et al., 2012). Their purpose is to include students with disabilities in classes (e.g., health, fitness, art) with same-age peers so they can develop friendships and learn skills that will be valued in employment settings (Papay & Bambera). Components of successful post-secondary programs for students with ID include the use of individualized supports and peer mentors; barriers to success include a lack of awareness or understanding of the benefits of college programs for students with ID, faculty concerns about extra work, and the perception that providing modifications for some, but not all, students is unfair (Kleinert et al.). For example, some parents as well as some IHE faculty may not understand why a student with ID would benefit from enrollment in a program on the campus of an IHE, so it is imperative that the anticipated outcomes (e.g., social skills, friendships with same-age peers, employment skills, leisure skills) are clear in materials and conversations both prior to and following enrollment.

Think College at the University of Vermont and Think College Johnson State College are examples of postsecondary programs on college campuses that are open to students with ID (Ryan, 2014). These programs are person-centered and serve students 18 years of age and older who have IQs in the range of 50–78. The students enroll in undergraduate courses with the support of student mentors and work on related employment outcomes. Students' goals, in addition to future employment, include forming friendships with same-age peers without disabilities.

Some IHEs offer support programs for degree-earning students with disabilities. Barnhill (2014) reported that seven of 30 surveyed IHEs (23%) offered summer transition programs to improve the success of students with ASD; these programs varied in length from 3 days to 6 weeks. Such programs can be crucial to academic success for students with ASD who may have high grade point averages but low social and adaptive skills.

> What types of postsecondary educational opportunities may be available to students with disabilities? How might this differ according to the type of disability or the age of the student? What are the benefits of these programs and what are the potential barriers to success?

You can employ various strategies to prepare students with disabilities for success when they transition to an IHE. These include visiting the disability office of an IHE and sharing what you learn with families, setting up opportunities for IHEs to present information to families, decreasing dependency on supports in your students, facilitating the use of assistive technology, providing documentation of accommodations made for students prior to transition, involving students in their IEP meetings so they will be aware of their strengths and challenges, and teaching learning and organizational strategies to students (Hamblet, 2014).

For students with ASD, you can provide instruction on practical skills, such as managing safety, transportation, finances, personal hygiene, and laundry, so the students can live in a dormitory where they will have the opportunity to make friends, rather than at home (Zeedyk, Tipton, & Blacher, 2014). You also can teach social skills (e.g., appropriate conversation, appropriate class behavior) so students will be more successful in making friends (Zeedyk et al.), with a special emphasis on conversational skills and listener awareness, which affect social interactions (Zager & Alpern, 2010). Because students in college will no longer have IEPs, instruction on self-advocacy will benefit students in advocating for the accommodations they need, and instruction on time management will help them deal with scheduling changes (Roberts, 2010).

Some of the strategies for helping students with ASD make the transition to postsecondary educational programs—such as helping them to learn more about college services, having them participate in the IEP meeting, developing their time management skills, and teaching self-advocacy—also apply to students with learning disabilities or ADHD; students with learning disabilities and ADHD also may benefit from enrolling in college courses and in college preparatory courses while still in secondary school (Connor, 2012). Parents who are considering transition to college for their children with ASD may want to consider that 2-year colleges may be smaller and less overwhelming and provide more access to support from peers from the student's secondary school; although 4-year colleges may be more diverse and offer more formal support services, classes also will be larger and more self-advocacy will be needed (Zeedyk et al., 2014).

Voice of a Leader

Lead by Establishing a Transition Program

Contrary to what some families or some students may believe, having a disability does not bar a student from participating in college life or other experiences typical of young adulthood. Institutions of higher education that enroll students with disabilities may have—or need—transition programs to help these students manage new expectations and challenges. In this section, Renee Hollinger Scott gives advice to teachers interested in establishing transition programs like these.

Q: *What recommendations do you have for a teacher who may want to establish a transition program like the one where you work?*

A: Research similar transition programs and talk to the teachers or leaders of those programs. Network with university faculty. Learn what resources your community has to offer (e.g., funding and waiver sources, adult agencies and service providers, supported employment providers). You will need to be able to provide parents with this information as well as connect students to resources for support after graduation.

Employment

Regardless of whether they attend a postsecondary educational program, employment is a desired outcome for all students with disabilities, just as it is for all students without disabilities. A number of issues related to employment are important for you to discuss with parents during the transition process. These include the need to focus on self-determination skills (e.g., self-management) and the need for future transportation, flexibility of work schedules, and the wage scale; parents also need to understand the differences between school services and adult services and between paid and unpaid work experiences (Moon, Simonsen, & Neubert, 2011; Shogren, Wehmeyer, Palmer, Rifenbark, & Little, 2015).

To prepare students with developmental disabilities to make the transition to employment settings (Cease-Cook, Fowler, & Test, 2015), you can expose them to potential types of employment through several means. One is conducting career exploration activities, such as tours of job sites and interviews with employees. You can also provide job shadowing experiences and set up work sampling experiences in the classroom, such as creating displays; in the school setting, such as posting menus; at after-school events, such as selling refreshments; or during extracurricular activities, such as assisting with sports teams. In addition to teaching community-based skills during secondary school (Moon et al., 2011), you also can engage students in service learning projects, as previously described, and advocate for 1) internships (formal paid or unpaid time-limited experiences), 2) apprenticeships (experiences learning a trade under a mentor), and 3) paid employment (part- or full-time work experiences at competitive wages) (Cease-Cook et al.).

Another possibility is to encourage parents to have their children engage in summer employment experiences and offer to assist them in finding those jobs. For example, Carter, Trainor, Citchman, Swedeen, and Owens (2011) reported that, of 220 students with disabilities engaged in summer employment jobs, students with emotional and behavioral disabilities most often found employment in cleaning services during the school year through a friend and drove to work, students with ID most often found employment in food services during the school year themselves or through a parent and rode to work with family, and students with LD most often found employment in food services prior to the school year through a parent and drove to work.

If employment is to be a successful outcome for students with disabilities, it is important to assess a student's skills and to facilitate a good match between the student and the job. Morgan and Openshaw (2011) recommended the use of a web-based job preference assessment (http://www.yesjobsearch.com/) to match a student's skills to specific jobs and a social network assessment (involving interviews with the student, family, and others) to find leads to and locate preferred employment sites through social contacts. Hall, Morgan, and Salzberg (2014) assessed job matches for four transitioning students by rotating them through jobs in the community, completing a web-based assessment to identify high- and low-preference jobs, rating the student's skills to find high and low matches, and then teaching the job tasks. They found that the students performed better (e.g., more on-task behavior) on preferred jobs.

> What factors should be considered in identifying employment goals for students with disabilities? What strategies can teachers implement to identify appropriate employment settings?

Once an assessment has been conducted, you can use direct instruction to teach employment skills. It is never too early to begin working on future employment skills with students. For example, Rouse, Everhart-Sherwood, and Alber-Morgan (2014) began teaching middle school students with MSDs to use picture prompts to complete job tasks and to assess their completed work by comparing it to a picture. Effective instructional strategies for teaching job skills include video modeling and video prompting and virtual simulations as well as the use of assistive devices (e.g., GPS and portable devices to assist in transportation; Kellems et al., 2015). Preparing students for employment may sometimes require going beyond teaching the skills necessary to perform specific job tasks. For example, community rehabilitation providers involved in helping students with disabilities transition to employment also have stated concern that students have the behavior, personal hygiene, safety, and toileting skills needed for employment (Moon et al., 2011); these skills may need to be addressed, depending on each student's unique profile. In addition, technical skills and social skills needed for employment need to be addressed (Ryndak, Alper, Hughes, & McDonnell, 2012).

BE A LEADER: SUPPORT STUDENTS AND FAMILIES DURING TRANSITIONS

Throughout this chapter, you have learned about ways you can be a leader in how you help students and families navigate transitions. These include the transitions that take place throughout a student's years in school as well as the transition from school to adulthood. In the latter instance, you can demonstrate leadership in helping to develop a student's transition plan and in using strategies that help to facilitate smooth transitions, such as forming family partnerships, fostering students' self-determination, helping students to find opportunities through peer connections and service learning activities, and helping students to form connections with adults who have disabilities. As a teacher leader, you can help your students to live full, rich lives in adulthood by helping students and families to understand and choose among the options available for guardianship, postsecondary education, and employment.

The following guidelines are offered to help you to expand your leadership skills in facilitating transitions for students with disabilities:

1. Investigate services and options for students with disabilities who make the transition from school to adulthood in your local community and state. Be prepared to provide information on postsecondary options that include education and employment.

2. Realize that transition is a lifelong process. Address it with students no matter what their age. This includes teaching self-determination skills to students with disabilities and planting the seeds of an independent future with families.

3. Consult with an attorney to gather information on guardianship and alternatives, or invite an attorney to a meeting to provide information for parents.

4. Examine your beliefs about cultural differences and how they may affect your attitudes toward families. Educate yourself on the cultures of the families with whom you work as you interact with them to develop appropriate transition goals for their children.

5. When developing a transition plan, involve the student to the fullest extent possible, using person-centered planning strategies.

6. Employ strategies that facilitate successful transitions. These include forming family partnerships, teaching self-determination skills, providing opportunities for service learning and peer mentoring, and consulting with adult role models with disabilities.

FOLLOW-UP ACTIVITIES

In Chapter 6, you've learned about effective ways to facilitate the transition process for students at any stage of their education, including those making the transition from school to adulthood. Showing leadership in this area requires that you work with a given student and his or her family to consider available options and form a transition plan that helps the student to reach his or her full potential. It also involves thinking about what any adult, with or without disabilities, needs to lead a productive, rewarding life. The activities below are designed to help you reflect upon these topics and apply them to your work with students in transition.

1. **Reflect upon periods of transitions in your own life (e.g., educational, personal).** List them. What were the strategies and supports that enabled you to make these transitions? How might the transition process be different for a person with disabilities and what strategies and supports might be helpful? Does the type of disability make a difference? Why or why not?

2. **Review and list the rights that you have as an independent citizen.** Which of those rights might be in jeopardy if a person is not his or her own guardian? Consider also that in 1990, Bannerman, Sheldon, Sherman, and Harchik wrote an article titled "Balancing the right to habilitation with the right to personal liberties: The rights of people with developmental disabilities to eat too many doughnuts and take a nap," in which they questioned the moral and legal issues that arise when people with disabilities are not allowed to make poor choices. Should people with disabilities have the same right to make these choices that people without disabilities have? Why or why not?

3. **Interview at least five different people about why they chose the career they chose and whether it was their first choice.** When did these people choose their career path and what influenced their choice? What skills did they have to obtain to be successful? Considering what you learned, how could you assist a person with a disability in finding a source of employment that matches his or her strengths and interests?

4. **Research IHEs in your community, state, or region.** What information can you find about supports or special programs that are available for students with disabilities? Interview a secondary special education teacher, a secondary guidance counselor, or a special education director to learn if there are transition programs for students with disabilities that are housed on the campuses of nearby IHEs. If you locate one, determine who is eligible to participate, the model for participating in classes, and the skills that are the focus of the program.

5. **Talk with a family of a young child with a disability about their dreams and concerns for their child's future.** Then, do the same with the family of an adolescent with a disability. What similarities do you discover? What differences? Did the type of disability or the culture seem to affect the responses of the families? If so, how?

6. **Talk with someone from an agency that works with adults with disabilities.** This could be an independent case manager or someone from vocational rehabilitation services. What can they tell you about funding for adult services? Working with Social Security? The range of adult options (e.g., competitive or supported employment, adult daycare, independent living or supported living, group homes)? Based on what you learn, what could you share with parents?

7 Advocate for Students

Learning Objectives

After reading this chapter, readers will be able to

- Explain why advocacy and self-advocacy are important skills for teachers, families, students, and others involved in special education and services for people with disabilities

- Describe how advocacy has played a vital role in the history of special education

- Describe how policies become law and how special education teachers can be involved in the process

- Identify and apply strategies for being an effective advocate for people with disabilities at the local, state, and national levels

- Know and use effective ways of communicating with policy makers

- Know and follow the cautions that special education teachers should remember and exercise when advocating in a public arena

Terms to Know

Advocacy

Self-advocacy

←——→

INTRODUCTION

Advocacy consists of presenting an argument to influence a cause (Whitby et al., 2013) as well as being visible and doing what it takes to stand up for others (Stanley, 2015). The new Teacher Leader Model Standards (TLEC, 2012) have identified public advocacy for education and the teaching profession as one of the responsibilities of a teacher leader (Kajitani, 2015). Special education teachers are the experts at what they do, are knowledgeable about the issues that affect their profession, and have a constitutional right to make their voices heard (Underwood, 2013). Many, however, may be reluctant to speak out as advocates due to being uncomfortable with this role, fearing discipline from administrators, suffering discomfort from colleagues, and taking time away from instruction (Whitby et al.). If you have sometimes been unsure of how best to advocate for students, you may have felt these concerns.

Not only is advocacy for students important, Kaufman and Ring (2011) noted that new special education teachers, in particular, benefit from learning **self-advocacy** skills that empower them to speak up for themselves because they are at risk for being overwhelmed by their new role as professionals, experiencing burnout due to being hired at a late date, and being placed in high-poverty schools with little support or mentoring. If you are relatively new to special education, you may have felt the need to advocate for yourself or wondered how to do so effectively.

In addition to advocating for yourself, you have the responsibility of being an advocate for the students and families with whom you work. For example, you can advocate for students with disabilities within the process of developing IEPs (Whitby et al., 2013) and advocate for more postsecondary options as students with disabilities make the transition to adulthood (Ryan, 2014). Indeed, many special education teachers already view advocacy as a central part of their work. When Urbach et al. (2015) interviewed special education teachers about their roles and responsibilities, advocacy was one area they identified. This included both self-advocacy and advocacy for students. Urbach and colleagues cited one teacher who commented, "I pushed and pushed until the administration finally learned that I wasn't going to shut up" (2015, p. 331) and another who explained, "I have the opportunity to stand up for children who tend, without me, to be left out or pushed aside" (2015, p. 331). In a similar study, Brolan et al. (2012) noted the purposes of, and best practices in, advocacy, citing quotations from advocates:

- One purpose of advocacy is to influence another person on someone's behalf; an advocate for the health of people with ID said, "I am here to speak for him. I am his voice" (Brolan et al., 2012, p. 1091).

- Another purpose of advocacy is "to assist the person who cannot speak up for themselves. To help them live a life like anyone else" (Brolan et al., 2012, p. 1091).

- Best practice in advocacy is to "to give opinions that are in [the other person's] best interests not the advocate's best interests. Walk in [the] other's shoes" (Brolan et al., 2012, p. 1092).

Advocacy for the rights of students with disabilities is the foundation of the field of special education. In 1950, parents organized as advocates for their children with ID through The Arc (known at that time as the Association for Retarded Children); by 1974, this group of advocates had grown to more than 225,000 members and significantly influenced the deinstitutionalization movement in the United States, the changes in language used to refer to people with ID, and the creation of the Education for All Handicapped Children Act of 1975 (PL 94-142; Segal, 2016). The continuing advocacy movement for people with disabilities is evident through changes in terminology (Ford, Acosta, & Sutcliffe, 2013) under the Bush administration in 2003 and under the Obama administration in 2009, with these administrations employing the term *intellectual disability* and using person-first language. Under the Bush administration, this change in terminology was reflected in the President's Committee for People with Intellectual Disabilities; under the Obama administration, *intellectual disability* was a term used in Rosa's Law of 2010 (PL 111-256).

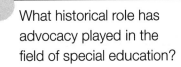

What historical role has advocacy played in the field of special education?

It is clear that advocacy is considered an appropriate, and perhaps vital, role you have as a special education teacher. This role requires you to be prepared to advocate for your own needs and those of your students and to model advocacy for your students with disabilities through working with professional organizations, becoming informed on issues, and communicating with policy makers (Mullen, 2014). This chapter describes strategies you can use to engage in advocacy.

CONNECTION TO PROFESSIONAL STANDARDS

Your role in engaging in advocacy on behalf of students with disabilities is supported by a number of professional standards listed under the Teacher Leader Model Standards (TLEC, 2012) and the CEC Standards for Professional Practice and Advanced Preparation Standards (CEC, 2015).

Teacher Leader Model Standards

Although not specific to special education, the Teacher Leader Model Standards address (TLEC, 2012) the need to engage in advocacy, which is listed under *Domain 7: Advocating for Student Learning and the Profession*. Advocacy involves "sharing information with colleagues . . . [on] local, state, and national trends and policies," "working with colleagues to identify and use research" for advocacy, "collaborating with colleagues to select appropriate opportunities to advocate for the rights and/or needs of students," and "advocating for access to professional resources." This includes advocating outside of the classroom setting.

Council for Exceptional Children Program Standards

The Special Education Standards for Professional Practice developed by CEC (2015) address advocacy under professional credentials and employment (2.0) through engaging in advocacy for appropriate and supportive teaching conditions (2.6) and resources (2.7) while also ensuring that individual public statements are not construed as the policy position of the agency (e.g., school district; 2.9) and documenting and reporting inadequacies to administrators (2.10). In addition, advocacy is addressed under research (7.0) through engaging in advocacy for sufficient resources to support research agendas to improve special education. The Advanced Preparation Standards address advocacy under program, services, and outcomes (3.0) through applying the knowledge from theories, EBPs, and the law to advocate for programs, supports, and services (3.3). Advocacy is also addressed under leadership and policy (5.0) through advocating for policies and practices to improve program, supports, and services (5.4) and the allocation of resources for preparation and professional development of personnel (5.5). The story of Sara Menlove Doutre and her family, described in the section that follows, illustrates how these standards for advocacy can be put into practice.

Voice of a Leader

Advocating as a Teacher and Parent

Sara Menlove Doutre is a former special education teacher who became an advocate after the birth of her daughter, Daisy. Sara and her mother, Dr. Ronda Menlove, are friends of mine whose work illustrates the importance of advocacy. Although Ms. Doutre's busy schedule did not allow time for an interview as this book was being completed, she has graciously agreed to have her family's story appear here. It is a powerful example of how the voice of a leader in special education can influence public policy.

Ms. Doutre's daughter Daisy became infected with cytomegalovirus (CMV) while Ms. Doutre was pregnant with her (May, 2013). As a result of the infection, Daisy became deaf by age 2. Initially, CMV was a new and unfamiliar topic to Ms. Doutre. Later, she learned that it also can cause mental disabilities and even death in children. As a result, Ms. Doutre advocated for state legislation that would require women to be told about CMV in pregnancy and educated on precautions they can take to prevent infection (e.g., washing hands, wiping saliva from children's toys, not sharing food and drinks with children, cleaning surfaces that come into contact with children's urine). The legislation would also require screening of young children for CMV if they failed two hearing screenings. Ms. Doutre's mother, Dr. Ronda Menlove, a professor and another former special education teacher, also got involved in the advocacy effort. During this time, she served as a Utah state representative, and she sponsored the bill.

The legislation ultimately passed in Utah due to the advocacy efforts of Ms. Doutre and Dr. Menlove. According to the National CMV Foundation (2016), Connecticut, Hawaii, Illinois, Texas, and Tennessee followed suit, and as of this writing, six other states were considering legislation as well.

Sometimes it takes a personal event to provide the impetus to advocate for a cause. This family's story illustrates the powerful impact a special education teacher can have in effecting change.

YOUR ROLE IN ADVOCACY

Publicly speaking out on issues is part of advocacy, but you can also engage in advocacy in more subtle ways. Whereas some teachers feel comfortable in a public arena, others prefer to engage in small acts of advocacy that still can have an impact. The important point is that teachers take a stand for themselves, their profession, and their students in an effective way. This can happen in the classroom, the school, the local community, or at a state or national level.

In stating that the three Ps of advocacy should be **p**urpose, **p**reparation, and **p**ersistence, Roberts noted an old saying: "If you are not at the table, you are on the menu" (2012, p. 61). To put this another way, if you do not speak out on behalf of your students, literally or figuratively representing them at the table where decisions are made, their needs are likely to be overlooked or subsumed by the needs of other groups. The same is true when it comes to advocating for your own interests as a teacher. The following sections describe some of the strategies you can use to advocate and how you can maximize their impact by facilitating advocacy in others.

Strategies for Being a Special Education Advocate

Through advocacy, you have the opportunity to offer solutions to problems, but you must be able to do this in a timely and practical way (Grob, 2014). This can be accomplished through working at a local level or at a state or national level.

Advocacy at the Local Level You have the opportunity to advocate for the students you teach on a daily basis, both within the student's daily routine and at special meetings, such as IEP meetings. Advocacy strategies recommended by Whitby et al. (2013) include the following:

- Working to build collegial relationships

- Communicating frequently in a positive way (not just at meetings)

- Listening to others and affirming that you hear what others are saying

- Finding commonalities that show areas of agreement

- Engaging in discussions using a "sandwich technique" (i.e., compliment, then criticize, then collaborate)

- Compromising to solve problems

- Controlling emotions by taking a break, as needed

- Offering expertise (e.g., sharing knowledge of EBPs and data to make decisions)

- Following up on issues and discussions

In addition, you can avoid problems that diminish your advocacy efforts. For example, avoid coming to an IEP meeting with goals and objectives prepared in advance without other team members' input, presuming that a special education setting is needed rather than inclusion in a general education setting, holding meetings without everyone present who should be there, continuing ineffective practices without using data to investigate alternatives, blaming parents when students do not learn, and using placements in restrictive environments simply because that is what has been done in the past (Cheatham et al., 2012).

In taking a public stand, special education teachers should be cautious (Underwood, 2013). Remember that you are entitled to have personal opinions and to speak out on issues of concern. At the same time, remember that when you speak out in a public forum, you are speaking for yourself and not as a representative of the school system for which you work. Public schools have the right to restrict a teacher's ability to speak out in any way that may harm the school's ability to perform its job. While a teacher may be free to voice opinions outside of the school setting, display political buttons and stickers, and engage in demonstrations, school districts can restrict these activities at school-sponsored functions.

Special education teachers also need to be aware of district policies when they actively participate in politics (Underwood, 2013). If you choose to run for public office, the school district may require a leave of absence if there is a conflict with the school schedule and your ability to perform your school responsibilities. Also, you cannot use school (state) resources for political activities or campaigns during school hours. Some elected political offices (e.g., school board member) may pose a conflict of interest and require resignation from the school system.

> What are some cautions to be aware of before speaking out in a public arena?

A different set of considerations applies within the boundaries of your classroom. While it is a good practice to maintain a classroom climate that is open for debate, be sure to maintain a neutral position on political issues and discuss political topics in a nonpartisan way with students—for example, when teaching students about the candidates in a current election during a civics lesson (Flanagan, 2014).

Advocacy at the State and National Levels   When the issues under discussion warrant your involvement, you can be an effective advocate at the state and national levels, because legislators are likely to listen to grassroots stories from people who are in the trenches on a daily basis. A single story can be more effective in changing policy than a signature on a mass-produced letter. Do not be intimidated by the prospect of approaching your elected legislators, because it is their job to listen to and represent the constituents who elected them (Flanagan, 2014). Remind yourself that simply having attended school does not necessarily make a legislator an expert on school policies (Flanagan). As a special education teacher, you are likely to know more about educational topics (e.g., assessment, appropriate class sizes, special education practices, standards) based on your professional preparation, familiarity with special education research, and daily involvement in your profession.

The foundation for effective advocacy with legislators is an understanding of the legislative process (Bond & Pope, 2013). The first step for creating a law takes place when a bill is submitted to a committee for review. The bill is usually revised before a hearing is held. During the hearing, you and other constituents have an opportunity to voice your opinions. Many hearings are open, and legislators want to hear from the public. At the end of the hearing, the bill goes to the legislators for a public vote. If the bill is passed, it is signed by the appropriate person (e.g., governor, president) and becomes a law. If the bill is defeated, it can be revised and resubmitted.

Several effective strategies can be used to communicate with state legislators (Collins, Ludlow, & Menlove, 2005). For example, you can make an effort to meet candidates and share information when the candidates are running for office; you can even assist with a campaign if you feel strongly about the legislator's ability to represent special education issues. Once legislators are elected, you can monitor the news for proposed bills related to special education and contact the appropriate legislator before these bills go up for a vote. Find out the committees to which legislators are assigned and send appropriate legislators short (i.e., one-page) summaries on issues likely to be discussed in committees related to special education.

For example, you can be a resource on the language that should be used in a bill as it is being drafted; recall the influence The Arc has had over the past 6 decades on changing language used to refer to disabilities and people who have disabilities. If you are reluctant to be a single voice, it can be helpful to align with an existing advocacy group and then share materials from that group. (Chapter 8 discusses different professional organizations that help to serve the needs of people with disabilities; you might consider aligning with one or more of those organizations.)

Strategies like the ones described here also work at the national level (Collins et al., 2005). Keep in mind that all elected legislators will have staffed home offices within their states. Although any citizen can make an appointment with a legislator, it can be helpful to be part of a national group that advocates for people with disabilities (e.g., American Council on Rural Special Education [ACRES], The Arc, CEC, TASH). These groups have materials that can be shared, and some have organized "days on the Hill" when groups travel to the state capitol or to Washington, D.C., to talk about issues with legislators or their staff members.

If you are making a personal trip to Washington, D.C., or are going with a group, it is helpful to do some advance preparation. For a small fee, you can order *Congress at Your Fingertips* (http://publishing.cqrollcall.com/) for information on contacting legislators, locating offices, and identifying the committees to which legislators are assigned. Much of this information also will be available on each legislator's web site (the current list of U.S. senators is available at https://www.senate.gov and list of U.S. representatives at https://www.house. gov). If making appointments to visit the Hill, schedule a time with the legislator's staff person assigned to educational issues. Most meetings will last 30 minutes. If more than one appointment is made, at least 30 minutes should be scheduled between meetings to allow time for getting from one office to another and going through security checks. Carrying a map to locate offices will save time, and carrying a cell phone to get additional directions or apologize if running late is also helpful. Once the meeting begins, show polite enthusiasm about the issues you present, stay focused on the topic, and share materials that can be left with the staff person. Sending a follow-up e-mail afterward will leave a good impression and remind the staff person that you can be a resource when legislative issues arise in future. If the school approves, you can invite legislators to visit your school to observe the issues firsthand (Flanagan, 2014).

Describe the legislative process that is used to establish a law. When and how can a special education teacher be involved in this process?

Other Ways to Advocate   If a legislative visit to a local or national office is not practical, you can exercise your rights as a citizen through other options. It may be helpful to form a partnership with universities (Bryan & Sims, 2011) because faculty may have an established forum for approaching legislators (as well as state agencies)—for example, a forum such as the Higher Education Consortium for Special Education (HECSE) or a protocol such as working with a university lobbyist. To begin forming this kind of partnership with a local university, you can contact the head of the university's special education department to set up a meeting to discuss issues of concern and to find a way to work with faculty members on advocacy activities (e.g., special events). For example, you can work with university faculty to plan an event for Light It Up Blue to promote awareness of ASD or partner with faculty on recruiting students to walk in the Buddy Walk sponsored by the National Down Syndrome Society to raise funds for associated advocacy activities.

If your time is too limited or you cannot locate local partners for advocacy activities, written communications can be effective. Opinion pieces written for local news outlets can draw attention to an issue. Because they reach a larger audience, they can have more impact on policy than writing for professional journals does. As with other means of expressing opinions in a public forum, you may write these pieces as long as you are speaking for yourself and not on behalf of the school system that employs you. If you are writing an opinion piece, you may find it helpful to follow a few simple rules that can be summarized as be brave, be brief, be quick, be conversational, and be prepared (Gasman, 2014). Begin by coming up with a topic and a few main points that can be addressed concisely (e.g., three main points covered within 800 words). The introduction must grab the readers' attention, and the conclusion must motivate readers to think differently. The topic should be timely, and your language should not contain jargon unfamiliar to a general audience. Once a piece is in press, be prepared to be critiqued and expect some readers to disagree with your position.

After your piece is published, be cautious and exercise restraint when you read counter-comments and e-mail responses from readers. If the topic is one that will stay current for some time to come, you might want to hold off on responding to reader commentary right away because it will likely be difficult to address opposing views objectively. If, after a few weeks have passed, the topic is still relevant, take time to look over reader responses. Select the most thoughtful and well-supported ones (including those that express opposing views) and respond to these readers in a way that encourages further dialogue.

> Describe several options for communicating on behalf of students with disabilities and the profession of special education. Why is a special education teacher like you likely to be an effective advocate?

In addition to submitting a written piece to a public outlet, you can easily submit written pieces to legislators' offices via e-mail or U.S. mail; directions for doing so are available on each legislator's web site. What is most important is to communicate often with legislators, whether through writing, phone calls, social media, or face-to-face visits (Bond & Pope, 2013). In communications, remember that your efforts may be better received if you rely on and share your knowledge as a professional, keep an open mind, and offer options rather than strict recommendations (Grob, 2014).

Helping Others Become Advocates

While you can be a leader through your individual advocacy efforts, power is in numbers. It is important to support the advocacy efforts of others, be a model for advocacy, and teach advocacy strategies. When you combine your efforts with those of others, more can be accomplished. Also, in the absence of advocacy from special education teachers, the advocacy skills of others can influence the lives of individuals with disabilities.

Families are most likely to serve as the first advocates for their children with disabilities. Whereas special education teachers work with students only a few hours each day for a few years, families work with their children throughout their lives (Ludlow, 2012); thus, families who are effective advocates have the opportunity to make a greater impact, as noted in Chapter 5. When Shogren (2012) interviewed Hispanic mothers of children with disabilities, she found them to be vocal advocates; on the other hand, when Thurston and Navarrete (2010) interviewed rural mothers of children with disabilities who were living at poverty level, they found that these mothers lacked the self-confidence or education to be advocates and recommended that teachers advocate for them. Keep in mind that families of children with disabilities may experience fatigue after battling districts to ensure that their children's needs are met (Hetherington et al., 2010); thus, a partnership between special education teachers and families can be advantageous when parents believe that they are fighting a losing battle or lack the skills to be effective advocates for their children.

Self-advocacy skills also are important for students with disabilities if they are to exercise self-determination in their lives, as discussed in Chapter 6. The acquisition of self-advocacy skills may require direct instruction (Collet-Klingenberg & Kolb, 2011; Roberts, 2010), and curricula are available to help you address these skills (Lee et al., 2011). Research has shown that school administrators also value instruction on self-advocacy by special education teachers but may be unaware if this is being addressed in classroom instruction (Carter, Lane et al., 2011); thus, you may want to make administrators and other staff aware of the importance of teaching self-advocacy skills to students with disabilities and how this is being addressed.

Chapter 3 discussed the importance of serving as a mentor to beginning teachers. As noted earlier in this chapter, novice teachers can benefit from learning to be self-advocates during their initial years of teaching because they are susceptible to burnout as they learn survival skills. One way to teach advocacy skills to new teachers is to involve them in advocacy projects early in their preparation, because "success with advocacy-based projects during educator preparation fosters efficacy for early-career grassroots advocacy efforts" (Hurley, 2016, p. 49). If you are involved with the clinical experiences of preservice special education teachers, you may want to consider involving them in advocacy projects (e.g., school meetings, presentations for parents' groups).

> As you come to the end of this chapter, what are some ways you think you can become involved in advocacy efforts on behalf of students with disabilities? How can you engage in self-advocacy?

In summary, it is vitally important to be a strong advocate for your students with disabilities and to work with families and students to strengthen their advocacy skills as well. In addition, when you choose to become a strong advocate, you can be a role model for colleagues, students without disabilities, and members of the community in demonstrating how strategies for effective advocacy can be applied.

BE A LEADER: ENGAGE IN ADVOCACY

In Chapter 7, you have learned about ways to lead by advocating—for your students and, when necessary, for yourself and other teachers as well. Advocacy can occur on a small or large scale, in public arenas at the local, state, or even national levels. As part of advocacy, it is often helpful to form connections with like-minded individuals or affiliate yourself with organizations that address the issues that concern you and your students. Advocacy may also include teaching others to become advocates.

The following guidelines are offered to expand your leadership skills in advocating for students with disabilities:

1. Before engaging in advocacy, prepare yourself by thoroughly reviewing the issue and establishing the best outlet for disseminating information on the issue.

2. Research organizations that are involved in advocacy and form partnerships in your advocacy efforts, including sharing materials.

3. Communicate efficiently and effectively with legislators. Consider e-mail, phone calls, and face-to-face visits as options. Remember to be brief and clear in your presentation and to have data, anecdotes, or other materials that support your stance on an issue.

4. Know and follow your employer's policies. Although it is the right of all citizens to speak out on issues, be aware of school district policies for voicing your opinions in a public arena.

5. When advocating on an issue, remember that you are serving as a role model for your students and their families as well as for colleagues.

6. Stay current and make use of daily experiences. Be timely in addressing current issues, and remember that describing a personal experience draws greater attention to an issue than voicing opinions does.

FOLLOW-UP ACTIVITIES

Advocating for students and teachers—and teaching them to become advocates as well—is a great way to demonstrate leadership. Chapter 7 has described strategies for engaging in advocacy at the local, state, and national levels. Doing so effectively involves being well informed and prepared, working with likeminded individuals and organizations, expressing ideas effectively in public forums and in private communications (e.g., with legislators), and keeping current about the issues that affect students with disabilities (and their families and teachers). The activities that follow are intended to help you get started on leading through advocacy efforts.

1. **Research one or more web sites that advocate for people with disabilities.** (For example, you might look up ACRES, Autism Society, CEC, National Down Syndrome Society, or TASH). Does the web site offer a description of past advocacy efforts? What forums are available in which you may choose to participate (e.g., visits to legislators, discussion groups, committees that draft policies and present position papers)? Check to see if there is a local chapter of any of the organizations in your community. If possible, attend a meeting or chat with a member to learn more about advocacy efforts.

2. **Identify a special education issue that you consider timely and important and on which you hold strong views.** (Examples include assessment, behavioral intervention and support, inclusion, supported living or employment, and transition.) Locate a minimum of five sources that support your position and recall a personal experience that led you to your conclusion. Then, draft a short

letter to the editor, an opinion piece for a news outlet, or a letter to a legislator about your stance on the issue. Share your finished product with a friend or colleague to determine how convincing you are and how you can improve your presentation of the issue. Be sure to use person-first language (e.g., "student with intellectual disability" instead of "special education student") and to avoid any jargon that might be unfamiliar to a novice reader.

3. **Compile a list of legislators who represent your community and state, using the Internet to conduct research.** Can you determine their stance on issues relevant to special education or the lives of people with disabilities? Can you find their contact information (e.g., local, state, national)? Is there information about the legislative committees on which they serve?

4. **Talk with a person with a disability or a family member to identify current issues related to education and disabilities.** What issues can you identify that are a concern for this individual or family? Has the person you interviewed ever been involved in advocacy or self-advocacy? If so, how? Can you identify possible solutions to the concerns that are raised that could be presented to community officials (e.g., school board, mayor) or to state or national legislators?

5. **Reflect upon how you serve as an advocate for your students with disabilities in the following environments:** 1) the faculty lounge, 2) IEP or transition meetings, 3) casual conversations with neighbors or friends, and 4) school meetings (e.g., PTA). What do you currently do to be an advocate and a leader in these environments? What else could you do?

6. **Recall a time when you took a stand for something that you believed was right, regardless of whether this was related to special education.** What was the cause? What did you do? What were the outcomes? As you reflect, determine whether the strategies you used were effective or whether you could have spoken or acted in a different way to be more convincing.

8 Connect With Disability-Related Organizations

Learning Objectives

After reading this chapter, readers will be able to

- State the benefits of belonging to and participating in a disability-related professional organization

- Identify various organizations related to special education and advocacy for people with disabilities

- Know how to share information with others through a professional organization

- Recommend professional organizations on special disability topics or specific types of disabilities to parents and colleagues

Terms to Know

Blind review

Universal design

INTRODUCTION

This book has addressed the many ways you can work individually to become a leader in special education. However, for several reasons, your pursuit of leadership may involve joining with others in the profession.

First, membership in a professional organization provides a way to keep up on current best practices in special education. Special education teachers often are isolated within their schools and districts because they are few in number and their responsibilities differ from those of general education teachers. They must take a leading role in developing, implementing, and monitoring IEPs; in developing and implementing transition plans; in assessing the function of challenging behaviors and creating positive behavior support plans; in identifying individual adaptations and accommodations that will allow students to engage with core content; and in working with families who need support to deal with the challenges of a child with special needs. Participating in graduate programs and professional development helps you to keep abreast of current practices, but these sources of information can be sporadically available or, depending on the geographic region, nonexistent. Belonging to a professional organization provides you with resources such as professional journals and other publications, webinars, and conferences that otherwise may not be available.

Second, belonging to a professional organization allows you to connect with a community of professionals who share your interests and can discuss solutions to challenges you face. These interests and challenges might include working with students with specific challenges such as ASD, implementing best practices such as inclusion, or understanding policy changes such as guidelines for alternate assessment. You may connect online in professional learning communities or meet face-to-face in special interest groups at professional conferences.

What are the ways in which a special education teacher can be involved in a professional organization? Based on the initial descriptions you've read, which types of involvement appeal to you the most and seem like the best fit for your leadership skills?

Third, becoming actively involved in a disability-related professional organization as a skilled special education teacher allows you to have an impact beyond the classroom and school in which you work. Local chapters of professional organizations can be the catalyst for your involvement in activities that will make a difference in the lives of students with disabilities and their families and create awareness of special education issues within the community and beyond. These activities might include things like participation in Buddy Walk for people with Down syndrome and Light It Up Blue for people with ASD. Local chapters of professional organizations also allow you to work with people outside of the educational system to make the community a more welcoming and supportive environment for people with disabilities. For example, you might work with family members, professionals such as case workers, and community partners such as the managers of businesses and corporations. You may find that participating in professional organizations also connects you with a network at the state, regional, or national level.

Finally, professional organizations can be an outlet for sharing your expertise and experience with others. Professional publications often provide an outlet for teachers to share through written pieces geared toward practitioners (e.g., *Teaching Exceptional Children*), even if they are not involved in academic research. If you do not yet have confidence in your ability to write professionally, educational conferences provide an outlet for teachers to present to each other, often in a casual and small setting of like-minded professionals (e.g., a state conference for the CEC). Some disability-related professional organizations also organize special campaigns to write letters to legislators regarding special education policies or even to visit with legislators or their staff at the state or national levels, providing you with the opportunity to share your firsthand experiences in the field and to state a rationale for supporting or opposing specific policies. When a special education teacher works with a professional organization in these capacities, the impact can be almost immeasurable.

This chapter provides an overview of disability-related organizations with which you can become involved. It also will review guidelines for sharing information with others in the field.

CONNECTION TO PROFESSIONAL STANDARDS

The teacher's role in participating in professional organizations is supported by a number of professional standards listed under the Teacher Leader Model Standards (TLEC, 2012) and the CEC Standards for Professional Practice and Advanced Preparation Standards (CEC, 2015).

Teacher Leader Model Standards

Although not specific to special education, the Teacher Leader Model Standards (TLEC, 2012) address the need to participate in professional organizations and use them as resources across several domains. According to standards listed under *Domain 2: Accessing and Using Research to Improve Practice and Student Learning*, teachers are to "keep abreast of the latest research," and organizations may act as a clearinghouse for this information through their publications (especially those that are peer-reviewed), resources, blogs, and newsletters. Under *Domain 3: Promoting Professional Learning for Continuous Improvement*, professional organizations can provide the forum for working with colleagues to "collect, analyze, and disseminate data" to others. Under *Domain 6: Improving Outreach and Collaboration with Families and Community*, professional organizations allow teachers the opportunity to "collaborate with families, communities, and colleagues to develop comprehensive strategies" to meet family and community needs. Finally, under *Domain 7: Advocating for Student Learning and the Profession*, professional organizations provide the opportunity for teachers to work at the local, state, or national level to advocate for educational policies "to meet the needs of all students."

Council for Exceptional Children Program Standards

The Special Education Standards for Professional Practice developed by CEC (2015) show that special education teachers can benefit from participating in professional organizations with professional colleagues (4.0) through collaboration with others to improve special education services (4.3) and outcomes (4.4). Although the Advanced Preparation Standards do not directly address participation in professional organizations, participation is addressed through advocating for programs, supports, and services (3.3); advocating for policies and practices to improve programs

(5.4); actively supporting the advancement of the profession (6.7); and collaborating to promote understanding and build consensus in the field (7.3). Samantha Matthews Orihuela, a special education teacher leader interviewed for this chapter, exemplifies how these standards can be applied in practice.

Voice of a Leader

Working With Community Organizations

Samantha Matthews Orihuela is a certified special education teacher who currently is completing the coursework and clinical hours to become a Board-Certified Behavior Analyst. She has been involved in classroom research (Matthews, Collins, Spriggs, & Kleinert, 2016) that addresses using systematic instruction to teach math core content to elementary students with moderate and severe disabilities. Ms. Orihuela has a strong interest in the inclusion of people with disabilities in their local community. She thus became involved as an active member on the board of a local professional organization that addresses the needs of people with Down syndrome and their families and she became involved in activities for people with disabilities through her faith community. Here, she describes the work she does with local organizations that provide support to students like the ones she teaches.

Q: *In what way have you worked with professional organizations for people with disabilities in your community?*

A: I worked with DSACK (Down Syndrome Association of Central Kentucky) as the elementary-age support group leader for several years. In this group, I would schedule a monthly event for individuals aged 5–13 to attend on a Saturday. Each month would have a theme. The event would last for 2–4 hours. It would include a game/social activity, craft, lesson, snack (that each kid would assist in preparing), and music or short video. At the end of the group, children would have social time to play with materials and interact with each other.

I became involved with DSACK after moving to Lexington for college at UK (University of Kentucky). While in high school, I was a member of GRADSA (Green River Area Down Syndrome Association) and was a peer tutor of an individual with Down syndrome for 4 years. Through our friendship and time in the community, I knew I wanted to continue working with individuals with Down syndrome.

At Southland Christian Church, we started a Sunday school program for children with disabilities ranging in age from 5 to 13 years. This class is called Kids R Special. [When we started] this class, the schedule was as follows: social time/check in, leveled groups (higher-functioning students read from an early reader Bible while lower-functioning students were read to from the Picture It Bible), craft related to the lesson, video about the lesson, snack, then dismissal. Individuals in this class ranged in ability level from severe/profound to mild intellectual disability. The ratio is 15 students to 1 lead teacher and 6 volunteers. [Author's note: Although Ms. Orihuela no longer runs Kids R Special, this program is still continuing and is now serving 15–20 kids per weekend.]

Q: *Has research played a role in work with a professional organization?*

A: Yes, I applied research to the games selected to improve social skills and communication functioning in both groups.

YOUR ROLE IN DISABILITY-RELATED PROFESSIONAL ORGANIZATIONS

Participating in professional organizations related to special education and disability can help you to become a more effective leader in many ways. They are a source of information to keep you informed on current best practices and new policies; they provide an outlet for you to interface with others within your community, state, and region and nationwide; and they provide a way for you to share your own expertise with others and, thus, have a greater impact on the field. This chapter provides an overview of specific organizations with which you can get involved, followed by information about how to disseminate information and make presentations through professional organizations and how to contribute articles to professional publications.

Disability-Related Professional Organizations

The following sections provide an overview of various disability-related professional organizations. The list is long, and it is not reasonable to belong to or participate in all of these organizations. Some can serve as a resource if you are interested in a specific topic based on the challenges related to the students with whom you work—for example, EBPs for students with significant disabilities. Others are organizations you may want to join to become more involved in, and have a greater impact upon, the profession of special education. Belonging to a professional organization can be expensive, although membership is tax-deductible as a professional expense, so you will want to investigate each organization to determine whether the benefits of membership are worth the cost. For example, examine the type, quality, and quantity of publications provided with membership; discounts on resource materials available through the organization; discounts on attending professional conferences and locations where the conferences are held; advocacy efforts of the organization; and whether the organization provides ways to network with others in the field, such as special interest groups that meet online. (Regarding membership fees, note also that some organizations offer different levels of membership with varying fees associated, and many organizations offer reduced membership fees for students.)

Each of the following sections provides information on a specific organization's mission and history, resources it provides, and whether the organization has local chapters or affiliates. As you read, you may wish to take notes or flag organizations that particularly interest you so you can conduct further investigation on your own before deciding on membership in specific organizations.

The decision to join a professional organization is a personal one and should be based on your interests as well as your desire and ability to participate. Although passive membership allows you to reap the benefits of gaining resources and remaining current, active membership allows you to share your expertise, create a broader circle of supportive colleagues, and have a greater impact upon the profession.

All of the organizations described here are nonprofit groups that are directed by boards and accept donations; however, some require dues to gain access to resources. Table 8.1 provides a quick overview of the benefits of each of these organizations.

Table 8.1. Overview of disability-related professional organizations

Name of organization	Holds annual conference	Publishes journal or other materials	Has regional, state, or local chapters	Has annual membership dues
AAPD: American Association of People with Disabilities		X		
AAIDD: American Association on Intellectual and Developmental Disabilities	X	X	X	X
ACRES: American Council on Rural Special Education	X	X		X
ACB: American Council of the Blind	X	X	X	
ABAI: Association for Behavior Analysis International	X	X	X	X
ASA: Autism Society of America	X	X	X	X
CHADD: Children and Adults with Attention-Deficit/ Hyperactivity Disorder		X	X	X
CLD: Council for Learning Disabilities	X	X	X	X
CEC: Council for Exceptional Children (see also the various divisions described in Chapter 8)	X	X	X	X[a]
LDA: Learning Disabilities Association of America	X	X	X	X
NADS: National Association for Down Syndrome		X		X
NAD: National Association of the Deaf	X	X	X	X
NDSS: National Down Syndrome Society	X		X	
NFB: National Federation of the Blind	X	X	X	X
NOD: National Organization on Disability				
TASH	X	X	X	X
The Arc			X	X
UCP: United Cerebral Palsy	X	X	X	

[a]Additional dues are charged for each additional division joined.

American Association of People with Disabilities The mission of the American Association of People with Disabilities (AAPD) is "to improve the lives of people with disabilities by acting as a convener, connector, and catalyst for change, increasing the political and economic power of people with disabilities" (AAPD, 2017). Founded in 1995 in Washington, D.C., to implement the Americans with Disabilities Act (ADA) of 1990 (PL 101-336), the organization is a resource that offers several publications, including one on school safety. AAPD promotes access to education from preschool through postgraduate work through advocacy and partnerships. The organization has issued policy statements on topics that include employment, faith, health, housing, inclusion, technology, transportation, and voting. AAPD offers summer internships, has a campaign to stop bullying, and opposes seclusion and restraint. The organization also supports a national network for youth with disabilities (ages 16–28 years), a national network to promote equal rights for people with ASD, and a national transition collaborative to support young people with disabilities as they enter adulthood.

American Association on Intellectual and Developmental Disabilities The American Association on Intellectual and Developmental Disabilities (AAIDD) "promotes progressive policies, sound research, effective practices, and universal human rights for people with intellectual and developmental disabilities" (AAIDD, 2017). The oldest and largest professional organization on disabilities, AAIDD has provided leadership in intellectual and developmental disabilities since it was founded in 1876. The organization publishes the *American Journal on Intellectual Disabilities*, *Intellectual and Developmental Disabilities*, *Inclusion*, a number of special-interest journals on specific topics, and a number of books on topics that include diversity and positive behavior supports. AAIDD has more than 5,000 members in the United States and in 55 other countries. Different levels of membership are offered (e.g., basic, premium) at varying fees; members also may join special interest groups (e.g., communication disorders, community services, education, families). Members who pay national dues receive access to training, publications, and supports that vary according to the level of dues paid, and they are considered members of local and regional chapters of the organization where they live as well. AAIDD hosts an annual conference. It should be noted that AAIDD has been instrumental historically in identifying and defining the terminology used in the field of ID.

American Council on Rural Special Education Members of the American Council on Rural Special Education (ACRES) "strive to provide leadership and support that will enhance services for individuals with exceptional needs, their families, and the professionals who work with them, and for the rural communities in which they live and work" (ACRES, 2017). Founded in 1981 as the only professional organization devoted to rural special education, ACRES has approximately 250 members, who pay annual dues. In return, members receive *Rural Special Education Quarterly* and a discount on the fee for attending the annual conference. ACRES also publishes periodic monographs on special topics such as distance education in special education, gives annual awards to outstanding rural education programs and agencies as well as special education researchers who have an impact on practices, provides scholarships for rural special educators, recognizes rural special education leaderships with an Eagle award, issues briefs on rural policies in special education, and advocates for rural special education with congressional leaders.

American Council of the Blind   The American Council of the Blind (ACB) "strives to increase the independence, security, equality of opportunity, and quality of life, for all blind and visually-impaired people" (ACB, 2013). Although the organization was officially founded in 1961, some of its more than 70 local chapters and state affiliates can trace their participation to the 1800s. ACB publishes *The Braille Forum* and hosts an annual conference.

Association for Behavior Analysis International   Founded for professionals and practitioners in the field of applied behavior analysis, the Association for Behavior Analysis International (ABAI) is "the primary membership organization for those interested in the philosophy, science, application, and teaching of behavior analysis" (ABAI, 2017), which can be applied to the educational and behavioral programming for students with a variety of disabilities, including ASD. ABAI has 23,000 members and 90 affiliated chapters. Dues vary depending on the type of membership. The organization publishes *The Analysis of Verbal Behavior*, *Behavior Analysis in Practice*, *The Behavior Analyst*, and *The Psychological Record;* offers books on behavioral topics; and hosts an annual conference.

Autism Society of America   The Autism Society of America (ASA) is devoted to improving the lives of all affected by autism through "work[ing] to increase public awareness about the day-to-day issues about people across the spectrum, advocate for appropriate services for individuals of every age, and provide the latest information regarding treatment, education, research, and advocacy" (ASA, 2016). Founded as a grass roots organization in 1965, ASA launched a nationwide awareness campaign for ASD in the 1970s and has become a leading source of information related to ASD. ASA has more than 120,000 members and more than 100 affiliates; membership dues vary depending on the type of membership. ASA publications include *Autism Advocate*, the *Living with Autism* and *Victims of Crime* series, and other resources. ASA also hosts an annual conference.

Children and Adults with Attention-Deficit/Hyperactivity Disorder   Children and Adults with Attention-Deficit/Hyperactivity Disorder (CHADD) "improves the lives of people affected by ADHD" (CHADD, 2017). Founded by parents in 1987, the organization has 12,000 members (of which 2,000 are professionals) and publishes *Attention Magazine* and *Attention Weekly*. CHADD also provides a database of 7,000 publications and serves as a clearinghouse on information for members. Dues vary according to the type of membership, with membership scholarships available. CHADD provides local face-to-face support groups, advocates for policies, offers webcasts and training, and conducts workshops for teachers and parents.

Council for Learning Disabilities   The Council for Learning Disabilities (CLD) is an "international organization composed of professionals who represent diverse disciplines" and "is committed to enhancing the education and quality of life for individuals with learning disabilities across the life span" (CLD, 2017). Members pay dues, with students paying a reduced rate, and CLD has a number of state chapters. The organization publishes *Learning Disability Quarterly, Intervention in School* *and Clinic*, and *LD Forum;* offers awards for research, service, and teaching; hosts an annual conference; and provides advocacy in the field.

Council for Exceptional Children   The mission of CEC is "to ensure, through excellence and advocacy, the educational success and quality of life for children and youth with exceptionalities and to enhance engagement of their families" (CEC, 2016). Founded in 1922 for educators, administrators, and advocates, CEC has 27,000 members, 18 special interest divisions, and state chapters. CEC membership dues vary according to the level of membership. Members of CEC receive *Teaching Exceptional Children, Exceptional Children,* and *TEC+* (online); membership in additional divisions requires additional dues and also provides access to additional journals. CEC and some of its divisions host national conferences, and members also may have access to state CEC and division conferences as well as webinars and workshops. CEC divisions of interest to special education teachers are described in the following subsections.

Council of Administrators of Special Education   The purpose of the Council of Administrators of Special Education (CASE) is to promote professional leadership and opportunities for advancement in the field of special education. For a fee, CASE members receive the *Journal of Special Education Leadership* and the *CASE Newsletter.*

Council for Children with Behavioral Disorders   The purpose of the Council for Children with Behavioral Disorders (CCBD) is to promote the education and welfare of children with behavioral and emotional disorders. For a fee, CCBD members receive *Behavioral Disorders, Beyond Behavior* magazine, and the *CCBD Newsletter.*

Division for Research   The purpose of the Division for Research (CEC-DR) is to advance research related to the education of individuals with disabilities and/or those who are gifted. For a fee, CEC-DR members receive the *Journal of Special Education* and the *CEC-DR Focus on Research* newsletter.

Division on Autism and Developmental Disabilities   The purpose of the Division on Autism and Developmental Disabilities (DADD) is to enhance the quality of life for people with ASD, ID, and other developmental disabilities. For a fee, DADD members receive *Education and Training in Autism and Developmental Disabilities, Focus on Autism and Other Developmental Disabilities,* and *DADD Express Newsletter.*

Division of Visual and Performing Arts Education   The purpose of the Division of Visual and Performing Arts Education (DARTS) is to focus on education in the arts (i.e., art, music, drama, dance) for students with disabilities. DARTS membership fees are comparatively low.

Division for Communicative Disabilities and Deafness   The purpose of the Division for Communicative Disabilities and Deafness (DCDD) is to improve education for students with communication disabilities or who are deaf or hard of hearing. For a fee, DCDD members receive *Communication Disorders Quarterly.*

Division on Career Development and Transition   The purpose of the Division on Career Development and Transition (DCDT) is to focus on career development and transition for students with disabilities and/or who are gifted. For a fee, DCDT members receive *Career Development for Exceptional Individuals* and the *DCDT Network* newsletter.

Division for Culturally and Linguistically Diverse Exceptional Learners   The purpose of the Division for Culturally and Linguistically Diverse Exceptional Learners (DDEL) is to advance educational opportunities for diverse students with disabilities and/or who are gifted and those who serve them. For a fee, DDEL members receive *Multiple Voices for Ethnically Diverse Exceptional Learners* and the *DDEL Newsletter.*

Division for Early Childhood   The purpose of the Division for Early Childhood (DEC) is to work on the behalf of young children with special needs and their families. For a fee, DEC members receive *Journal of Early Intervention* and *Young Exceptional Children* magazine.

Division of International Special Education and Services   The purpose of the Division of International Special Education and Services (DISES) is to focus on special education in countries outside of the United States. For a fee, DISES members receive the *Journal of International Special Needs Education* and the *DISES Newsletter.*

Division for Learning Disabilities   The purpose of the Division for Learning Disabilities (DLD) is to improve services for people with learning disabilities. For a fee, DLD members receive *Learning Disabilities Research and Practice* and *DLD Times Newsletter.*

Division for Physical, Health and Multiple Disabilities   The purpose of the Division for Physical, Health and Multiple Disabilities (DPHMD) is to advocate for a quality education for students with physical disabilities, multiple disabilities, and special health care needs. For a fee, DPHMD members receive *Physical Disabilities: Education and Related Services* and the *DPHMD Newsletter.*

Division on Visual Impairments and Deafblindness   The purpose of the Division on Visual Impairments and Deafblindness (DVIDB) is to advance the education of students with visual impairments and deafblindness. For a fee, DVIDB members receive *Visual Impairment and Deafblind Education Quarterly.*

The Association for the Gifted   The purpose of The Association for the Gifted (TAG) is to provide information about gifted and talented children and their needs. For a fee, TAG members receive the *Journal for the Education of the Gifted* and the *TAG Update* newsletter.

Technology and Media Division   The purpose of the Technology and Media Division (TAM) is to address the use of technology and media for individuals with disabilities and/or who are gifted. For a fee, TAM members receive the *Journal of Special Education Technology* and the *TAM Connector* newsletter.

Learning Disabilities Association of America   The mission of the Learning Disabilities Association of America (LDA) is to "create opportunities for success for all individuals affected by learning disabilities and to reduce the incidence of learning disabilities in future generations" (LDA, 2017). LDA began in 1963 as a resource for parents, was incorporated in 1964, and established its headquarters in 1973. LDA has chapters at the state and local level; draws more than 3,000 people to its annual conference; advocates for people with learning disabilities; publishes *Learning Disabilities: A Multidisciplinary Journal* and *LD Source*, and is a source for various guides, books, webinars, and workshops. Geared toward teachers, parents, adults with learning disabilities, and professionals, this organization charges membership dues that may vary depending on the state.

National Association for Down Syndrome The purpose of the National Association for Down Syndrome (NADS) is to support "all persons with Down syndrome in achieving their full potential" (NADS, 2016). Founded by parents in Chicago in 1961, NADS remains based in Chicago but offers a variety of resources nationally that include publications, videos, and the *NADS News*. Dues vary.

National Association of the Deaf The mission of the National Association of the Deaf (NAD) "is to preserve, protect and promote the civil, human and linguistic rights of deaf and hard of hearing people in the United States of America" (NAD, 2017). Established as an advocacy group in 1880, NAD has thousands of members across state affiliates, publishes e-news, and hosts national and state conferences. Dues vary; for a small additional fee, members can join a special interest group section (e.g., advocacy).

National Down Syndrome Society The mission of the National Down Syndrome Society (NDSS) "is to be the national advocate for the value, acceptance and inclusion of people with Down syndrome" (NDSS, 2017). NDSS began in 1979 and now has 385 local affiliates. NDSS acts as an advocate, partners in research, provides resources (e.g., videos, webinars), and hosts conferences. Its Buddy Walk to raise awareness of Down syndrome began in 1995 and has grown from 17 to 250 events nationwide. Although there are no national dues, NDSS takes donations and participates in fundraising.

Based on the descriptions you have read so far, what is the mission, purpose, or focus of most professional organizations in the field of special education and disability? What is the reason that most of these professional organizations came into being?

National Federation of the Blind The purpose of the National Federation of the Blind (NFB) is "the complete integration of the blind into society on a basis of equality" (NFB, 2017). Founded in 1940, the organization is open to the blind and the sighted. The NFB provides education, information, referrals, scholarships, aids, and equipment; publishes *NFB-Newsline online*, *Braille Monitor*, *Journal of Blindness Innovation and Research*, *Future Reflections*, and books and audio/video materials; and hosts state and national conferences. Each year, the NFB selects an educator of the year and a distinguished educator of blind students. The NFB has 50,000 members with local chapters and divisions, including one for educators. Dues are comparatively low for members at large, but individuals also can join local affiliates.

National Organization on Disability   The National Organization on Disability (NOD) "promotes the full participation and contributions of America's 57 million people with disabilities in all aspects of life" (NOD, 2017.) In addition, "NOD focuses on increasing employment opportunities for the 80-percent of working-age Americans with disabilities who are not employed (NOD)." Formed in 1982 by people from across 48 states, NOD conducts surveys and advocates for policies in regard to people with disabilities. There are no dues, and information on events and best practices is disseminated from the NOD web site.

TASH   TASH "advocates for human rights and inclusion for people with significant disabilities and support needs—those most vulnerable to segregation, abuse, neglect and institutionalization. TASH works to advance inclusive communities through advocacy, research, professional development, policy, and information and resources for parents, families and self-advocates" (TASH, 2017). Founded in the 1970s as the American Association for the Education of the Severely and Profoundly Handicapped or AAESPH, TASH is now known by its current acronym alone. TASH is noted for its history of affecting policies for people with significant disabilities and publishes *Research and Practice in Severe Disabilities*, *Connections*, and books. In addition, TASH hosts a national conference, regional themed conferences, and webinars and also presents annual awards. Current national agenda items include inclusive education, community living, employment, diversity and cultural competency, and human rights. TASH membership consists of families, advocates, and professionals; dues vary according to the type of membership, and those who pay national dues become members of state chapters.

The Arc   The Arc "promotes and protects the human rights of people with intellectual and developmental disabilities and actively supports their full inclusion and participation in the community throughout their lifetimes" (The Arc, 2017.) Started as a grassroots organization by parents in 1950, The Arc began as the National Association for Retarded Children and has had several name changes over time. The Arc now has 140,000 members and 700 chapters and provides several publications, toolkits, online resources, and fact sheets. Membership dues vary.

United Cerebral Palsy   United Cerebral Palsy (UCP) "continues to work closely with its affiliates on issues that open doors for people with disabilities. From home ownership to health care reform, inclusive education to competitive employment, UCP has established itself as a leader in the disability community and as a strong voice for individuals with disabilities and their families" (UCP, 2017). Formed in 1949 by parents, UCP is now one of the largest nonprofits and assists thousands of people, providing information and resource guides and publishing *Ability* magazine. UCP has affiliates and hosts an annual conference.

Table 8.2 provides the URLs for the web sites of each organization; you can use this list to learn more about specific organizations with which you might want to get involved. (Note that URLs are current at the time of this book's publication but subject to change in future; if necessary, type an organization's name into a search engine to find the current URL for its web site.)

←——————————————————————————————————————→

Table 8.2. Web sites of disability-related professional organizations

Name of organization	Web site URL
AAPD: American Association of People with Disabilities	http://www.aapd.com
AAIDD: American Association on Intellectual and Developmental Disabilities	http://aaidd.org/
ACRES: American Council on Rural Special Education	https://acres-sped.org/
ACB: American Council of the Blind	http://www.acb.org/
ABAI: Association for Behavior Analysis International	https://www.abainternational.org/welcome.aspx
ASA: Autism Society of America	http://www.autism-society.org/
CHADD: Children and Adults with Attention-Deficit/Hyperactivity Disorder	http://www.chadd.org/
CLD: Council for Learning Disabilities	https://www.council-for-learning-disabilities.org/
CEC: Council for Exceptional Children	http://www.cec.sped.org/
CASE: *Council of Administrators of Special Education*	http://www.casecec.org/
CCBD: *Council for Children with Behavioral Disorders*	http://www.ccbd.net/home
CEC-DR: *Division for Research*	http://www.cecdr.org/home
DADD: *Division on Autism and Developmental Disabilities*	http://www.daddcec.org/
DARTS: *Division of Visual and Performing Arts Education*	http://community.cec.sped.org/darts/home
DCDD: *Division for Communicative Disabilities and Deafness*	http://community.cec.sped.org/dcdd/home
DCDT: *Division on Career Development and Transition*	http://community.cec.sped.org/dcdt/home

DDEL:
   *Division for Culturally and Linguistically Diverse
      Exceptional Learners*
	http://community.cec.sped.org/ddel/home

DEC: *Division for Early Childhood*	http://www.dec-sped.org/
DISES: *Division of International Special Education and Services*	http://www.dises-cec.org
DLD: *Division for Learning Disabilities*	http://teachingld.org/

DPHMD:
   *Division for Physical, Health and Multiple
      Disabilities*
	http://community.cec.sped.org/dphmd/home

DVIDB: *Division on Visual Impairments and Deafblindness*	http://community.cec.sped.org/dvi/home
TAG: *The Association for the Gifted*	http://cectag.com
TAM: *Technology and Media Division*	http://www.tamcec.org/

(continued)

←——→

Table 8.2.   *(continued)*

Name of organization	Web site URL
LDA: Learning Disabilities Association of America	http://ldaamerica.org/
NADS: National Association for Down Syndrome	http://www.nads.org/
NAD: National Association of the Deaf	http://nad.org/
NDSS: National Down Syndrome Society	http://www.ndss.org/
NFB: National Federation of the Blind	https://nfb.org/
NOD: National Organization on Disability	https://www.nod.org/
TASH	http://tash.org/
The Arc	http://www.thearc.org/
UCP: United Cerebral Palsy	http://ucp.org/

Voice of a Leader

Advocating Through Disability-Related Organizations

Regardless of which professional organization(s) you might choose to join, doing so provides you with opportunities to advocate for people with disabilities—locally, in your state or region, and nationally. In the following interview, Samantha Matthews Orihuela describes how advocacy is interwoven with her involvement in disability-related professional organizations.

Q: How have you advocated for people with disabilities as part of a professional organization?

A: I have handed out information to OB/GYN [obstetrician/gynecologist] offices that abortion is not the only option if you know your child will have a disability, and gone to ARC (admission and release committee) meetings for friends and family members to ensure that they are getting the highest level of education and related services they are entitled to. I have worked with local businesses to raise awareness of children with disabilities by having them sponsor activities, such as Lunch and Learns, as well as CBI (community-based instruction) and Buddy Walk dinner nights. I have arranged for individuals to be in social settings (bowling, restaurants, etc.) with typical peers and adults.

DISSEMINATING INFORMATION THROUGH A PROFESSIONAL ORGANIZATION

The previous chapters of this book presented seven different pathways you can take to become a leader in special education. If you choose to follow any of these paths, joining a professional organization that addresses disability-related concerns can be a way to strengthen your impact. For example, Chapter 4 focused on how you can share information with others through conducting professional development and consultations; professional organizations provide an excellent outlet for reaching a large audience. Chapter 7 focused on advocacy and provided guidelines for affecting policy through communication with legislators, including working with professional advocacy organizations (e.g., Collins et al., 2005; Ford et al., 2013). Both of these examples of leadership involve sharing information with an audience and reaching a broader audience as a result of being affiliated with a professional organization.

This section provides guidelines for disseminating information to others in the profession by making presentations through professional organizations and contributing articles to professional publications. Although this topic was briefly introduced in Chapter 1, the following guidelines provide more detail.

Presenting at a Professional Conference

Presenting at a professional conference may seem intimidating. Remember, however, that the audience members have gathered because they are interested in the topic and because they value what a speaker has to share about it. Although attendance at professional development sessions may be required, attendance at a professional conference is likely to be voluntary. People come to a conference because they want to learn.

They can learn from you. You have expertise in your field, and presenting complex information to an audience is something you already do as a matter of course with students, families, IEP teams, and so forth. If you have never presented at a professional conference before or feel nervous about doing so, you can start with a smaller, local group and gradually build up to larger audiences.

As a special education teacher, you may have a lot to share based on your daily experiences. Groups whose membership includes parents may want to learn strategies from a special education teacher so they can better work with their children with disabilities in the home environment. If you are an experienced special education teacher, other teachers may want to know what you have found to work or not work with children with specific types of disabilities or when teaching specific types of content. Community professionals and volunteers may want to know how they can partner with schools to provide better services.

The best place to do a presentation for the first time is through a local forum. To give an effective presentation, the first key is to acknowledge that you have the experience and knowledge to be the expert on a specific topic. The second key, as noted in Chapter 1, is to have data to support whatever ideas you present—for example, evidence that a specific practice did or did not work.

After delivering a presentation to a local organization, you can analyze what went well and what did not. Even the most seasoned speaker can learn from the experience. You may then look for opportunities to present at a state conference (e.g., your state's CEC chapter), a regional conference (e.g., a regional TASH conference), or even a national conference that welcomes special education teachers.

There are several ways to make moving to a larger arena a less intimidating experience. First determine if you want to present alone or with a group of colleagues. For example, several special education teachers may decide to do a group presentation on a specific topic where each has a set time limit in which to address the topic or provide a part of the presentation sequence (e.g., introduction, issues, research results, discussion). You also may have relationships with faculty members from special education programs at IHEs who are willing to co-present on an issue of concern, a topic from a graduate course, or the results of collaborative research.

Once you have decided upon an individual or group presentation, you can determine the best format. Poster and roundtable discussion formats are a simple way of sharing information on a topic without preparing a formal presentation to take place in front of an audience. Panel presentations allow you to share experiences and opinions on a topic without preparing visual materials. The most formal presentation will be one in which you stand and present on the topic with prepared audio and/or visual materials for a specified amount of time and then take questions from the audience. In this case, the audience will be limited to those with a special interest in the topic and not to all who are attending the conference, which means attendance may be as few as one person or as many as 50.

How to Prepare a Proposal for a Professional Conference

The first step in preparing a proposal for a professional conference is to read the Call for Proposals put out by the professional organization, usually available on its web site. The Call for Proposals should list the conference theme, specific strands presenters may address (e.g., research, technology, diversity), the types of presentation formats presenters may use, and the length allotted for each.

Whether the proposal is to be submitted in hard copy or online, type it first as a document on your computer. In most cases, the organization will specify a desired word count and the parts or sections your proposal should include. Typically, you will need to provide the following details:

- Basic information (names of presenters, contact information)
- A title that will entice participants to come to the presentation at the conference—it should be short, descriptive, and interesting
- A very concise description of the presentation, to be printed in the conference program
- An in-depth description of the presentation (e.g., a few paragraphs) that explains the rationale for it, tells how it will relate to the conference theme, describes exactly what will be presented, and lists its objectives and expected outcomes
- Your choice of presentation format (e.g., single presenter, multiple presenters, panel, roundtable discussion, poster)
- Any special equipment that may be needed

Once your proposal is submitted, it will go out to peers for a review; a notice of acceptance or rejection will follow this. In some cases, you may be asked to change from one presentation format to another based on space and scheduling.

How to Prepare for a Conference Presentation

Once a presentation proposal for a professional conference is accepted, you will have a specified amount of time to prepare your materials and practice your presentation delivery. Needed materials may include a PowerPoint presentation, a handout, hands-on activity materials, modeling materials, or a poster. When preparing your presentation and the corresponding materials, it is important to bear in mind that people with disabilities are likely to attend presentations. Thus, you will need to apply the principles of **universal design** to create content that is accessible to everyone regardless of ability. For example, posters or slides should use large, clear lettering that contrasts with a simple background.

Once the materials are prepared, do a practice session to time the length of the presentation, whether you are presenting alone or with others. It is important to allow time for audience participation through questions and discussion. Be sure to provide contact information in case participants have additional questions or want to continue dialogue once the presentation is over. Finally, it is important to stick to your allotted time and be prepared to leave when it is up, so as to allow the next presenter sufficient time to set up.

The most important point to remember is that you should be the expert on a topic and have something of interest to share. Although presenting in front of an audience for the first time can be intimidating, it becomes easier over time.

Voice of a Leader

Find Opportunities to Lead in Disability-Related Organizations

Many different organizations serve the needs of people with disabilities, and each offers different types of opportunities for leadership. Samantha Matthews Orihuela offers these tips for thinking about how to get involved.

Q: What recommendations do you have for a special education teacher who wants to become active in a professional organization for people with disabilities?

A: Select an organization that represents the disability you feel is your "calling." I feel this has been the biggest influence on my life and career. Working with individuals with Down syndrome has impacted me in a way that I could never fully express; it is truly a blessing to be a part of so many amazing individuals' lives. Research the organization to make sure it does what it claims, and be willing to assist in any capacity. Become a board member when an opening is available. It gives you the opportunity to impact decision making and be aware of the group mission and upcoming events and needs.

Contributing Articles to Professional Publications

Another way to disseminate information to a larger audience is to contribute articles to professional publications, such as journals, in your field. The first rule in writing for publication is to be familiar with the various professional outlets offered by professional organizations. Some publish academic research studies in peer-reviewed journals, some publish practitioner pieces in peer-reviewed journals, and some publish newsletters with items left to the discretion of the editor. Most professional organizations publish guidelines for submission on their web sites and within their publications and list the types of articles that they accept (e.g., research studies, literature reviews, position papers, program models, articles about promising practices, professional book reviews). They also state guidelines for the length of

What is the connection between EBPs and the work that professional organizations in the field of special education and disability do? How do these organizations help to promote the use of EBPs?

submitted manuscripts and the submission format. Most submissions (but not all) now involve an online process.

If you want to contribute to a professional publication, the beginning point is to have a good idea. As examples, a sample issue of *Teaching Exceptional Children* contained articles that focused on how special education teachers can manage stress (Ansley, Houchins, & Varjas, 2016), how to help parents address challenging behaviors in the home (Chai & Lieberman-Betz, 2016), how special education teachers can address literacy instruction (Claravall, 2016), how to teach students with significant disabilities to use switches (Schaefer & Andzik, 2016), and how to manage the effects of hearing loss when teaching literacy (Werfel & Hendricks, 2016). After coming up with your idea, you can search for outlets that publish that sort of piece. (See the previous section for the publications that various professional organizations publish.) If you are writing for a journal for the first time, consider asking for guidance from an experienced coauthor who is familiar with the formatting and submission process.

How to Prepare a Manuscript for Submission   Once you have determined the idea you want to write about and have selected an outlet for publication, the writing process begins. The exact manuscript format will vary depending on the type of article you are writing and the specific guidelines of the publication. However, your manuscript will likely need to include the following components:

- A cover page that lists the article title (again, something descriptive that will catch a reader's eye) as well as the authors and their affiliations (if multiple authors are listed, the order of authorship should reflect the nature of their contributions, with the person who does most of the writing and conceptualization listed first; include an author note indicating who will be the contact person regarding the manuscript—yourself or a coauthor)

- The abstract, a paragraph that briefly tells the reader what the article is about and lists a few key words that describe the content

- An introduction that ends by stating the article's purpose

- The main body of the manuscript (e.g., research methods and results, points to be made on a topic, description of a practice)

- A discussion with concluding comments

The best way to prepare a manuscript in the appropriate format is to find an article that is similar in structure to the one that is being written and analyze its content and the amount of space devoted to each section.

In 2013, Ludlow and Dieker wrote a set of easy-to-follow guidelines for writers wishing to publish in *Teaching Exceptional Children*, a practitioner journal published by CEC. However, the steps they recommend are broadly applicable to other professional publications in special education as well. These steps include 1) identifying a practice that should be shared; 2) reviewing the journal guidelines for writing and submission; 3) reading recently published issues for format, style, and content; 4) finding an exemplar article to use as a model; 5) preparing an outline; 6) writing a first draft; 7) adding examples of the practice; 8) adding figures and tables as resources; 9) writing a final draft; and 10) proofreading for grammar, spelling, and format.

Most journals in the field of special education require formatting in accordance with the American Psychological Association (APA). Guidelines are provided in the *Publication Manual of the American Psychological Association* (APA, 2010), which can be purchased in bookstores or through the APA web site; basic APA guidelines may also be included in the free writing resources many colleges and university writing programs provide online. For the beginning professional writer, it may be easiest to first write without worrying about format and then work with someone experienced in APA format, such as an English teacher or university faculty member, to reformat the manuscript.

When the article is complete, it is ready for submission. You (or whoever has been selected as the corresponding author) will need to prepare a submission letter to accompany the manuscript stating that it is the original work of the author(s), is not currently under review by another journal, and has not been published elsewhere.

What to Expect in the Review Process

Once a manuscript is submitted for publication, it usually goes through a review process that may take several weeks to several months. The editor will select several reviewers from a list of professionals with expertise in the topic and then send the manuscript to them. In most cases, they will conduct a **blind review,** meaning they will not see the cover sheet with your identifying information. Each reviewer builds a written case for a publication decision, which may be to 1) accept the manuscript for publication, 2) accept it with revisions, 3) ask the authors to revise and resubmit the manuscript, or 4) reject it as not appropriate for the journal.

List the ways in which a professional organization in special education can maximize the impact you might have on your profession. As you near the end of this chapter, do you have any definite ideas about which organizations you might like to get involved with and how?

Once all of the reviews are obtained, the editor of the publication will contact you or your designated coauthor and will share the publication decision and the reviews. If your article has been accepted, celebrate! If you have been asked to revise and resubmit, accept that some more work is needed. Do not be discouraged if your manuscript has been rejected, because there are a number of possible reasons. These include an insufficient rationale for the manuscript, insufficient detail for others to implement the practice, a topic not suited to the journal's readership, an article that does not contribute to what is already known, or the article's having been published elsewhere (Ludlow & Dieker, 2013). You may choose to make further revisions and then submit to another outlet.

BE A LEADER: CONNECT WITH
DISABILITY-RELATED PROFESSIONAL ORGANIZATIONS

This book has presented many different paths to leadership. Regardless of which path or paths you choose to pursue, you can have a greater impact on the special education community by getting involved with professional organizations that serve the needs of people with disabilities. Chapter 8 provided an overview of various national organizations in this field, including their mission, ongoing work, and publications; more in-depth information about these topics as well as membership, fees, conferences, special projects, and so forth is available through each organization's web site. Keep in mind that in addition to the professional organizations discussed in this chapter, many more exist at the local, state, and regional levels to address educational and disability-related issues.

Your involvement with a professional organization can take many forms: becoming a member, participating in sponsored events, networking with other members, attending or presenting at conferences, or contributing to its publications. The following guidelines are offered to help you expand your leadership skills by actively participating in disability-related organizations:

1. Narrow your focus. Have a good idea of the area of special education in which you are most interested as you investigate professional organization membership.

2. Explore the web site of a professional organization in depth before you become a member. This will help you to determine whether it will meet your needs as a source of information, ideas for engaging in advocacy, networking and discussion groups, and local conferences or professional development opportunities. It will also help you to determine whether the organization's beliefs and practices are in agreement with your personal philosophy.

3. Research the organization's decision makers. Search the web site for a list of the board of directors and their credentials; if local chapters do not have this available, contact the national offices for this information.

4. Review associated publications. Search online or visit the library of an IHE to peruse copies of the publications produced by professional organizations. This will help you to determine the value of the content for your own professional growth; if you are considering submitting a manuscript, it also gives you a chance to analyze the types of articles published.

5. Review topics discussed at this organization's conferences. Many professional organizations' web sites allow you to download programs from conferences held in previous years. Doing so can help you to determine whether future conferences would be of value for you to attend or an appropriate outlet for you to make a presentation. Note that most organizations vary the site of the conferences that they host from year to year.

6. Look for local opportunities, too. Contact organizations at the local level to determine if there are ways you can volunteer (e.g., information fair, fundraising, advocacy efforts, family support groups).

FOLLOW-UP ACTIVITIES

Many different professional organizations exist to serve the interests and needs of people with disabilities and educators who work with people with disabilities. This chapter provides information about high-profile national organizations with a large membership; you may know of or participate in smaller, lesser-known organizations as well.

As a busy special education teacher with many responsibilities, you will likely not have the time and energy to get involved with every organization related to your professional interests. Thus, the following activities are designed to help you explore your interests and reflect on what you hope to achieve so that you can narrow your focus and determine the best place to direct your efforts.

1. **Think about the organizations in which you have participated in the past.** What prompted you to join? How was the experience valuable to you as a person or as a professional? Make a list of activities that you would want a professional organization to offer if you were to join.

2. **Review the list of disability-related organizations in this chapter.** What do they have in common? How do they differ?

3. **Contact someone who is involved in a disability-related professional organization.** If this is someone you know locally, find out why the person became involved. What activities does the organization offer that interest you? Would these activities also be of interest to your colleagues or to the families of your students? If your contact is involved with professional organizations at the state or national level, how did the person become involved? Does the person value the resources that are available? Does the person take advantage of webinars or conferences? Does the person actively participate in any way? If you do not know anyone locally who is involved in a professional organization, contact someone who is listed on the organization's web site and ask whether there are local chapters or affiliates with someone you can contact.

4. **Scan several issues of a professional journal geared toward practitioners.** Can you find information on the authors (e.g., teachers, university faculty, project directors)? Do the authors cite professional references to support the content of the articles? Can you locate author guidelines? Who is on the editorial board?

5. **Use the Internet to research conferences that will be held in your state in the coming year.** If you identify one or more conferences of interest to you, look for answers to these questions: Where will the event be held? How long will it last? Will there be presentations of interest to teachers? Are presentations by teachers welcomed or encouraged? What does it cost to attend? Is it possible to earn professional development credits for attending? Who will be the keynote speaker and what is the topic of the keynote address? What are the conference strands (e.g., inclusion, diversity, assessment)? Will vendors be available to demonstrate products? Check whether there are any funds available from your school district to support teachers who want to attend or present at a professional conference.

Afterword

This text has been meant to inspire you as a teacher to engage in leadership activities. No one else has had the unique experiences that you have, and your contribution to the leadership of your school and profession is valuable.

My own personal journey is an example of how leadership can develop over time. When I graduated from my university program in special education, I felt well prepared to take a job as a teacher in a small rural community. At that point, I was one of two teachers certified in low-incidence disabilities in a large school district, something that is not uncommon in rural America today. What surprised me was the number of people who turned to me for advice, including teachers, parents, and members of the community. I was only 24 years old and had just left my student teaching experience, but already I was being consulted as if I were an expert who knew everything there was to know about special education. Now that I have been in my profession for more than 40 years and have worked with countless special education teachers, I do not think my experience is uncommon. Special education teachers are often thrust into leadership as experts even before they have accumulated a large body of experiences.

In writing each chapter of this book, I reflected on how my own leadership skills developed. I still can remember how nervous I was when I conducted my first IEP meeting, when I gave my first professional presentation at a state conference, when I responded to a request to serve on a community board for people with disabilities, when I volunteered to serve on a committee in a professional organization, when I conducted my first classroom research study, when I offered advice to a parent and a teacher in the role of a consultant, and when I first met with legislators to discuss special education needs. I do not think I felt competent in any of these roles in the beginning, but in each instance, I was willing to take a tiny step forward because I realized my education and my experiences had equipped me with the ability to provide leadership in my profession. As I have tried to convey in this book, taking the first step requires initiative, but one step can lead to another until your competence as a leader develops. No one becomes a leader overnight, but reflection on what worked well and what did not can provide the impetus for developing strong leadership skills.

At this point in my career, I have been blessed to mentor many special education teachers and nurture their leadership skills. Of the eight special education teacher leaders featured in this book, six were my undergraduate and then graduate students.

I watched them grow from students who wanted to become teachers to competent leaders who see sharing their expertise as both an obligation and an opportunity to influence others in their profession and beyond. In addition, nine of these special teachers have conducted research with the students in their classrooms, adding to their ability to influence practices in their profession. I have watched them grow from turning to me for advice to using their own analytical skills to solve problems and lead others. These teachers are just like you. They are accumulating a wealth of experiences that can be shared with others to make a difference in the lives of students with disabilities. If they can become leaders, you can, too.

References

Abell, M., Collins, B. C., Kleinert, H., & Pennington, R. (2014). Providing support for rural teachers of students with low incidence disabilities who are completing the Kentucky teacher internship program. *Rural Special Education Quarterly, 33*(3), 14–18.

Able, H., Sreckovic, M. A., Schultz, T. R., Garwood, J. D., & Sherman, J. (2015). Views from the trenches: Teacher and student supports needed for full inclusion of students with ASD. *Teacher Education and Special Education, 38*(1), 44–57.

Agran, M., & Hughes, C. (2013). "You can't vote—you're mentally incompetent": Denying democracy to people with severe disabilities. *Research and Practice in Severe Disabilities, 38*(1), 58–62.

Agran, M., & Krupp, M. (2010). A preliminary investigation of parents' opinions about safety skills instruction: An apparent discrepancy between importance and expectation. *Education and Training in Autism and Developmental Disabilities, 45*(2), 303–311.

Alnahdi, G. (2013). Transition services for students with mild intellectual disability in Saudi Arabia. *Education and Training in Autism and Developmental Disabilities, 48*(4), 531–544.

American Association of People with Disabilities. (2017). *Our focus.* Retrieved from http://www.aapd.com/our-focus/

American Association on Intellectual and Developmental Disabilities. (2017). *Mission.* Retrieved from https://aaidd.org/about-aaidd/mission#.WaB3yVHlrcc

American Council of the Blind. (2013). *About the American Council of the Blind.* Retrieved from http://acb.org/about

American Council on Rural Special Education. (2017). *About us.* Retrieved from http://www.acres-sped.org/about

American Psychological Association. (2010). *Publication manual of the American Psychological Association* (6th ed.). Washington, DC: Author.

Americans with Disabilities Act (ADA) of 1990, PL 101-336, 42 U.S.C. §§ 12101 *et seq.*

Anderson, K. A., McDonald, T. A., Edsall, D., Smith, L. E., & Taylor, J. L. (2014). Postsecondary expectations of high-school students with autism spectrum disorders. *Focus on Autism and Other Developmental Disabilities, 31*(1), 16–26.

Angell, M. E., Stoner, J. B., & Fulk, B. M. (2010). Advice from adults with physical disabilities on fostering self-determination during the school years. *Teaching Exceptional Children, 42*(3), 64–75.

Ansley, B. M., Houchins, D., & Varjas, K. (2016). Optimizing special educator wellness and job performance through stress management. *Teaching Exceptional Children, 48*(4), 176–185.

Association for Behavior Analysis International. (2017). *About.* Retrieved from https://www.abainternational.org/about-us.aspx

Autism Society of America. (2016). *Improving the lives of all affected by autism.* Retrieved from https://www.autism-society.org/

Bader, S. H., Barry, T. D., & Hann, J. A. H. (2015). The relation between parental expressed emotion and externalizing behaviors in children and adolescents with an autism spectrum disorder. *Focus on Autism and Other Developmental Disabilities, 30*(1), 23–34.

Banda, D. R. (2015). Review of sibling interventions with children with autism. *Education and Training in Autism and Developmental Disabilities, 50*(3), 303–315.

Bannerman, D. J., Sheldon, J. B., Sherman, J. A., & Harchik, A. E. (1990). Balancing the right to habilitation with the right to personal liberties: The rights of people with developmental disabilities to eat too many doughnuts and take a nap. *Journal of Applied Behavior Analysis, 23,* 79–89.

Barnhill, G. P. (2014). Supporting students with Asperger syndrome on college campuses: Current practices. *Focus on Autism and Other Developmental Disabilities, 31*(1), 3–15.

Bartholomew, A., Papay, C., McConnell, A., & Cease-Cook, J. (2015). Embedding secondary transition in the Common Core State Standards. *Exceptional Children, 47*(6), 329–335.

Bartholomew, A., Test, D. W., Cooke, N. L., & Cease-Cook, J. (2015). Effects of teaching self-determination skills using the common core state standards. *Education and Training in Autism and Developmental Disabilities, 50*(4), 433–445.

Barton, E. E., Chen, C., Pribble, L., Pomes, M., & Kim, Y. (2013). Coaching preservice teachers to teach play skills to children with disabilities. *Teacher Education and Special Education, 36*(4), 330–349.

Barton, E. E., & Wolery, M. (2010). Training teachers to promote pretend play in young children with disabilities. *Exceptional Children, 77*(1), 85–106.

Bell, E. C. (2012). Mentoring transition-age youth with blindness. *Journal of Special Education, 46*(3), 170–179.

Bellini, S., Henry, D., & Pratt, C. (2011). From intuition to data: Using logic models to measure professional development outcomes for educators working with students on the autism spectrum. *Teacher Education and Special Education, 34*(1), 37–51.

Benedict, A. E., Brownell, M. T., Park, Y., Bettini, E. A., & Lauterback, A. A. (2014). Taking charge of your professional learning: Tips for cultivating special educator expertise. *Teaching Exceptional Children, 46*(6), 147–157.

Berry, A. B., Petrin, R. A., Gravelle, M. L., & Farmer, T. W. (2012). Issues in special education teacher recruitment, retention, and professional development: Considerations in supporting rural teachers. *Rural Special Education Quarterly, 39*(4), 3–11.

Bethune, K. S., & Wood, C. L. (2013). Effects of coaching on teachers' use of function-based interventions for students with severe disabilities. *Teacher Education and Special Education, 36*(2), 97–114.

Bezdek, J., Summers, J. A., & Turnbull, A. (2010). Professionals' attitudes on partnering with families of children and youth with disabilities. *Education and Training in Autism and Developmental Disabilities, 45*(3), 356–365.

Billingsley, B., Israel, M., & Smith, S. (2011). Supporting new special education teachers: How online resources and Web 2.0 technologies can help. *Teaching Exceptional Children, 43*(5), 20–29.

Billingsley F., White, O. R., & Munson, R. (1980). Procedural reliability: A rationale and example. *Behavioral Assessment, 2,* 229–241.

Bond, N., & Pope, S. (2013). Advocacy throughout the year: Taking a stand for the teaching profession. *Kappa Delta Pi Record, 49*(2), 64–69.

Bottge, B. A., Toland, M. D., Gassaway, L., Butler, M., Choo, S., Griffen, A. K., & Ma, X. (2015). Impact of enhanced anchored instruction in inclusive math classrooms. *Exceptional Children, 81*(2), 158–175.

Bouck, E. C., & Joshi, G. (2012). Functional curriculum and students with mild intellectual disability: Exploring post school outcomes through the LSTS2. *Education and Training in Autism and Developmental Disabilities, 47*(2), 139–153.

Bremer, C. D., Kachgal, M., & Schoeller, K. (2003). Self-determination: Supporting successful transition. *NCSET Research to Practice Brief 2*(1). Retrieved from www.ncset.org/publications/viewdesc .asp?id=962

Britton, N. S., Collins, B. C., Ault, M. J., & Bausch, M. E. (2015). Using a constant time delay procedure to teach support personnel to use a simultaneous prompting procedure. *Focus on Autism and Other Developmental Disabilities,* 1–12. doi:10.1177/1088357615587505

Brock, M. E., & Carter, E. W. (2015). Effects of a professional development package to prepare special education paraprofessionals to implement evidence-based practice. *Journal of Special Education, 49*(1), 38–51.

Brock, M. E., Huber, H. B., Carter, E.W., Juarez, A. P., & Warren, Z. E. (2014). Statewide assessment of professional development needs related to educating students with autism spectrum disorders. *Focus on Autism and Other Developmental Disabilities, 29*(2), 67–79.

Brock, M. E., & Schaefer, J. M. (2015). Location matters: Geographic location and education placement of students with developmental disabilities. *Research and Practice for Persons with Severe Disabilities, 40*(2), 154–164.

Brolan, C. E., Boyle, F. M., Dean, J. H., Gomez, M. T., Ware, R. S., & Lennox, N G. (2012). Health advocacy: A vital step in attaining human rights for adults with intellectual disability. *Journal of Intellectual Disability Research, 56*(11), 1087–1097.

Browder, D. M., Jimenez, B. A., Mims, P. J., Knight, V. F., Spooner, F., Lee, A., & Flowers, C. (2012). The effects of a "tell-show-try-apply" professional development package on teachers of students with severe developmental disabilities. *Teacher Education and Special Education, 35*, 212–227.

Browder, D. M., Spooner, F., & Jimenez, B. (2011). Standards-based individualized education plans and progress monitoring. In D. M. Browder & F. Spooner (Eds.). *Teaching students with moderate and severe disabilities.* New York, NY: Guilford.

Brown, F., & Snell, M. E. (2011). Measuring student behavior and learning. In M. E. Snell & F. Brown (Eds.). *Instruction of students with severe disabilities* (7th ed.). Boston, MA: Pearson.

Brown, G., & Traniello, D. A. (2010). The path to aversive interventions: Four mothers' perceptions. *Research and Practice for Persons with Severe Disabilities, 35*(3–4), 128–136.

Brown, P., Stephenson, J., & Carter, M. (2014). Multicomponent training of teachers of students with severe disabilities. *Teacher Education and Special Education, 37*(4), 347–362.

Bryan, C., & Sims, S. (2011). Advocacy in action: K–12 and university partnerships: Bridging the advocacy gap. *Strategies: A Journal for Physical and Sport Educators, 25*(1), 36–37.

Byrd, E. S. (2011). Educating and involving parents in the response to intervention process: The school's important role. *Teaching Exceptional Children, 43*(3), 32–39.

Capizzi, A. M., Wehby, J. H., & Sandmel, K. N. (2010). Enhancing mentoring of teacher candidates through consultative feedback and self-evaluation of instructional delivery. *Teacher Education and Special Education, 33*(3), 191–212.

Carter, E. W., Boehm, T. L., Biggs, E. E., Annandale, N. H., Taylor, C. E., Loock, A. K., & Liu, R. Y. (2015). Known for my strengths: Positive traits of transition-age youth with intellectual disability and/or autism. *Research and Practice in Severe Disabilities, 40*(2), 101–119.

Carter, E. W., Brock, M. E., & Trainor, A. A. (2014). Transition assessment and planning for youth with severe intellectual and developmental disabilities. *Journal of Special Education, 47*(4), 245–255.

Carter, E. W., Lane, K. L., Jenkins, A. B., Magill, L., Germer, K., & Greiner, S. M. (2011). Administrator views on providing self-determination instruction in elementary and secondary schools. *Journal of Special Education, 49*(1), 52–64.

Carter, E. W., Moss, C. K., Asmus, J., Fesperman, E., Cooney, M., Brock, M. E.,…Vincent, L. B. (2015). Promoting inclusion, social connections, and learning through peer support arrangements. *Teaching Exceptional Children, 48*(1), 9–18.

Carter, E. W., Swedeen, B., Cooney, M., Walter, M., & Moss, C. K. (2012). "I don't have to do this by myself?" Parent-led community conversations to promote inclusion. *Research and Practice for Persons with Severe Disabilities, 37*(1), 9–23.

Carter, E. W., Swedeen, B., & Moss, C. K. (2012). Engaging youth with and without significant disabilities in inclusive service learning. *Teaching Exceptional Children, 44*(5), 46–54.

Carter, E. W., Trainor, A. A., Citchman, N., Swedeen, B., & Owens, L. (2011). Community-based summer work experiences of adolescents with high-incidence disabilities. *Journal of Special Education, 45*(2), 89–103.

Cease-Cook, J., Fowler, C., & Test, D. W. (2015). Strategies for creating work-based learning experiences in schools for secondary students with disabilities. *Exceptional Children, 47*(6), 352–358.

Chai, A., & Lieberman-Betz, R. (2016). Strategies for helping parents of young children address challenging behaviors in the home. *Teaching Exceptional Children, 48*(4), 186–194.

Cheatham, G. A., Hart, J. E., Malian, I., & McDonald, J. (2012). Six things to never say or hear during an IEP meeting: Educators as advocates for families. *Teaching Exceptional Children, 44*(3), 50–57.

Chen, P.-Y., & Schwartz, I. S. (2012). Bullying and victimization experiences of student with autism spectrum disorders in elementary schools. *Focus on Autism and Other Developmental Disabilities, 27*(4), 200–212.

Childre, A. L. (2014). Preparing special educators highly qualified in content: Alternative route certification for unlicensed teachers in rural Georgia. *Rural Special Education Quarterly, 33*(1), 23–32.

Childre, A. L., & Van Rie, G. L. (2015). Mentor teacher training: A hybrid model to promote partnering in candidate development. *Rural Special Education Quarterly, 34*(1), 10–16.

Children and Adults with Attention-Deficit/Hyperactivity Disorder. (2017). *Mission and history: Mission statement.* Retrieved from http://www.chadd.org/About-CHADD/Mission-and-History.aspx

Cimera, R. E., Burgess, S., & Bedesem, P. L. (2014). Does providing transition services by age 14 produce better vocational outcomes for students with intellectual disability? *Research and Practice in Severe Disabilities, 39*(1), 47–54.

Claravall, E. R. (2016). Integrating morphological knowledge in literacy instruction: Framework and principles to guide special education teachers. *Teaching Exceptional Children, 48*(4), 195–203.

Collet-Klingenberg, L. L., & Kolb, S. M. (2011). Secondary and transition programming for 18–21 year old students in rural Wisconsin. *Rural Special Education Quarterly, 30*(2), 19–27.

Collier-Meek, M. A., Fallon, L. M., Sanetti, L. M. H., & Maggin, D. M. (2013). Focus on implementation: Strategies for problem-solving teams to assess and promote treatment fidelity. *Teaching Exceptional Children, 45*, 52–59.

Collins, B. C. (2012). *Systematic instruction for students with moderate and severe disabilities.* Baltimore, MD: Paul H. Brookes Publishing Co.

Collins, B. C., Ault, M. J., & Leahy, M. (2016). *The effectiveness of a graduate course in preparing special education teachers as leaders.* Unpublished manuscript.

Collins, B. C., Branson, T. A., Hall, M., & Rankin, S. W. (2001). Teaching secondary students with moderate disabilities in an inclusive academic classroom setting. *Journal of Developmental and Physical Disabilities, 13*, 41–59.

Collins, B. C., Evans, A., Galloway, C. G., Karl, A., & Miller, A. (2007). A comparison of the acquisition and maintenance of teaching functional and core content in special and general education settings. *Focus on Autism and Other Developmental Disabilities, 22*, 220–233.

Collins, B. C., & Griffen, A. (1996). Teaching students with moderate disabilities to have safe responses to product warning labels. *Education and Treatment of Children, 19*, 30–45.

Collins, B. C., Hager, K. D., & Galloway, C. C. (2011). The addition of functional content during core content instruction with students with moderate disabilities. *Education and Training in Developmental Disabilities, 46*, 22–39.

Collins, B. C., Karl, J., Riggs, L., Galloway, C. C., & Hager, K. D. (2010). Teaching core content with real-life applications to secondary students with moderate and severe disabilities. *Teaching Exceptional Children, 43*(1), 52–59.

Collins, B. C., Ludlow, B. L., & Menlove, R. (2005). Tips for becoming a rural special education advocate. *Rural Special Education Quarterly, 24*(4), 32–35.

Conderman, G., & Hedin, L. (2012). Purposeful assessment practices for co-teachers. *Teaching Exceptional Children, 44*(4), 18–27.

Conderman, G., Johnston-Rodriguez, S., Harman, P., & Walker, D. (2012). Honoring voices from beginning special educators for making changes in teacher preparation. *Teacher Education and Special Education, 36*(1), 65–76.

Connor, D. J. (2012). Helping students with disabilities transition to college: 21 tips for students with LD and/or ADHD. *Teaching Exceptional Children, 45*(5), 16–25.

Conroy, P. W. (2012). Collaborating with cultural and linguistically diverse families of students in rural schools who receive special education services. *Rural Special Education Quarterly, 31*(3), 20–24.

Cook, B. G., & Cook, S. C. (2011). Unraveling evidence-based practices in special education. *Journal of Special Education, 47*(2), 71–82.

Cook, B. G., Shepherd, K. G., Cook, S. C., & Cook, L. (2012). Facilitating the effective implementation of evidence-based practices through teacher–parent collaboration. *Teaching Exceptional Children, 44*(3), 22–30.

Cook, C. R., Mayer, G. R., Wright, D. B., Kraemer, B., Wallace, M. D., Dart, E., Collins, T., & Resotri, A. (2012). Exploring the link among behavior intervention plans, treatment integrity, and student outcomes under natural educational conditions. *Journal of Special Education, 46*(1), 3–16.

Council for Exceptional Children. (2015). *What every special educator must know: Professional ethics and standards* (7th ed.). Reston, VA: Author.

Council for Exceptional Children. (2016). *About CEC.* Retrieved from http://www.celebrateexceptional.org/about-cec/

Council for Exceptional Children, Interdivisional Research Group (2014). Evidence-based special education in the context of scarce evidence-based practices. *Teaching Exceptional Children, 47*(2), 81–84.

Council for Learning Disabilities. (2017). *Mission statement.* Retrieved from https://www.council-for-learning-disabilities.org/

Courtade, G. R., Browder, D. M., Spooner, F., & DeBiase, W. (2010). Training teachers to use an inquiry-based task analysis to teach science to students with moderate and severe disabilities. *Education and Training in Autism and Developmental Disabilities, 45*(3), 378–399.

Courtade, G. R., Test, D. W., & Cook, B. G. (2015). Evidence-based practices for learners with severe intellectual disability. *Research and Practice for Persons with Severe Disabilities, 39*(4), 305–318.

Creech-Galloway, C., Collins, B. C., Knight, V., & Bausch, M. E. (2014). Using simultaneous prompting with an iPad to teach the Pythagorean theorem to adolescents with moderate and severe disabilities. *Research and Practice in Severe Disabilities, 38*, 222–232.

Currie-Rubin, R., & Smith, S. J. (2010). Understanding the roles of families in virtual learning. *Teaching Exceptional Children, 46*(5), 117–126.

Danielson, C. (1996). *Enhancing professional practice: A framework for teaching.* Alexandria, VA: ASCD.

De Boer, A. A., & Munde, V. S. (2015). Parental attitudes toward the inclusion of children with profound intellectual and multiple disabilities in general primary education in the Netherlands. *Journal of Special Education, 49*(3), 179–187.

deFur, S. (2012). Parents as collaborators: Building partnership with school- and community-based providers. *Teaching Exceptional Children, 44*(3), 58–67.

Diliberto, J. A., & Brewer, D. (2014). Six tips for successful IEP meetings. *Teaching Exceptional Children, 47*(2), 128–135.

Donnellan, A. M., & Miranda, P. L. (1984). Issues related to professional involvement with families of individuals with autism and other severe handicaps. *Journal of the Association for Persons with Severe Handicaps, 9,* 16–24.

Education for All Handicapped Children Act of 1975, PL 94-142, 20 U.S.C. §§ 1400 *et seq.*

Edwards, C. C., & Da Fonte, A. (2012). The 5-point plan: Fostering successful partnership with families of students with disabilities. *Teaching Exceptional Children, 44*(3), 6–13.

Erbas, D. (2010). A collaborative approach to implement positive behavior support plans for children with problem behaviors: A comparison of consultation versus consultation and feedback approach. *Education and Training in Autism and Developmental Disabilities, 45*(1), 94–106.

Espiner, D., & Guild, D. (2012). Capturing what matters most: Engaging students and their families in educational planning. *Teaching Exceptional Children, 44*(5), 56–67.

Falvey, M. A., Forest, M., Pearpoint, J., & Rosenberg, R. (1997). *All my life's a circle.* Toronto, Ontario, Canada: Inclusion.

Fenty, N. S., McDuffie-Landrum, K., & Fisher, G. (2013). Using collaboration, co-teaching, and question answer relationship to enhance content area literacy. *Teaching Exceptional Children, 44*(6), 28–37.

Flanagan, N. (2014). Send this to your legislator! *Kappan, 95*(7), 35–36.

Ford, M., Acosta, A., & Sutcliffe, T. J. (2013). Beyond terminology: The policy impact of a grassroots movement. *Intellectual and Developmental Disabilities, 51*(2), 108–112.

Francis, G., Gross, J. M. S., Turnbull, R., & Parent-Johnson, W. (2013). Evaluating the effectiveness of the family employment awareness training in Kansas: A pilot study. *Research and Practice in Severe Disabilities, 38*(1), 44–57.

Freeman, J., & Sugai, G. (2013). Identifying evidence-based special education interventions from single-subject research. *Teaching Exceptional Children, 45*(5), 6–12.

Friend, M., & Cook, L. (1992). *Interaction: Collaboration skills for school professionals.* White Plains, NY: Longman.

Friend, M., Embury, D. C., & Clarke, L. (2015). Teaching versus apprentice teaching: An analysis of similarities and differences. *Teacher Education and Special Education, 38*(2), 79–87.

Gagnon, J. C., Houchins, D. E., & Murphy, K. M. (2012). Current juvenile corrections professional development practices and future directions. *Teacher Education and Special Education, 35*(4), 333–344.

Gasman, M. (2014). How to write an opinion essay and why you should do it now. *Kappan, 96*(1), 28–29.

Gast, D. L. (2010). *Single subject research methodology in behavioral sciences.* New York, NY: Routledge.

Gersten, R., Fuchs, L. S., Compton, D., Coyne, M., Greenwood, C., & Innocenti, M. S. (2005). Quality indicators for group experimental and quasi-experimental research in special education. *Exceptional Children, 72*(2), 149–164.

Giangreco, M. F., Cloninger, C. J., & Iverson, V. S. (2011). *Choosing outcomes and accommodations for children (COACH): A guide to educational planning for students with disabilities* (3rd ed.). Baltimore, MD: Paul H. Brookes Publishing Co.

Gonsoulin, S., Zablocki, M., & Leone, P. E. (2012). Safe schools, staff development, and the school-to-prison pipeline. *Teacher Education and Special Education, 35*(4), 309–319.

Good, C. P., McIntoch, K., & Gietz, C. (2012). Integrating bullying prevention into schoolwide positive behavior support. *Teaching Exceptional Children, 44*(5), 48–56.

Gothberg, J. E., Peterson, L. Y., Peak, M., & Sedaghat, J. M. (2015). Successful transition of students with disabilities to 21st-century college and careers: Using triangulation and gap analysis to address non-academic skills. *Exceptional Children, 47*(6), 344–351.

Greeff, A. P., & van der Wah, K. (2010). Resilience in families with an autistic child. *Education and Training in Autism and Developmental Disabilities, 45*(3), 347–355.

Griffen, A. K., Schuster, J. W., & Morse, T. E. (1998). The acquisition of instructive feedback: A comparison of continuous versus intermittent presentation schedules. *Education and Training in Mental Retardation and Developmental Disabilities, 33*(1), 42–61.

Griffen, M. M., McMillan, E. D., & Hodapp, R. M. (2010). Family perspectives on post-secondary education for students with intellectual disabilities. *Education and Training in Autism and Developmental Disabilities, 45*(3), 339–346.

Griffen, M. M., Taylor, J. L., Urbano, R. C., & Hodapp, R. M. (2014). Involvement in transition planning meetings among high school students with autism spectrum disorders. *Journal of Special Education*, *47*(4), 256–264.

Grob, G. F. (2014). How to become an effective advocate without selling your soul. *American Journal of Evaluation*, *35*(3), 391–397.

Hager, K. D., Baird, C. M., & Spriggs, A. D. (2012). Remote teacher observation at the University of Kentucky. *Rural Special Education Quarterly*, *31*(4), 3–8.

Hagner, D., Kurtz, A., Cloutier, H., Arakelian, C., Brucker, D. L., & May, J. (2012). Outcomes of a family-centered transition process for students with autism spectrum disorders. *Focus on Autism and Other Developmental Disabilities*, *27*(1), 42–50.

Haines, S. J., Gross, J. M. S., Blue-Banning, M., Francis, G. L., & Turnbull, A. P. (2015). Parent perceptions of time spent meaningfully by you. *Research and Practice for Persons with Severe Disabilities*, *40*(3), 227–239.

Hall, J., Morgan, R. L., & Salzberg, C. L. (2014). Job-preference and job-matching assessment results and their association with job performance and satisfaction among young adults with developmental disabilities. *Education and Training in Autism and Developmental Disabilities*, *49*(2), 301–312.

Hall, L. J. (2015). Sustaining evidence-based practices by graduate special educators of students with ASD: Creating a community of practice. *Teacher Education and Special Education*, *38*(1), 28–43.

Hamblet, E. C. (2014). Nine strategies to improve college transition planning for students with disabilities. *Teaching Exceptional Children*, *46*(3), 53–59.

Harn, B., Parisi, D., & Stoolmiller, M. (2013). Balancing fidelity with flexibility and fit: What do we really know about fidelity of implementation in schools? *Exceptional Children*, *79*(2), 181–193.

Hart, D., Grigal, M., & Weir, C. (2010). Expanding the paradigm: Postsecondary education options for individuals with autism spectrum disorders and intellectual disabilities. *Focus on Autism and Other Developmental Disabilities*, *25*(3), 134–150.

Hebert, E. B. (2014). Factors affecting parental decision-making regarding interventions for their child with autism. *Focus on Autism and Other Developmental Disabilities*, *29*(2), 111–124.

Heinrich, S., Collins, B. C., Knight, V., & Spriggs, A. D. (2016). Embedded simultaneous prompting procedure to teach STEM content to high school students with moderate disabilities in an inclusive setting. *Education and Training in Autism and Developmental Disabilities*, *51*(1), 41–54.

Hetherington, S. A., Durant-Jones, L., Johnson, K., Nolan, K., Smith, E., Taylor-Brown, S., & Tuttle, J. (2010). The lived experiences of adolescents with disabilities and their parents in transition planning. *Focus on Autism and Other Developmental Disabilities*, *25*(3), 163–172.

Heward, W. L. (2013). *Exceptional children: An introduction to special education* (10th ed.). Boston, MA: Pearson.

Hochman, J. M., Carter, E. W., Bottema-Ceite, K., Harvey, M. N., & Gustafson, J. R. (2015). Efficacy of peer networks to increase social connections among high school students with and without autism spectrum disorder. *Exceptional Children*, *82*(1), 96–116.

Hodgetts, S., Nicholas, D., & Zwaigenbaum, L. (2013). Home sweet home? Families' experiences with aggression in children with autism spectrum disorders. *Focus on Autism and Other Developmental Disabilities*, *28*(3), 166–174.

Hoppey, D., & McLeskey, J. (2013). A case study of principal leadership in an effective inclusive school. *Journal of Special Education*, *46*(4), 245–256.

Horner, R. H., Carr, E. G., Halle, J., McGee, G., Odom, S., & Wolery, M. (2005). The use of single-subject research to identify evidence-based practice in special education. *Exceptional Children*, *72*(2), 165–179.

Horrocks, E. L., & Morgan, R. L. (2011). Effects of inservice teacher training on correct implementation of assessment and instructional procedures for teachers of students with profound multiple disabilities. *Teacher Education and Special Education*, *34*(4), 283–319.

Houchins, D. E., & Shippen, M. E. (2012). Welcome to a special issue about the school-to-prison pipeline: The pathway to modern institutionalization. *Teacher Education and Special Education*, *35*(4), 265–270.

Houchins, D. E., Shippen, M. E., & Murphy, K. M. (2012). Evidence-based professional development considerations along the school-to-prison pipeline. *Teacher Education and Special Education*, *35*(4), 271–283.

Hudson, M. E., Browder, D. M., & Wood, L. A. (2013). Review of experimental research on academic learning by students with moderate and severe intellectual disability in general education. *Research and Practice for Persons with Severe Disabilities*, *38*(1), 17–29.

Hughes, C., Bernstein, R. T., Kaplan, L. M., Reilly, C. M., Brigham, N. L., Cosgriff, J. C., & Boykin, M. P. (2013). Increasing conversational interactions between verbal high school students with autism and their peers without disabilities. *Focus on Autism and Other Developmental Disabilities, 28*(4), 241–254.

Hughes, C., Cosgriff, J. C., Agran, M., & Washington, B. H. (2013). Student self-determination: A preliminary investigation of the role of participation in inclusive settings. *Education and Training in Autism and Developmental Disabilities, 48*(1), 3–17.

Hughes, C., Golas, M., Cosgriff, J., Brigham, N., Edwards, C., & Cashen, K. (2011). Effects of a social skills intervention among high school students with intellectual disabilities and autism and their general education peers. *Research and Practice for Persons with Severe Disabilities, 36*(1–2), 46–61.

Hughes, C., Harvey, M., Cosgriff, J., Reilly, C., Heilingoetter, J., Brigham, N., Kaplan, L., & Bernstein, R. (2013). A peer-delivered social interaction intervention for high school students with autism. *Research and Practices for Persons with Severe Disabilities, 389*(1), 1–16.

Hume, K., Sreckovic, M., Snyder, K., & Carnahan, C. R. (2014). Smooth transitions: Helping students with autism spectrum disorder navigate the school day. *Teaching Exceptional Children, 47*(1), 35–45.

Hunt, J. H., Powell, S., Little, M. E., & Mike. A. (2015). The effects of e-mentoring on beginning teacher competencies and perceptions. *Teacher Education and Special Education, 36*(4), 286–297.

Hurley, K. S. (2016). Grassroots efforts: If you plant them, they will grow? *Strategies: A Journal for Physical and Sport Educators, 29*(1), 47–49.

Individuals with Disabilities Education Improvement Act (IDEA) of 2004, PL 108-446, 20 U.S.C. §§ 1400 *et seq.*

Israel, M., Kamman, M. L., McCray, E. D., & Sindelar, P. T. (2014). Mentoring in action: The interplay among professional assistance, emotional support, and evaluation. *Exceptional Children, 81*(1), 45–63.

Jameson, J. M., Riesen, T., Polychronis, S., Trader, B., Mizner, S., Martinis, J., & Hoyle, D. (2012). Guardianship and the potential of supported decision making with individuals with disabilities. *Research and Practice in Severe Disabilities, 37*(3), 160–169.

Jasper, A. D., & Taber Doughty, T. (2015). Special educators and data recording: What's delayed recording got to do with it? *Focus on Autism and Other Developmental Disabilities, 30*(3), 143–153.

Jimenez, B. A., Browder, D. M., & Dibiase, W. (2012). Inclusive inquiry science using peer-mediated embedded instruction for students with moderate intellectual disability. *Exceptional Children, 78*(3), 301–317.

Johnson, L. D., Wehby, J. H., Symons, F. J., Moore, T. C., Maggin, D. M., & Sutherland, K. S. (2014). An analysis of preference relative to teacher implementation of intervention. *Journal of Special Education, 48*(3), 214–224.

Jones, N. D., Youngs, P., & Frank, K. A. (2013). The role of school-based colleagues in shaping the commitment of novice special and general education teachers. *Exceptional Children, 79*(3), 365–383.

Kajitani, A. (2015). How do you know whether you're a teacher leader? *Kappa Delta Pi Record, 51*(3), 121–125.

Karl, J., Collins, B. C., Hager, K. D., Schuster, J. W., & Ault, M. J. (2013). Teaching core content embedded in a functional activity to students with moderate cognitive disabilities using a simultaneous prompting procedure. *Education and Training in Autism and Developmental Disabilities, 48*(3), 363–378.

Kaufman, R. C., & Ring, M. (2011). Pathways to leadership and professional development: Inspiring novice special educators. *Teaching Exceptional Children, 43*(5), 52–60.

Kellems, R. O., Grigal, M., Unger, D. D., Simmons, T. J., Bauder, D., & Williams, C. (2015). Technology and transition in the 21st century. *Exceptional Children, 47*(6), 336–343.

Kellems, R. O., & Morningstar, M. E. (2010). Tips for transition. *Teaching Exceptional Children, 43*(3), 60–68.

Kelly, A., & Tincani, M. (2013). Collaborative training and practice among applied behavior analysts who support individuals with autism spectrum disorder. *Education and Training in Autism and Developmental Disabilities, 48*(1), 120–131.

Klein, E., & Hollingshead, A. (2015). Collaboration between special and physical for all students. *Teaching Exceptional Children, 47*(3), 163–171.

Kleinert, H., Towles-Reeves, E., Quenemoen, R., Thurlow, M., Fluegge, L., Weseman, L., & Kerbel, A. (2015). Where students with the most significant cognitive disabilities are taught: Implications for general curriculum access. *Exceptional Children, 81*(3), 312–328.

Kleinert, H. L., Jones, M. M., Sheppard-Jones, K., Harp, B., & Harrison, E. M. (2012). Students with intellectual disabilities going to college? Absolutely! *Teaching Exceptional Children, 44*(5), 26–33.

Kleinert, J. O., Harrison, E., Mills, K. R., Dueppen, B. M., & Trailor, A. M. (2014). Self-determined goal selection and planning by students with disabilities across grade bands and disability categories. *Education and Training in Autism and Developmental Disabilities, 49*(3), 464–477.

Kozleski, E. B., Yu, T., Satter, A. L., Francis, G. L., & Haines, S. J. (2015). A never ending journey: Inclusive education is a principle of practice, not an end game. *Research and Practice for Persons with Severe Disabilities, 40*(3), 211–226.

Kretlow, A. G., & Bartholomew, C. C. (2010). Using coaching to improve the fidelity of evidence-based practices: A review of studies. *Teacher Education and Special Education, 33*(4), 279–299.

Kretlow, A. G., Wood, C. L., & Cooke, N. L. (2011). Using in-service and coaching to increase kindergarten teachers' accurate delivery of group instructional units. *Journal of Special Education, 44*(4), 234–246.

Kunnavatana, S. S., Bloom, S. E., Samaha, A. L., Lignugaris/Kraft, B., Dayton, E., & Harris, S. K. (2013). Using a modified pyramidal training model to teach special education teachers to conduct trial-based functional analyses. *Teacher Education and Special Education, 36*(4), 267–285.

Lalvani, P. (2012). Parents' participation in special education in the context of implicit educational ideologies and socioeconomic status. *Education and Training in Autism and Developmental Disabilities, 47*(4), 474–486.

Leach, D. (2010). *Bringing ABA into your inclusive classroom: A guide to improving outcomes for student autism spectrum disorders.* Baltimore, MD: Paul H. Brookes Publishing Co.

Learning Disabilities Association of America. (2017). *Vision and mission: LDA's mission.* Retrieved from https://ldaamerica.org/about-us/vision-and-mission/

Lee, S., Wehmeyer, M. L., & Shogren, K. A. (2015). Effect of instruction with the self-determined learning model of instruction on student with disabilities: A meta-analysis. *Education and Training in Autism and Developmental Disabilities, 50*(2), 237–247.

Lee, Y., Wehmeyer, M. L., Palmer, S. B., Williams-Diehm, K., Davies, D. K., & Stock, S. E. (2011). The effect of student-directed transition planning with a computer-based reading support program on the self-determination of students with disabilities. *Journal of Special Education, 45*(2), 104–117.

Lingo, A. S., Barton-Arwood, S. M., & Jolivette, K. (2011). Teachers working together: Improving learning outcomes in the inclusive classroom—practical strategies and examples. *Teaching Exceptional Children, 43*(3), 6–13.

Lo, L. (2012). Demystifying the IEP process for diverse parents of children with disabilities. *Teaching Exceptional Children, 44*(3), 15–20.

Ludlow, B. (2011). Collaboration. *Teaching Exceptional Children, 43*(3), 4.

Ludlow, B. (2012). Teachers + families = success for all students. *Teaching Exceptional Children, 44*(3), 4.

Ludlow, B. L., & Dieker, L. (2013). How to write for "Teaching Exceptional Children." *Teaching Exceptional Children, 45*(6), 58–65.

Machalicek, W., O'Reilly, M. F., Rispoli, M., Davis, T., Lang, R., Franci, J. H., & Chan, J. M. (2010). Training teachers to assess the challenging behaviors of students with autism using video tele-conferencing. *Education and Training in Autism and Developmental Disabilities, 45*(2), 203–215.

Maddox, L. L., & Marvin, C. A. (2012). A preliminary evaluation of a statewide professional development program on autism spectrum disorders. *Teacher Education and Special Education, 36*(1), 37–50.

Mallory, B. L. (2010). An ecocultural perspective on family support in rural special education. *Rural Special Education Quarterly, 29*(2), 12–17.

Marshall, J., Kirby, R. S., & Gorski, P. A. (2016). Parent concern and enrollment in intervention services for young children with developmental delays: 2007 national survey of children health. *Exceptional Children, 82*(2), 251–268.

Matthews, S. D., Collins, B. C., Spriggs, A. D., & Kleinert, H. (2016). *Including nontargeted information when teaching multiple exemplars of geometric shapes to young children with moderate intellectual disabilities.* Manuscript submitted for publication.

May, H. (2013, January 25). Bill: Alert Utah families that common virus endangers babies. *The Salt Lake Tribune.* Retrieved from http://archive.sltrib.com/article.php?id=55663401&itype=CMSID

Mazzotti, V. L., & Rowe, D. A. (2015). Teaching transition skills in the 21st century. *Teaching Exceptional Children, 47*(6).

Mazzotti, V. L., Wood, C. L., & Test, D. W. (2012). Effects of computer-assisted instruction on students' knowledge of the self-determined learning model of instruction and disruptive behavior. *Journal of Special Education, 45*(4), 216–226.

McDonnall, M. C., Cavenaugh, B. S., & Giesen, J. M. (2012). The relationship between parental involvement and mathematics achievement for students with visual impairments. *Journal of Special Education, 45*(4), 204–215.

McDonnell, J., Jameson, J. M., Riesen, T., Polychronis, S., Crockett, M. A., & Brown, B. E. (2011). A comparison of on-campus and distance teacher education programs in severe disabilities. *Teacher Education and Special Education, 34*(2), 106–118.

McIntosh, K., Mercer, S. H., Hume, A. E., Frank, J. L., Turri, M. G., & Mathews, S. (2013). Factors related to sustained implementation of schoolwide positive behavior support. *Exceptional Children, 79*(3), 293–311.

McLeskey, J., Landers, E., Williamson, P., & Hoppey, D. (2012). Are we moving toward educating students with disabilities in less restrictive settings? *Journal of Special Education, 46*(3), 131–140.

McLeskey, J., Waldron, N. L., & Redd, L. (2014). A case study of a highly effective inclusive elementary school. *Journal of Special Education, 48*(1), 59–70.

Meadan, H., Halle, J. W., & Eata, A. T. (2010). Families with children who have autism spectrum disorders: Stress and support. *Exceptional Children, 77*(1), 7–36.

Meadan, H., Meyer, L. E., Snodgrass, M. R., & Halle, J. W. (2013). Coaching parents of young children with autism in rural areas using internet-based technologies: A pilot program. *Rural Special Education Quarterly, 32*(3), 3–10.

Meadan, H., Shelden, D. L., Appel, K., & DeGrazia, R. L. (2010). Developing a long-term vision: A road map for students' futures. *Teaching Exceptional Children, 43*(3), 8–14.

Millar, D. S. (2011). Guardianship alternatives: Their use affirms self-determination of individuals with intellectual disabilities. *Education and Training in Autism and Developmental Disabilities, 48*(3), 291–303.

Millar, D. S. (2014a). Addition to transition assessment resources: A template for determining the use of guardianship alternatives for students who have intellectual disability. *Education and Training in Autism and Developmental Disabilities, 49*(2), 171–188.

Millar, D. S. (2014b). Extending transition to address guardianship alternatives: An issue concerning students who have intellectual disability. *Education and Training in Autism and Developmental Disabilities, 49*(3), 449–463.

Miller-Warren, V. (2016). Parental insights on the effects of the secondary transition planning process on the postsecondary outcomes of graduates with disabilities. *Rural Special Quarterly, 35*(1), 31–36.

Miracle, S. A., Collins, B. C., Schuster, J. W., & Grisham-Brown, J. (2001). Peer versus teacher delivered instruction: Effects on acquisition and maintenance. *Education and Training in Mental Retardation and Developmental Disabilities, 36*, 375–385.

Miranda, A., Tarraga, R., Fernandez, I., Colomer, C., & Pastor, G. (2015). Parenting stress in families of children with autism spectrum disorder and ADHD. *Exceptional Children, 82*(1), 81–95.

Moon, S., Simonsen, M. L., & Neubert, D. A. (2011). Perception of supported employment providers: What students with developmental disabilities, families, and educators need to know for transition planning. *Education and Training in Autism and Developmental Disabilities, 46*(1), 94–105.

Moorehead, T., & Grillo, K. (2013). Celebrating the reality of inclusive STEM education: Co-teaching in science and mathematics. *Teaching Exceptional Children, 45*(4), 50–57.

Morgan, R. L., & Openshaw, K. P. (2011). Targeted transition assessment leading to job placement for young adults with disabilities in rural areas. *Rural Special Education Quarterly, 30*(2), 19–27.

Morningstar, M. E., & Benitez, D. T. (2013). Teacher training matters: The results of a multistate survey of secondary special educators regarding transition from school to adulthood. *Teacher Education and Special Education, 36*(1), 51–64.

Morningstar, M. E., Shogren, K. A., Lee, H., & Born, K. (2015). Preliminary lessons about supporting participation and learning in inclusive classrooms. *Research and Practice for Persons with Severe Disabilities, 40*(3), 173–191.

Moyson, T., & Roeyers, H. (2011). The quality of life of siblings of children with autism spectrum disorder. *Exceptional Children, 78*(1), 41–55.

Mullen, C. A. (2014). Advocacy for child wellness in high-poverty environments. *Kappa Delta Pi Record, 50*(4), 157–163.

Murawski, W. W. (2012). 10 tips for using co-planning time more efficiently. *Teaching Exceptional Children, 44*(4), 8–15.

Murphy, M. A., McCormick, K. M., & Rous, B. S. (2013). Rural influences on the use of transition practices by preschool teachers. *Rural Special Education Quarterly, 32*(1), 29–37.

Musti-Rao, S., Hawkins, R. O., & Tan, C. (2011). A practitioner's guide to consultation and problem solving in inclusive settings. *Teaching Exceptional Children, 44*(1), 18–26.

National Association for Down Syndrome. (2016). *About us: Our mission.* Retrieved from http://www .nads.org/about-us/

National Association of the Deaf. (2017). *Bylaws.* Retrieved from https://www.nad.org/about-us/bylaws/

National CMV Foundation. (2016). *CMV legislation.* Retrieved from https://www.nationalcmv.org/cmv-research/legislation.aspx

National Down Syndrome Society. (2017). Our Mission. Retrieved from https://www.ndss.org

National Federation of the Blind. (2017). *About the National Federation of the Blind.* Retrieved from https://nfb.org/about-the-nfb

National Organization on Disability. (2017). *About: Mission.* Retrieved from http://www.nod.org/about/

No Child Left Behind Act of 2001, PL 107-110, 115 Stat. 1425, 20 U.S.C. §§ 6301 *et seq.*

Odom, S. L., Cox, A. W., Brock, M. E., & National Professional Development Center on ASD. (2013). Implementation science, professional development, and autism spectrum disorders. *Exceptional Children, 79*(2), 233–251.

Olcay-Gul, W., & Tekin-Iftar, E. (2016). Family generated and delivered social story intervention: Acquisition, maintenance, and generalization of social skills in youths with ASD. *Education and Training in Autism and Developmental Disabilities, 51*(1), 67–78.

Papay, C., Unger, D. D., Williams-Diehm, K., & Mitchell, V. (2015). Begin with the end in mind: Infusing transition planning and instruction into elementary classrooms. *Exceptional Children, 47*(6), 310–318.

Papay, C. K., & Bambera, L. M. (2011). Postsecondary education for transition-age students with intellectual and other developmental disabilities: A national survey. *Education and Training in Autism and Developmental Disabilities, 46*(1), 78–93.

Parette, H. P., Meadan, H., Doubet, S., & Hess, J. (2010). Supporting families of young children with disabilities using technology. *Education and Training in Autism and Developmental Disabilities, 45*(4), 552–565.

Parish, S. L., Rose, R. A., & Andrews, M. E. (2010). TANF's impact on low-income mothers raising children with disabilities. *Exceptional Children, 76*(2), 234–253.

Park, J. H., Alber-Morgan, S. R., & Fleming, C. (2011). Collaborating with parents to implement behavioral interventions for children with challenging behaviors. *Teaching Exceptional Children, 43*(3), 22–30.

Pence, A. R., & Dymond, S. K. (2015). Extracurricular school clubs: A time for fun and learning. *Teaching Exceptional Children, 47*(5), 281–288.

Pennington, R., Grau, R., Bobo, J., Lorence, D., Tomcheck, S., Stewart, J., & Wooldridge, D. (2013). Building statewide support for Kentucky families of individuals with ASD. *Rural Special Education Quarterly, 32*(2), 3–7.

Peterson, L. Y., Burden, J. P., Sedaghat, J. M., Gothberg, J. E., Kohler, P. D., & Coyle, J. L. (2010). Triangulated IEP transition goals: Developing relevant and genuine annual goals. *Exceptional Children, 43*(6), 46–57.

Ploessl, D. M., & Rock, M. L. (2015). eCoaching: The effects on co-teachers' planning and instruction. *Teacher Education and Special Education, 37*(3), 191–215.

Plotner, A. J., Mazzotti, V. L., Rose, C. A., & Carlson-Britting, K. B. (2013). Factors associated with enhanced knowledge and use of secondary transition evidence-based practices. *Teacher Education and Special Education, 39*(1), 28–46.

Podvey, M. C., Hinojosa, J., & Koenig, K. G. (2013). Reconsidering insider status for families during the transition from early intervention to preschool special education. *Journal of Special Education, 46*(4), 211–222.

Povenmire-Kirk, T., Bethune, L. K., Alverson, C. Y., & Kahn, L. G. (2015). A journey, not a destination: Developing cultural competence in secondary transition. *Exceptional Children, 47*(6), 301–309.

Rakap, S., Jones, H. A., & Emery, A. K. (2015). Evaluation of a web-based professional development program (Project ACE) for teachers of children with autism spectrum disorders. *Teacher Education and Special Education, 38*(3), 221–239.

Raskauskas, J., & Modell, S. (2012). Modifying anti-bullying programs to include students with disabilities. *Teaching Exceptional Children, 44*(5), 60–67.

Rieger, A., & McGrail, J. P. (2015). Relationships between humor styles and family functioning in parents of children with disabilities. *Journal of Special Education, 49*(3), 188–196.

Riggs, L., Collins, B. C., Kleinert, H., & Knight, V. (2013). Teaching principles of heredity to high school students with moderate and severe disabilities. *Research and Practice in Severe Disabilities, 38*(1), 30–43.

Roberts, J. L. (2012). Teachers as advocates: If not you—who? *Gifted Child Today, 35*(1), 59–61.

Roberts, K. D. (2010). Topic areas to consider when planning transition from high school to postsecondary education for students with autism spectrum disorders. *Focus on Autism and Other Developmental Disabilities, 25*(3), 158–162.

Robertson, J. S., & Singleton, J. D. (2010). Comparison of traditional versus alternative preparation of special education teachers. *Teacher Education and Special Education, 33*(3), 213–224.

Robinson, S. E. (2011). Teaching paraprofessionals of students with autism to implement pivotal response treatment in inclusive school settings using a brief video feedback training package. *Focus on Autism and Other Developmental Disabilities, 26*(2), 105–118.

Rock, M. L., Schumacker, R. E., Gregg, M., Howard, P. W., Gable, R. A., & Zigmond, N. (2014). Longer term effects of eCoaching through online bug-in-ear technology. *Teacher Education and Special Education, 37*(2), 161–181.

Rodrigues, R. J., Blatz, E. T., & Elbaum, B. (2014). Parents' views of schools' involvement efforts. *Exceptional Children, 81*(1), 79–95.

Rood, C. E., Kanter, A., & Causton, J. (2015). Presumption of incompetence: The systematic assignment of guardianship within the transition process. *Research and Practice for Persons with Severe Disabilities, 39*(4), 319–328.

Rosa's Law of 2010, PL 111-256, 20 U.S.C. §§ 1400 *et seq.*

Rouse, C. A., Everhart-Sherwood, J. M., & Alber-Morgan, S. R. (2014). Effects on self-monitoring and recruiting teacher attention on pre-vocational skills. *Education and Training in Autism and Developmental Disabilities, 49*(2), 313–327.

Rowe, D. A., Mazzotti, V. L., Hirano, K., & Alverson, C. Y. (2015). Assessing transition skills in the 21st century. *Exceptional Children, 47*(6), 301–309.

Rowe, D. A., & Test, D. W. (2010). The effects of computer-based instruction on the transition planning process knowledge of parents of students with disabilities. *Research and Practice in Severe Disabilities, 35*(3–4), 102–115.

Ryan, J. B., Hughes, E. M., Katsiyannis, A., McDaniel, M., & Sprinkle, C. (2011). Research-based educational practices for students with autism spectrum disorders. *Teaching Exceptional Children, 43*(3), 56–64.

Ryan, S. M. (2014). An inclusive rural postsecondary education program for students with intellectual disabilities. *Rural Special Quarterly, 33*(2), 18–28.

Rye, J. A., Selmer, S. J., Pennington, S., Vanhorn, L., Fox, S., & Kane, S. (2013). Elementary school garden programs enhance science education for all learners. *Teaching Exceptional Children, 44*(6), 58–65.

Ryndak, D. L., Alper, S., Hughes, C., & McDonnell, J. (2012). Perceptions of supported employment providers: What students with developmental disabilities, families, and educators need to know for transition planning. *Education and Training in Autism and Developmental Disabilities, 47*(2), 127–138.

Ryndak, D. L., Taub, D., Jorgensen, C. M., Gansier-Gerdin, J., Arndt, K., Sauer, J.,…Allcock, H. (2014). Policy and impact on placement, involvement, and progress in general education: Critical issues that require rectification. *Research and Practice for Persons with Severe Disabilities, 39*(1), 65–74.

Ryndak, D. L., Ward, T., Alper, S., Montgomery, J. W., & Storch, J. F. (2010). Long-term outcomes of services for two persons with significant disabilities with differing educational experiences: A qualitative consideration of the impact of educational experiences. *Education and Training in Autism and Developmental Disabilities, 45*(3), 323–338.

Sansosti, F. J., Lavik, K. B., & Sansosti, J. M. (2012). Family experiences through the autism diagnostic process. *Focus on Autism and Other Developmental Disabilities, 27*(2), 81–92.

Sawyer, M. (2015). BRIDGES: Connecting with families to facilitate and enhance involvement. *Teaching Exceptional Children, 47*(3), 172–179.

Schaefer, J. M., & Andzik, N. R. (2016). Switch on the learning: Teaching students with significant disabilities to use switches. *Teaching Exceptional Children, 48*(4), 204–212.

Scheeler, M. C., Congdon, M., & Stansberry, S. (2010). Providing immediate feedback to co-teachers through bug-in-ear technology: An effective method of peer coaching in inclusion classrooms. *Teacher Education and Special Education, 33*(1), 83–96.

Scheeler, M. C., McKinnon, K., & Stout, J. (2012). Effects of immediate feedback delivered via webcam and bug-in-ear technology on preservice teacher performance. *Teacher Education and Special Education, 35*(1), 77–90.

Schmidt, M., Gage, A. M., Gage, N., Cox, P., & McLeskey, J. (2015). Bringing the field to the supervisor: Innovation in distance supervision for field-based experiences using mobile technologies. *Rural Special Education Quarterly, 34*(1), 37–43.

Scott, R., Collins, B. C., Knight, V., & Kleinert, H. (2013). Teaching adults with moderate intellectual disabilities ATM use via the iPod. *Education and Training in Autism and Developmental Disabilities, 48*(2), 190–199.

Segal, R. (2016). *The National Association for Retarded Citizens.* Retrieved from http://www.thearc.org/who-we-are/history/segal-account

Seo, H. (2014). Promoting the self-determination of elementary and secondary students with disabilities: Perspectives of general and special educators in Korea. *Education and Training in Autism and Developmental Disabilities, 49*(2), 277–289.

Shaw, S. F., Dukes, L. L., & Madaus, J. W. (2012). Beyond compliance: Using the summary of a performance to enhance transition planning. *Teaching Exceptional Children, 44*(5), 6–12.

Shippen, M. E., Patterson, D., Green, K. L., & Smitherman, T. (2012). Community and school practices to reduce delinquent behavior: Intervening on the school-to-prison pipeline. *Teacher Education and Special Education, 35*(4), 296–308.

Shogren, K. (2012). Hispanic mothers' perceptions of self-determination. *Research and Practice for Persons with Severe Disabilities, 37*(3), 170–184.

Shogren, K. A., McCart, A. B., Lyon, K. J., & Sailor, W. S. (2015). All means all: Building knowledge for inclusive schoolwide transformation. *Research and Practice for Persons with Severe Disabilities, 40*(3), 173–191.

Shogren, K. A., Plotner, A. J., Palmer, S. B., Wehmeyer, M. L., & Pack, Y. (2014). Impact of the self-determined learning model of instruction on teacher perceptions of student capacity and opportunity for self-determination. *Education and Training in Autism and Developmental Disabilities, 49*(3), 440–448.

Shogren, K. A., Wehmeyer, M. L., Palmer, S. B., Rifenbark, G. G., & Little, T. D. (2015). Relationships between self-determination and post school outcomes for youth with disabilities. *Journal of Special Education, 48*(4), 256–267.

Sileo, J. M. (2011). Co-teaching: Getting to know your partner. *Teaching Exceptional Children, 45*(5), 32–38.

Simonsen, B., Myers, D., & DeLuca, C. (2010). Teaching teachers to use prompts, opportunities to respond, and specific praise. *Teacher Education and Special Education, 33*(4), 300–318.

Sindelar, P. T., Brownell, M. T., & Billingsley, B. (2010). Special education teacher education research: Current status and future directions. *Teacher Education and Special Education, 33*(1), 8–24.

Sindelar, P. T., Dewey, J. F., Rosenberg, M. S., Corbett, N. L., Denslow, D., & Loftfinia, B. (2012). Cost effectiveness of alternative route special education teacher preparation. *Exceptional Children, 79*(1), 25-42.

Spaulding, L. S., & Flanagan, J. S. (2013). DIS$_2$ECT: A framework for effective inclusive science instruction. *Teaching Exceptional Children, 44*(6), 6–14.

Spooner, F., Browder, D. M., & Mims, P. J. (2011). Evidence-based practices. In D. M. Browder & F. Spooner (Eds.). *Teaching students with moderate and severe disabilities.* New York, NY: Guilford.

Stanley, S. L. G. (2015). The advocacy efforts of African American mothers of children with disabilities in rural special education: Considerations for school professionals. *Rural Special Education Quarterly, 34*(4), 3–17.

Steinbeck, J. (1937). *Of Mice and Men.* London, England: Penguin.

Stephenson, J., Carter, M., & Arthur-Kelly, M. (2011). Professional learning for teachers without special education qualifications working with students with severe disabilities. *Teacher Education and Special Education, 34*(1), 7–20.

Stockall, N. S. (2014). When an aide really becomes an aid: Providing professional development for special education paraprofessionals. *Teaching Exceptional Children, 46*(6), 197–205.

Stodden, R. A., & Mruzek, D. W. (2010). An introduction to post-secondary education and employment of person with autism and developmental disabilities. *Focus on Autism and Other Developmental Disabilities, 25*(3), 131–133.

Suhrheinrich, J. (2011). Training teachers to use pivotal response training with children with autism: Coaching as a critical component. *Teacher Education and Special Education, 34*(4), 339–349.

Suppo, J., & Floyd, K. (2012). Parent training for families who have children with autism: A review of the literature. *Rural Special Education Quarterly, 31*(2), 12–26.

Suppo, J. L., & Mayton, M. R. (2014). Expanding training opportunities for parents of children with autism. *Rural Special Education Quarterly, 33*(3), 19–28.

Swain-Bradway, J., Pinkney, C., & Flannery, K. B. (2015). Implementing schoolwide positive behavior interventions and supports in high schools: Contextual factors and stages of implementation. *Teaching Exceptional Children, 47*(5), 245–255.

Swedeen, B., Carter, E. W., & Molfenter, N. (2010). Getting everyone involved: Identifying transition opportunities for youth with severe disabilities. *Teaching Exceptional Children, 43*(3), 38–49.

Szidon, K., Ruppar, A., & Smith, L. (2015). Five steps for developing effective transition plans for high school students with autism spectrum disorder. *Teaching Exceptional Children, 47*(3), 147–152.

Taber-Doughty, R., & Jasper, A. D. (2012). Does latency in recording data make a difference? Confirming the accuracy of teachers' data. *Focus on Autism and Other Developmental Disabilities, 27*(3), 168–176.

TASH. (2017). *About TASH.* Retrieved from https://tash.org/

Teacher Leadership Exploratory Consortium. (2012). *Teacher Leader Model Standards.* Retrieved from http://www.teacherleaderstandards.org/index.php

Tekin-Iftar, E., Collins, B. C., Spooner, F., & Olcay-Gul, S. (2017). Teaching teachers to use systematic instruction to teach core content to students with ASD. *Teacher Education and Special Education, 40*(3), 225–245. doi:10.1177/0888406417703751

Test, D. W., Kemp-Inman, A., Diegelmann, K., Hitt, S. B., & Bethune, L. (2015). Are online sources for identifying evidence-based practices trustworthy? An evaluation. *Exceptional Children, 82*(1), 58–80.

Test, D. W., Mason, C., Hughes, C., Konrad, M., Neale, M., & Wood, W. M. (2004). Student involvement in individualized education program meetings. *Exceptional Children, 70*(4), 381–412.

The Arc. (2017). *Mission and values: Mission statement.* Retrieved from http://www.thearc.org/who-we-are/mission-and-values

Thurston, L. P., & Navarrete, L. A. (2010). Rural, poverty-level mothers: A comparative study of those with and without children who have special needs. *Rural Special Education Quarterly, 30*(1), 39–46.

Turnbull, A., Zuna, N., Hong, J. Y., Hu, X., Kyzar, K., Obremski, S.,…Stowe, M. (2010). Knowledge-to-action guides: Preparing families to be partners in making educational decisions. *Teaching Exceptional Children, 42*(3), 42–53.

Underwood, J. (2013). Do you have the right to be an advocate? *Kappan, 95*(1), 26–31.

United Cerebral Palsy. (2017). *History of UCP.* Retrieved from http://ucp.org/about/history/

Urbach, J., Moore, B. A., Klingner, J. K., Galman, S., Haagerm, D., Brownell, M. T., & Dingle, M. (2015). "That's my job": Comparing the beliefs of more and less accomplished special educators related to their roles and responsibilities. *Teacher Education and Special Education, 38*(4), 323–336.

Valerie, L. M., & Foss-Swanson, S. (2012). Using family message journals to improve student writing and strengthen the school–home partnership. *Teaching Exceptional Children, 44*(3), 41–48.

Valimarsdottir, H., Halldorsdottir, L. Y., & Sigurdardotter, Z. G. (2010). Increasing the variety of foods consumed by a picky eater: Generalization of effects across caregivers and settings. *Journal of Applied Behavior Analysis, 43*, 101–105.

Vannest, K. J., Parker, R., & Dyer, N. (2011). Progress monitoring in grade 5 science for low achievers. *Journal of Special Education, 44*(4), 221–223.

Vannest, K. J., Soares, D. A., Smith, S. L., & Williams, L. E. (2012). Progress monitoring to support science learning for all students. *Teaching Exceptional Children, 44*(6), 66–72.

Votava, K., & Chiasson, K. (2015). Perceptions of Part C coordinators on family assessment in early intervention. *Rural Special Education Quarterly, 34*(2), 17–24.

Watt, S. J., Therrien, W. J., Kaldenberg, E., & Taylor, J. (2013). Promoting inclusive practices in inquiry-based science classrooms. *Teaching Exceptional Children, 45*(4), 40–48.

Wehmeyer, M. L., Palmer, S. B., Shogren, K., Williams-Diehm, K., & Soukup, J. H. (2013). Establishing a causal relationship between intervention to promote self-determination and enhanced student self-determinations. *Journal of Special Education, 46*(4), 195–210.

Wells, J. C., & Sheehey, P. H. (2012). Person-centered planning: Strategies to encourage participation and facilitate communications. *Teaching Exceptional Children, 44*(3), 33–39.

Wells, J. C., Sheehey, P. H., & Moore, A. N. (2012). Postsecondary expectations for a student in a rural middle school: Impact of person-centered planning on team member agreement. *Rural Special Quarterly, 31*(3), 25–33.

Werfel, K. L., & Hendricks, A. E. (2016). Identifying minimal hearing loss and managing its effects on literacy learning. *Teaching Exceptional Children, 48*(4), 213–217.

Westling, D. L., Fox, L., & Carter, E. W. (2015). *Teaching students with severe disabilities.* Boston, MA: Pearson.

Whetstone, P., Abell, M., Collins, B. C., & Kleinert, H. L. (2012). Teacher preparation in moderate and severe disabilities: A state tool for intern support. *Teacher Education and Special Education, 36*(1), 28–36.

Whitby, J. S., Marx, T., McIntire, J., & Weinke, W. (2013). Advocating for students with disabilities at the school level: Tips for special educators. *Teaching Exceptional Children, 45*(5), 32–39.

White, S. E. (2014). Special education complaints filed by parents of students with autism spectrum disorders in the Midwestern United States. *Focus on Autism and Other Developmental Disabilities, 29*(2), 80–87.

Williams-Diehm, K. L., Brandes, J. A., Chesnut, P. W., & Haring, K. A. (2014). Student and parent IEP collaboration. *Rural Special Education Quarterly, 33*(1), 3–11.

Witmer, S. E., Nasamran, A., Parikh, P. J., Schmitt, H. A., & Clinton, M. C. (2015a). The relation between parental expressed emotion and externalizing behaviors in children and adolescents with an autism spectrum disorder. *Focus on Autism and Other Developmental Disabilities, 30*(2), 67–85.

Witmer, S. E., Nasamran, A., Parikh, P. J., Schmitt, H. A., & Clinton, M. C. (2015b). Using parents and teachers to monitor progress among children with ASD: A review of intervention research. *Focus on Autism and Other Developmental Disabilities, 30*(2), 67–85.

←——→

Zager, D., & Alpern, C. S. (2010). College-based inclusion programming for transition-age students with autism. *Focus on Autism and Other Developmental Disabilities, 25*(3), 151–157.

Zeedyk, S. M., Tipton, L. A., & Blacher, J. (2014). Educational supports for high functioning youth with ASD: The postsecondary pathway to college. *Focus on Autism and Other Developmental Disabilities, 31*(1), 37–48.

Zhang, D., Landmark, L., Grenwelge, C., & Montoya, L. (2010). Culturally diverse parents' perspectives on self-determination. *Education and Training in Autism and Developmental Disabilities, 45*(2), 175–186.

Zheng, U., Maude, S. P., Brotherson, M. J., Summer, J. A., Palmer, S. B., & Erwin, E. J. (2015). Foundations for self-determination perceived and promoted by families of young children with disabilities in China. *Education and Training in Autism and Developmental Disabilities, 50*(1), 109–122.

Glossary

AB design A simple single-subject experimental design in which baseline condition (A) is followed by intervention (B), providing an indication that an intervention may be effective based on whether there is a therapeutic change in data from baseline condition to intervention; appropriate for indicating the effectiveness of interventions for both academic and social behaviors.

ABAB (withdrawal) design A single-subject experimental design in which baseline condition (A) is followed by intervention (B), providing an indication that an intervention may be effective based on whether the data reflect a counter-therapeutic change in data each time the baseline condition is in effect and a therapeutic change in data each time the intervention is implemented; appropriate for determining the effectiveness of a behavioral intervention on a social behavior.

Adapted alternating treatments design A single-subject experimental design in which one intervention (A) is compared to another intervention (B) by alternating which intervention is in effect for similar equivalent behaviors until one intervention appears to be more effective or efficient than the other; appropriate for comparing the effect of two or more interventions on an academic behavior (e.g., vocabulary words).

Advocacy The act of being visible in standing up for others while presenting an argument to influence a cause.

Alternating treatments design A single-subject experimental design in which one intervention (A) is compared to another intervention (B) by alternating which intervention is in effect for a single behavior until one intervention appears to be more effective or efficient than the other; appropriate for comparing the effect of two or more behavioral interventions on a social behavior (e.g., being out of seat).

Alternative teaching A model of co-teaching in which one teacher (e.g., general or special education teacher) takes the lead in teaching a lesson to a class of students while the other focuses on assisting with specific components of the lesson (e.g., explaining vocabulary words).

Apprentice teaching A model in which a master teacher or mentor delivers instruction alongside a beginning teacher, with both being accountable for teaching and learning.

Asynchronous mentoring A process by which an experienced teacher or mentor works with a beginning teacher at a distance using online materials that are archived for use as needed.

←———→

Blind review   A process in which a person's identity if concealed while his or her work is being assessed.

Chained task   A skill made up of a series of discrete (one-step) behaviors or responses that are linked in a sequence (e.g., writing a paragraph, tying a shoe).

Coaching   A process by which an experienced teacher provides support and feedback to a less-experienced teacher; this can include synchronous mentoring using technology (e.g., bug-in-the-ear, webcam) that makes it possible to provide instant feedback as instruction takes place.

Collaboration   A process in which two individuals (e.g., general and special education teachers) engage in shared decision making as they work toward a common goal.

Conceptual model   A theoretical framework that provides the underpinnings for a project.

Co-teaching   A process of collaboration between two teachers (e.g., general and special education) in which both have an active role in the planning and delivery of a lesson or instructional unit; it may consist of team teaching, parallel teaching, alternative teaching, or station teaching.

Cultural competence   A state in which individuals (e.g., teachers) have nonjudgmental awareness and sensitivity toward those (e.g., students, families) from different backgrounds.

Discrete task   A skill consisting of one response or step that can be recorded as a single behavior that is correct or incorrect.

Duration data   Data on how long (e.g., seconds, minutes) a single behavior occurs. These data can be summarized as either the number of minutes (or other time units) or as the percentage of time a behavior occurs.

eCoaching   A form of synchronous mentoring using technology (e.g., bug-in-the-ear, webcam) that makes it possible for an experienced teacher or mentor to provide instant feedback to a beginning teacher as instruction takes place.

Effectiveness   How well an intervention or procedure works (i.e., whether it results in performance at a preset criterion).

Efficiency   How quickly (number of sessions, number of minutes) a procedure or intervention results in criterion performance, how many errors a student makes over time in the process of learning, or how much effort or cost goes into implementation.

Event recording   Trial-by-trial data collected as a student performs a discrete task (e.g., works a math problem correctly, raises a hand before speaking).

Evidence-based practices   Interventions that have been determined to be effective by a sufficient body of high-quality research studies.

Facilitator   An experienced person (e.g., teacher) with the skills to lead a group toward consensus.

Family partnerships   Intentional relationships between individuals (e.g., teachers) and family members (e.g., parents, siblings) in which both share a common vision and have distinct roles with shared responsibility and decision making in reaching common goals.

Fidelity   A measure of believability that an intervention has been implemented in an accurate and consistent manner as planned or specified.

Formative data   Responses that are recorded as instruction occurs or as an intervention is implemented.

Frequency data   Responses that are recorded each time they occur; doing so results in an accurate measure of the occurrence of a behavior. These data can be summarized as the number of times a behavior occurs within a specified amount of time.

Generalization   The ability to use acquired skills across settings, people, or materials that were not used in training.

Graphic facilitator   A skilled and experienced person (e.g., teacher) who captures the discussion of a group meeting on a chart.

Guardianship   A legal process in which a court appoints an adult (or an agency) to make decisions on a person's behalf when that person is incapable of making his or her own decisions; may be plenary (full guardianship), partial (limited guardianship), or temporary (in effect for a specified amount of time).

Inclusion   An educational model in which all students of the same age, with or without disabilities, are educated in the same general education setting; active involvement and interaction of students is required, not just physical placement.

Interval data collection   Data collection in which responses are recorded if they occur at or during specific units of time; doing so results in an estimate of the occurrence of a behavior.

Latency data   A measure of how long it takes to begin performing a behavior.

Logic model   A framework that serves as a tool in planning and implementing a project by identifying 1) resources or inputs, 2) activities, 3) outputs, and 4) outcomes or impact.

Maintenance   The ability to continue to use acquired skills over a period of time.

Momentary time sampling   Data collection in which responses are recorded if they occur at the end of a specified interval of time; doing so results in an estimate of the occurrence of a behavior.

Multi-treatment design   A flexible single-subject experimental design in which baseline condition (A) is followed by two or more interventions (e.g., B, C, D), allowing the effectiveness of each intervention to be compared to the one that follows it; interventions may be repeated within the design (e.g., A-B-C-B-C).

Multiple baseline design   A single-subject experimental design in which a series of AB designs is implemented in a time-lagged fashion to show that an intervention is effective each time it is implemented following continuous collection of baseline data; the intervention may be implemented across students, behaviors, or settings.

Multiple probe design   A single-subject experimental design in which a series of AB designs is implemented in a time-lagged fashion to show that an intervention is effective each time it is implemented following intermittent collection of baseline data; the intervention may be implemented across students, behaviors, or settings.

Natural supports   Assistance (e.g., peers, materials) already found in a setting without being added that allows a student with a disability to be part of that setting and its activities.

Parallel teaching   A model of co-teaching in which two teachers (e.g., general and special education teacher) deliver the same lesson at the same time to two different groups of students within a single classroom.

←——→

Partial guardianship   A legal process in which a court appoints an adult (or an agency) to make a specified number of decisions, but not all, on a person's behalf when that person is incapable of making some of his or her own decisions.

Partial-interval data collection   Data collection in which responses are recorded once if there is an occurrence at any point in a specified interval of time; doing so results in an estimate of the occurrence of a behavior.

Partnerships   Intentional relationships between individuals (e.g., teachers and parents) in which both have distinct roles with shared responsibility and decision making in reaching common goals.

Permanent products   Artifacts (e.g., tests, worksheets, essays) that provide evidence of the acquisition of a skill.

Person-centered planning   An approach to assessment and development of student programs (e.g., transition plans) to attain desirable student future outcomes through a long-term vision based on student input.

Plenary guardianship   A legal process in which a court appoints an adult (or an agency) to make all decisions on a person's behalf when that person is incapable of making his or her own decisions.

Primary support   A level of assistance that is effective for the majority of students (typically about 80%–90%) within a schoolwide positive behavior support system to promote a positive social and learning environment.

Process facilitator   A skilled and experienced person (e.g., teacher) who oversees the steps and content of a group meeting.

Promising practice   An intervention that shows signs of possibly being effective but has not been investigated.

Research-based practice   An intervention that appears to be effective based upon a limited body of empirical support but has not been fully investigated.

Response to intervention   A general education initiative in which specialized intervention is provided to students who are at risk of being identified for special education services.

Schoolwide positive behavior support system   A systemwide approach in which different levels of intervention (i.e., primary, secondary, tertiary) are provided to students and staff to promote a positive social and learning environment for all.

Secondary support   A level of assistance that is needed for a small group of students within a schoolwide positive behavior support system when primary supports are not enough to promote a positive social and learning environment; typically about 10%–13% of the school population receives this level of support.

Self-advocacy   The act of being visible in standing up for oneself while presenting an argument to influence a cause.

Self-determination   A strategy for facilitating successful transitions based on competencies that provide students with more control over their lives—for example, choice making, decision making, problem solving, goal setting and attainment, self-observation, self-evaluation, self-reinforcement, self-awareness, self-advocacy, and self-knowledge.

Service learning   A strategy that allows instructional objectives to be addressed as students engage in community projects; it can involve peers with and without disabilities and occur within academic classes, elective classes, or extracurricular activities.

Side-by-side coaching   A form of mentoring in which an experienced teacher or mentor provides feedback to a beginning teacher as the teacher delivers instruction.

Station teaching   A model of co-teaching in which two teachers (e.g., general and special education teachers) circulate across learning centers, providing student support and facilitating learning as needed.

Summative data   Responses that are recorded at the end of a session or unit of study.

Supervisory coaching   A form of mentoring in which an experienced teacher or mentor provides feedback to a beginning teacher after observing the teacher conducting instruction.

Supported decision making   An alternative strategy to having a person with a disability lose legal rights through guardianship; this model provides the assistance needed for a person to actively participate in making his or her own decisions.

Synchronous mentoring   A process in which an experienced teacher or mentor works with a beginning teacher at a distance in a virtual, real-time online environment.

Task analytic data   Responses recorded on the number of steps completed on a chained task.

Team teaching   A model of co-teaching in which two teachers (e.g., general and special education teachers) deliver instructional content together during a lesson.

Temporary guardianship   A legal process in which a court appoints an adult (or an agency) to make decisions on a person's behalf for a specified amount of time when that person is incapable of making his or her own decisions.

Tertiary support   A level of assistance that is needed for a minimal number of students within a schoolwide positive behavior support system when primary and secondary supports are not enough to promote a positive social and learning environment. Typically about 1%–5% of the school population receives this level of support.

Transition   A lifelong process in which a person progresses from one stage of life to another.

Triangulated goal   In transition planning, a projected outcome that takes three variables into consideration: 1) postsecondary goals, 2) industry standards, and 3) educational standards.

Triangulation   In transition planning, an approach for writing goals that takes three variables into consideration: 1) postsecondary goals, 2) industry standards, and 3) educational standards.

Universal design   A format in which content is accessible to all regardless of ability.

Whole-interval data collection   Data collection in which responses are recorded if a behavior occurs for an entire specified interval of time; doing so results in an estimate of the occurrence of a behavior.

Index

Throughout this index, a *t* indicates a table and an *f* indicates a figure on that page.

AB research design, 12–13
ABAB (withdrawal) design, 13–14
Activities outside the classroom, engaging students in, 32–34
Adapted alternating treatments design, 15–16
Administrators, school, 16, 27, 59, 114, 121
Adulthood, making transition plan for, 96–100
Advice, sharing while mentoring, 49
Advocacy, 114, 117
Advocating for students, leadership in
    cautions in, 117–118
    follow-up activities for, 122–123
    helping others with, 120–121
    interview with a leader in, 116
    national groups for, 119
    overview of, 114–115, 121–122
    professional standards and, 115–116
    strategies for, 117–120
    teacher role in, 116–117
Alternating treatments design, 15
Alternative teaching, 30
American Association of People with Disabilities (AAPD), 130*t*, 131, 137*t*
American Association on Intellectual and Developmental Disabilities (AAIDD), 130*t*, 131, 137*t*
American Council of the Blind (ACB), 130*t*, 132, 137*t*
American Council on Rural Special Education (ACRES), 130*t*, 131
American Psychological Association (APA), formatting guidelines of, 143
Americans with Disabilities Act (ADA) of 1990 (PL 101-336), 131
Anti-bullying programs, 35, 131
Apprentice teaching, 52
The Arc, 114, 119, 130*t*, 136, 138*t*
Articles, contributing, 120, 141–143
Assessment data, for transition planning, 97
Association for Behavior Analysis International (ABAI), 130*t*, 132, 137*t*
Asynchronous mentoring, 50–51

Attention-deficit/hyperactivity disorder (ADHD), 74, 109, 132
Autism Society of America (ASA), 130*t*, 132, 133, 137*t*
Autism spectrum disorder (ASD)
    bullying of students with, 35
    challenging behaviors and, 74, 76, 82–83, 101
    peer tutors/buddies and, 33
    postsecondary educational programs, 107–109
    professional development and, 58, 67–68
    professional organizations for, 130*t*, 132, 133, 137

Baseline data, recording, 13, 14
Behavior, challenging, 5, 69, 74, 75, 84, 101
    see also Stress, families and
Behavior management
    data collection and, 11–12
    documenting effectiveness of, 12–16
    evidence-based practices and, 6–7
    leadership in, 5
    mentoring newly licensed teachers in, 45, 49–50
    procedures and strategies in, 9–10
    promising practices and, 7
    schoolwide systems of support, 34–35
    using data analysis to guide, 4–5
    see also Positive behavior interventions and supports (PBIS)
Blind review, 143
BRIDGES framework, 85, 101
Bug-in-the-ear technology, 30, 51
Bullying, 35, 131

Chained task, 11
Charts, 81, 98
Children and Adults with Attention-Deficit/ Hyperactivity Disorder (CHADD), 130*t*, 132, 137*t*
CLD, *see* Council for Learning Disabilities (CLD); Cultural and linguistic diversity (CLD)
Coaching, 29–30, 49–52, 67–68, 70, 83
Co-assessing, inclusive environments and, 30–31
Collaboration, 28, 30
Collaborative conference presentations, 17–18